A Kassen

Dimensions Variable

Mousse Publishing

Central Heating Fountains

The radiators of the exhibition space are disconnected, and the central heating pipes are connected to two bronze fountains which loop back into the system.

Kling & Bang, Reykjavik, Iceland, 2019

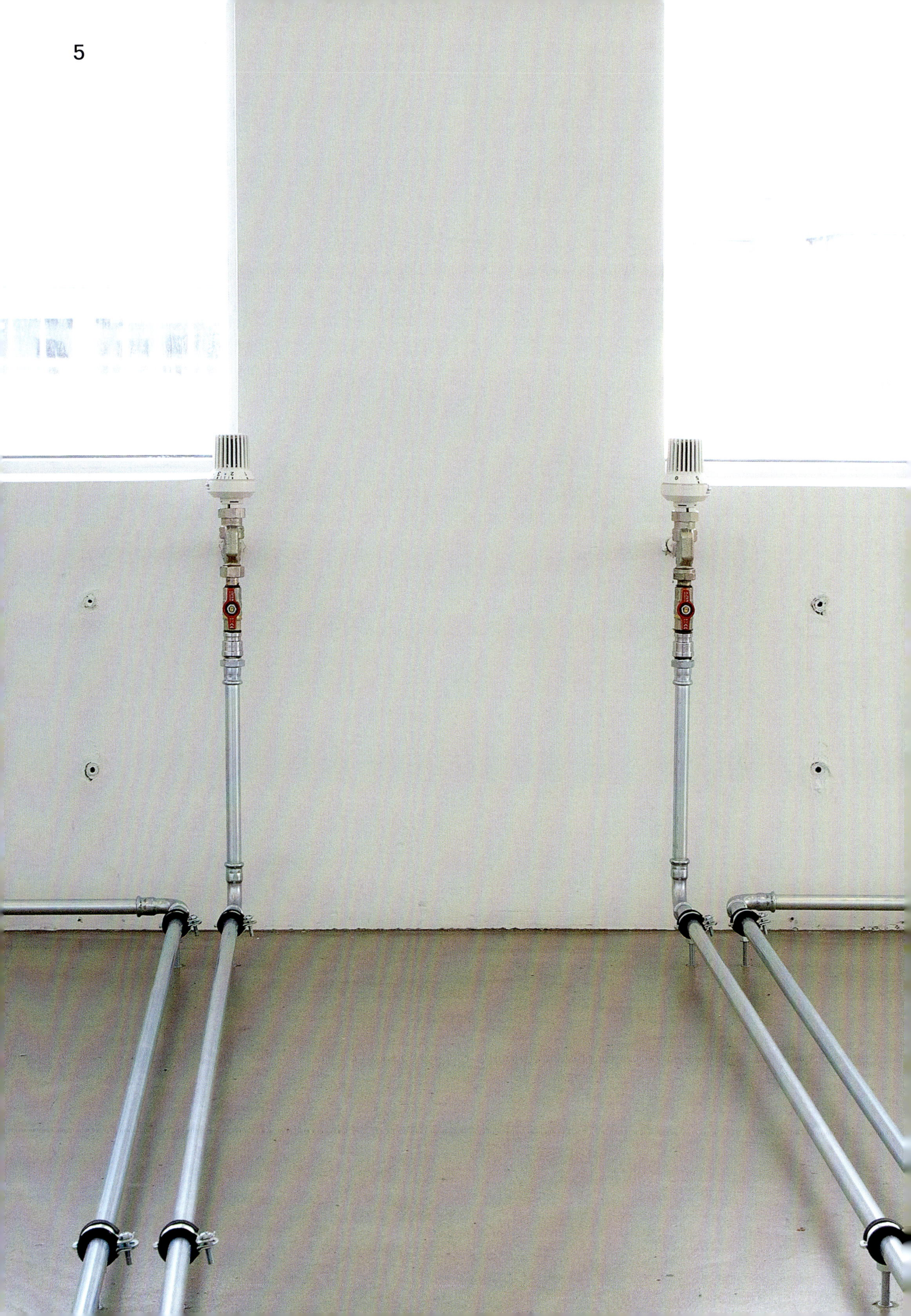

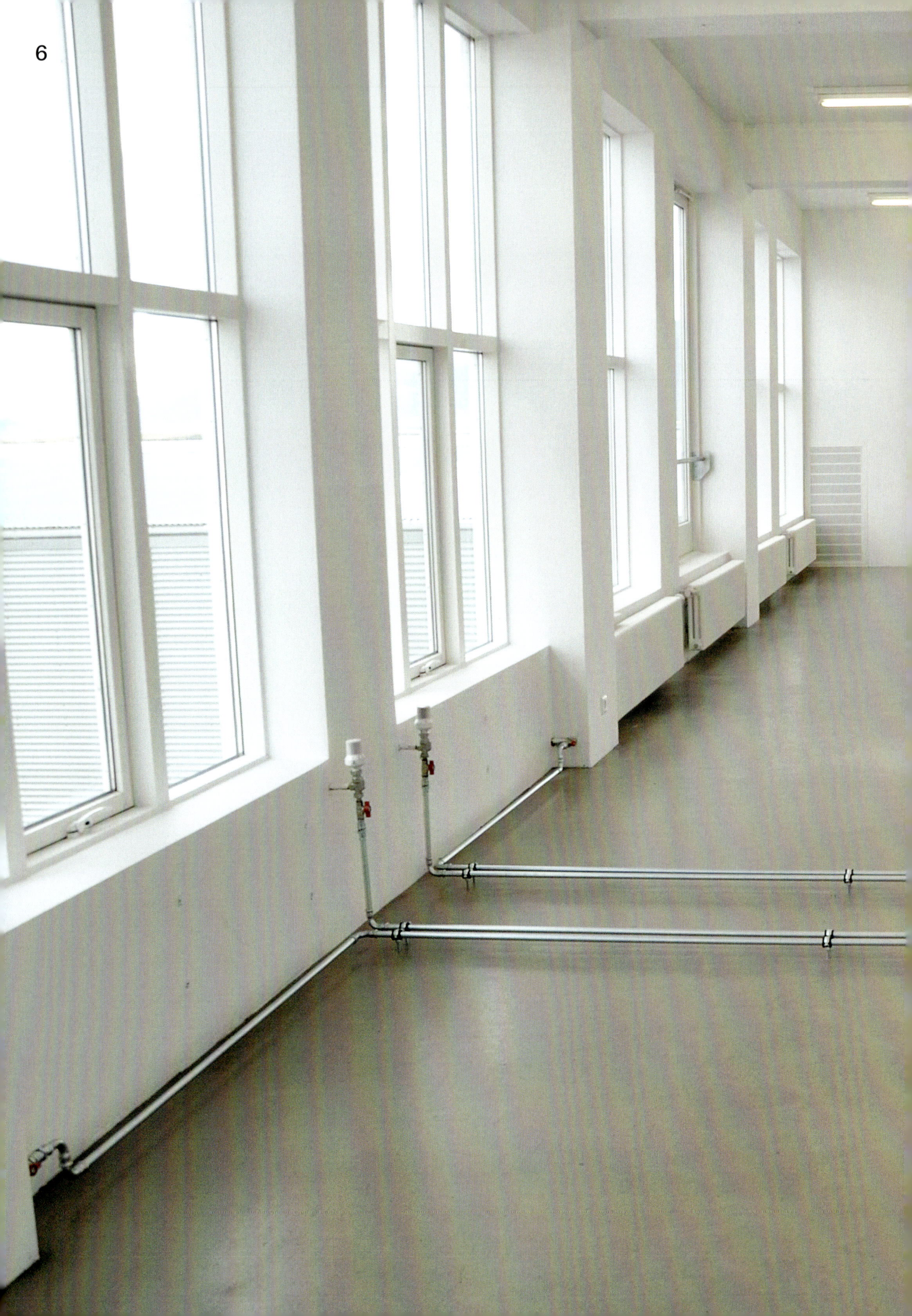

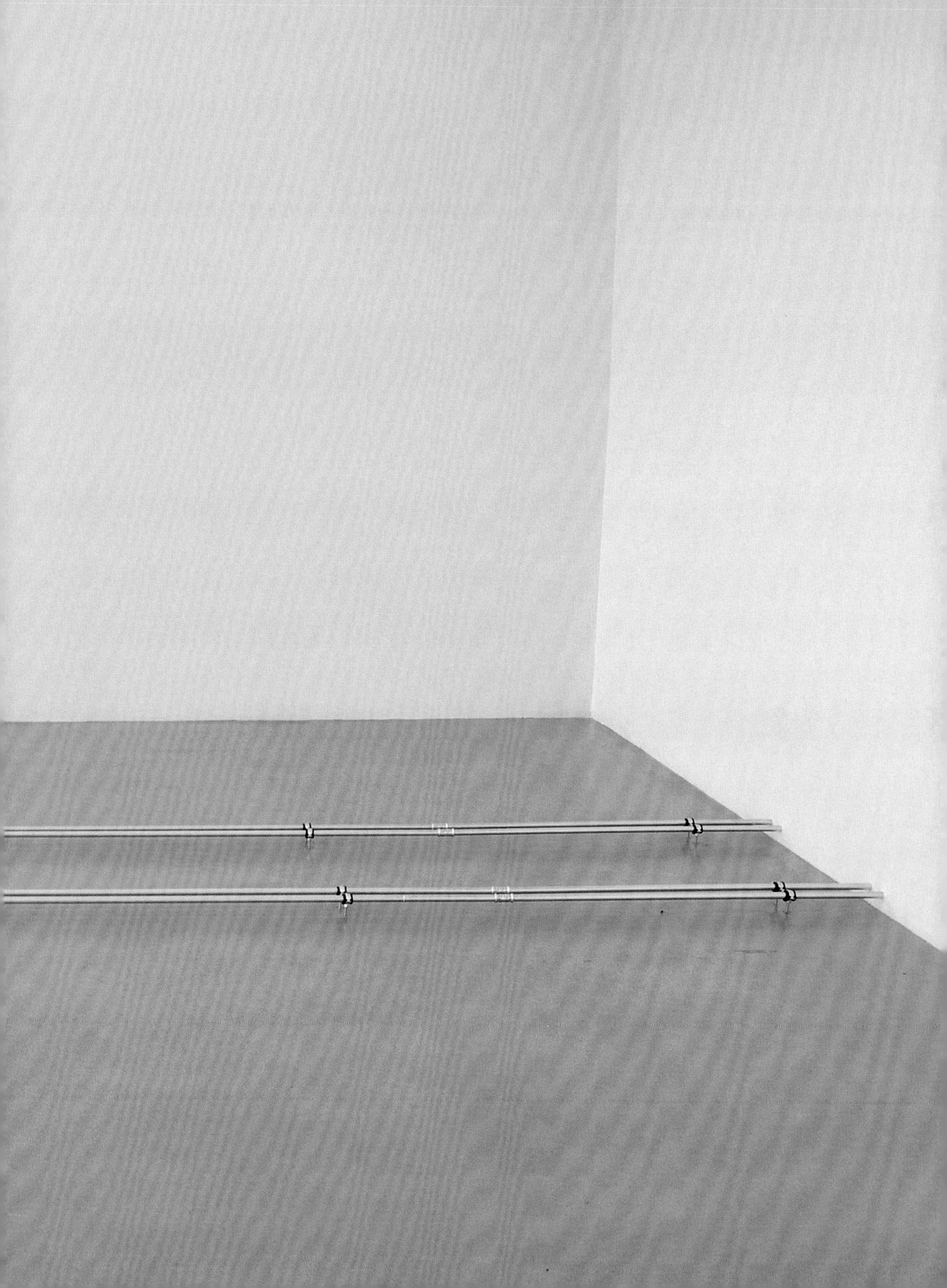

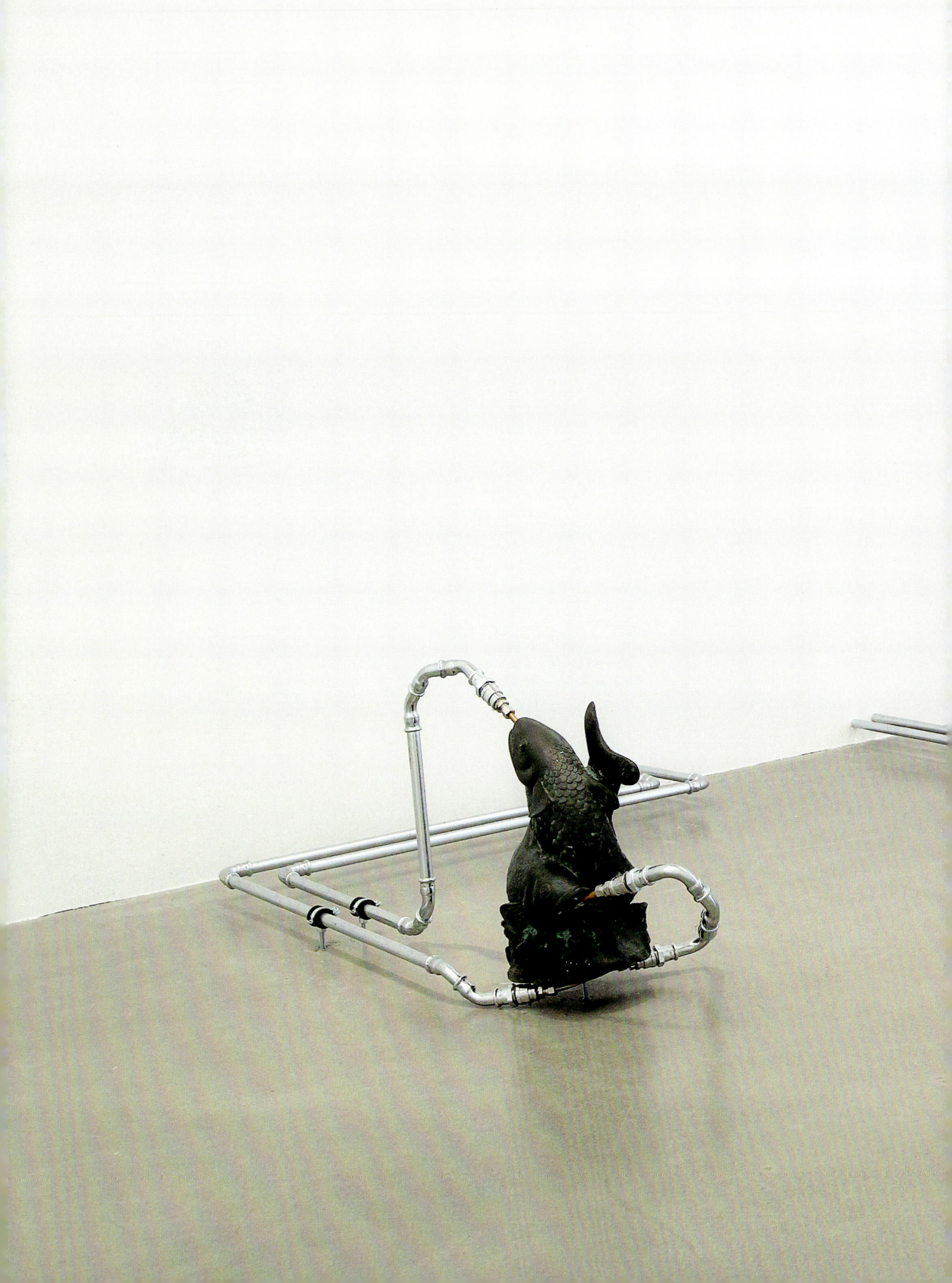

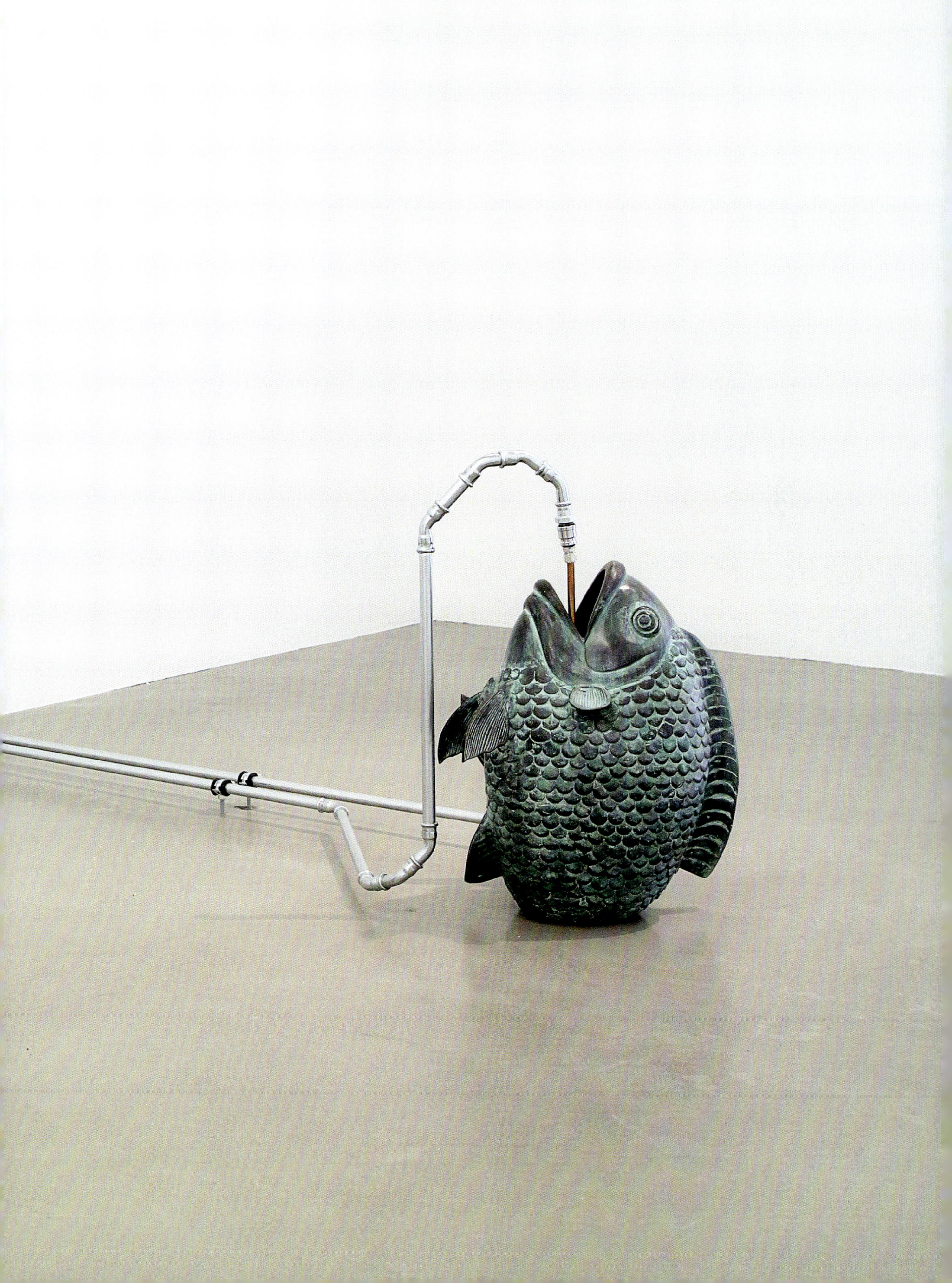

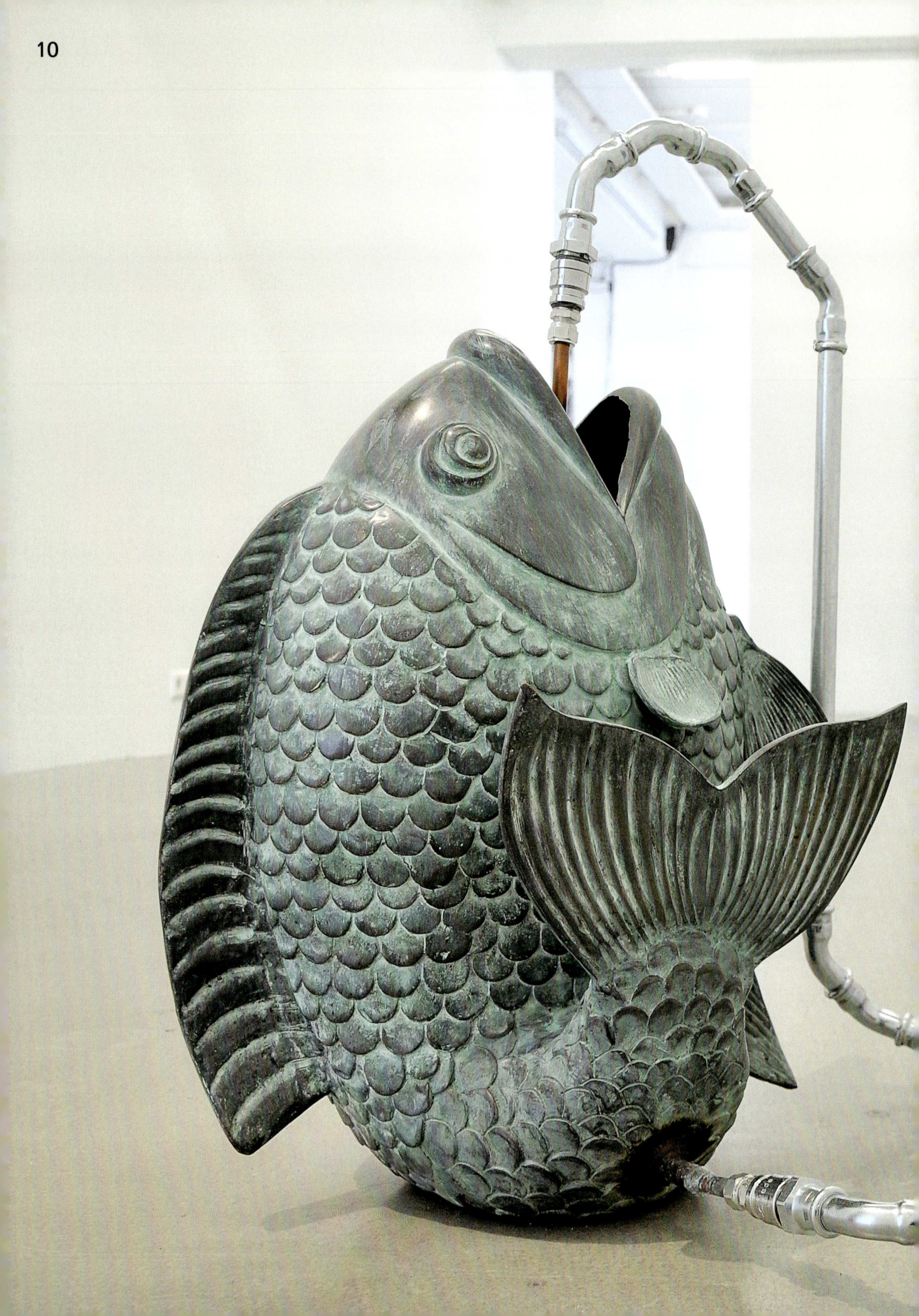

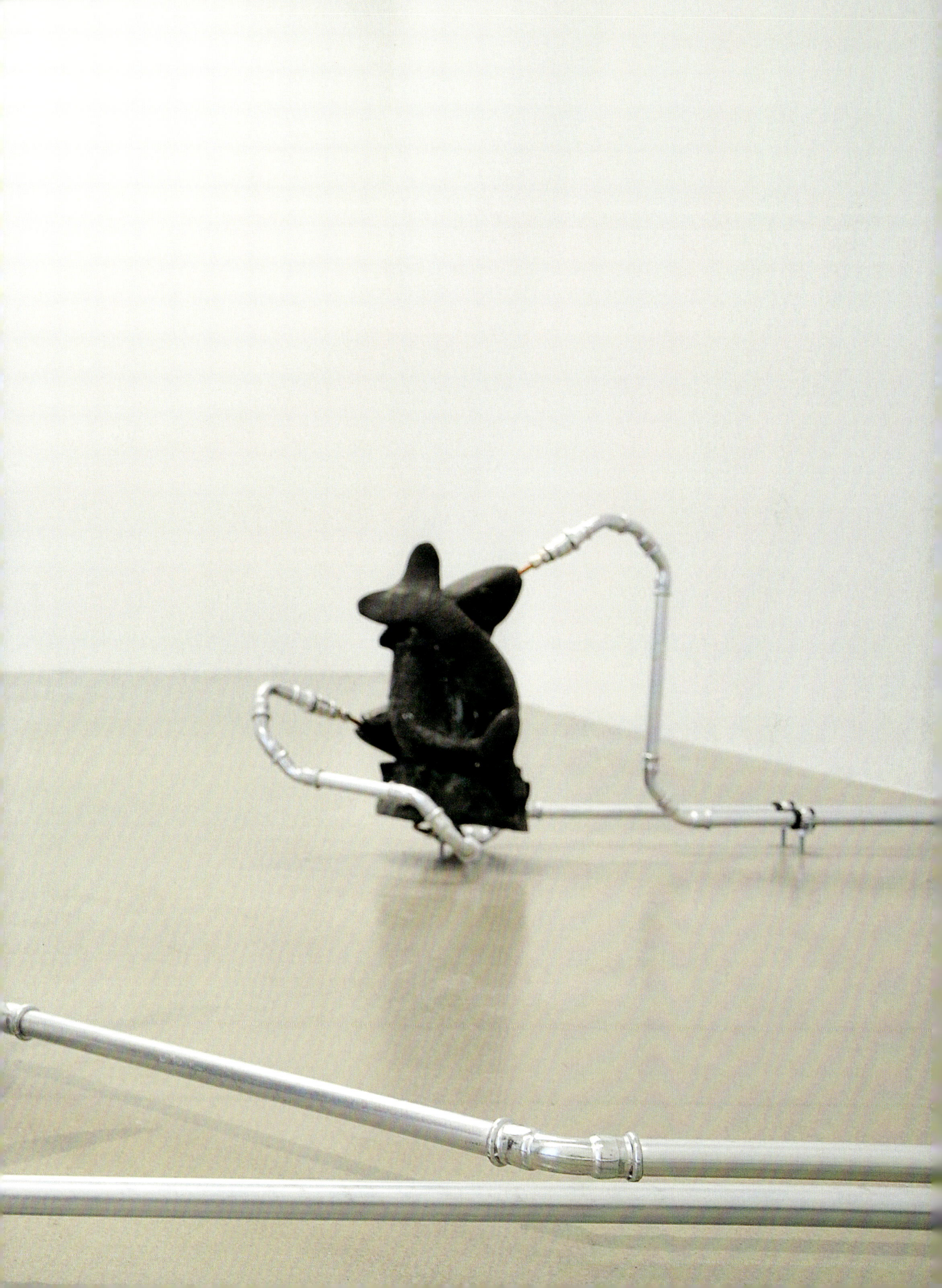

Mother & Child

Jonatan Habib Engquist

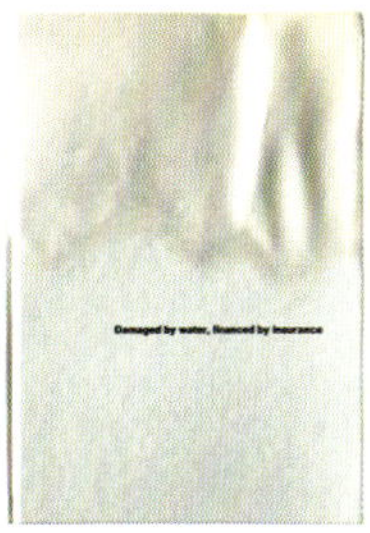

"How many times will he have to fold the sky to fit it in his pocket?" asks Eric Chevillard in the novel *The Crab Nebula* (*La Nébuleuse du crabe*). Chevillard is a writer who often comes to mind when thinking of the smart, crafty, and sometimes facetious practice of artist group A Kassen. In Danish, their name refers to the state unemployment benefit system, their 2008 catalog *Damaged by water, financed by insurance* is just that. Entrepreneurial cultural fragility exemplified. Tongue in cheek and yet as it is. Technically, their works range from performative installations to sculptures and photography, often including ready-mades, or more specifically, things made for something very different from what A Kassen is doing. These things often appear to be something other than what they are for this reason—or, to be more precise: things which, by being shown as they are, appear to be something that they are not and yet potentially could be. Just as Chevillard's novels present characters that are truly bizarre whilst also familiar, A Kassen insist on creating situations that are at once genuinely strange and curiously mundane. This is often done by parodying conventions, deconstructing narratives and meaning, and skillfully combining absurdity and hopelessness with humor.

The protagonist of Chevillard's 1997 novel *On the Ceiling* (*Au plafond*) only wears gray clothes. He does not have an exceptional appearance, is of average height, and has a most ordinary face. But he manages wherever he goes to have people stare at him. As much as he wants to avoid attention, he is forced to stoop in order to pass through doorways. He must wear clothes that button down the front and can only travel in cabriolets. So what is a person who constantly wears an upside-down chair on his head to do? The answer, it appears, is to move onto the ceiling. When the protagonist moves in with his girlfriend and her family, the bedroom is too small to accommodate everyone; a home is created on the more spacious ceiling.

In A Kassen's exhibition at the site of Kling & Bang gallery —and in the ceiling of The Living Art Museum, among other places—the floor has become a ceiling. As we enter the exhibition space, we encounter the figurative life-sized bronze statue
p. 16–19 titled *View from Below (Standing Woman)* (2019). It has been installed on the floor of Kling & Bang. So far, one could say that the whole thing is quite conventional. Perhaps even conservative, with the sculpture base on the gallery floor. However, the sculpture is placed on the floor upside-down so that its base aligns with the floor, thus only permitting us to appreciate its bottom from above; we can merely see the inside of the cast. Due to its size, this sculpture sticks out from the ceiling of the neighboring gallery downstairs, The Living Art Museum, where it protrudes from the upper interior surface like a stalactite or outlandish chandelier. Downstairs, the ceiling has become a floor. Because the floor is a roof.

As we move into the gallery on the floor-ceiling-floor, we are confronted with two bronze fish. It is the kind of item that

p. 4–11 you might expect to see spurting water in an Italian piazza or a bourgeoisie garden. Though in *Central Heating Fountains* (2019), the fountain has been integrated into the pipes of the building. The two water-spitting bronze fish have been connected to the existing central heating system and spit into the pipes in order to create a kind of closed-loop that effectively elongates the existing pipes from one side of the gallery to the other. The water pumped through the fountain fish can't be seen, but it circulates in the same manner as it would in any other fountain and simultaneously helps to heat the space.

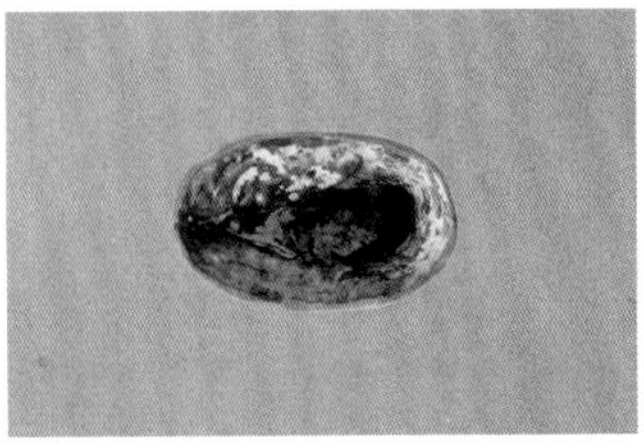

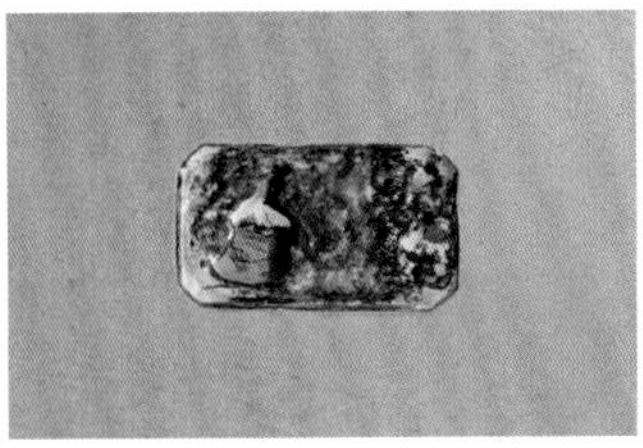

View from Below (Mother & Child) (2019) and *View from Below (Il porcellino)* (2019) are installed similarly to the bronze sculpture in the first room of the gallery. Only this time, due to their smaller size, it is impossible to see anything but the inside of the sculptures. And in the end, these *View from Below* can only really be viewed from above. Behind these inside-out sculptures, we find a series of photographs titled
p. 24–27 *Oceans Underneath* (2019), which portray shards of a broken globe. The depicted pieces, taken against a blue background, present the underside of the areas of the oceans on the globe. The placement next to *View from Below (Mother & Child)* and *View from Below (Il porcellino)* suggests that this is a photograph from underneath the representation of what lies below (and what lays above it). I am again tempted to speak of folding up the ocean in order to fit it in a pocket but abstain, as there thankfully is one classic art installation in this exhibition that seems to be able to be taken at face value and simply understood for what it is. And it's a giveaway! A poster stack; a pile of hand-out posters placed on a wooden transport pallet
p. 20–23 on the floor. But don't be fooled. It turns out that *Exhibition Poster* (2019) is perhaps the most site skewing site-specific piece of them all. It can be described as a portable mirror image of what lies above. It is a printed photograph that depicts the ceiling directly above the pallet. Again, it would seem that we need to look down in order to look up. To see what lays below in order to perceive what lies above. The ceiling above is the floor of Olafur Elisason's studio. A Kassen's exhibition seems to be taking place everywhere except in the gallery. Or, it would seem that it is spreading out while leaving many of the conventional exhibiting spaces of the gallery empty. Or perhaps they are exhibiting the venue. It is both in Kling & Bang and making itself part of the building at large. We can, of course, take the poster with us, expanding the exhibition even further. Perhaps place it on a wall. With the floor-image of the ceiling-floor of the upstairs neighbors placed on a wall somewhere else, we merely displace the space, turning a mirror into a wormhole.

The narrator in *On the Ceiling* initially has high hopes for the theoretically splendid new accommodation: "neutral, virgin space open to the unconstrained application." But after a while, the ceiling also becomes familiar, and it begins to look a lot like the floor, as it too is affected by the bothersome narrow-mindedness of the more densely populated world below. From the narrator's viewpoint, up on the ceiling, the conventional use of space and furniture is restricting, as a chair "imposes a direction on our gaze, given the inability to unscrew our neck," and makes "restless crowds of scatterbrained individuals [. . .] into an audience." A Kassen have solved the issue by simply dissolving the dichotomy between inside and outside, warping the functions of walls, floors, and ceilings. In a modest yet by far one of the more complex installations at Kling & Bang, they invite both the audience—and neighbors—to settle with them in the rafters.

View from Below

A statue is installed upside down penetrating the floor. The bottom of the statue is visible from the gallery, while the figure protrudes into The Living Art Museum floor below.

Kling & Bang, Reykjavik, Iceland, 2019

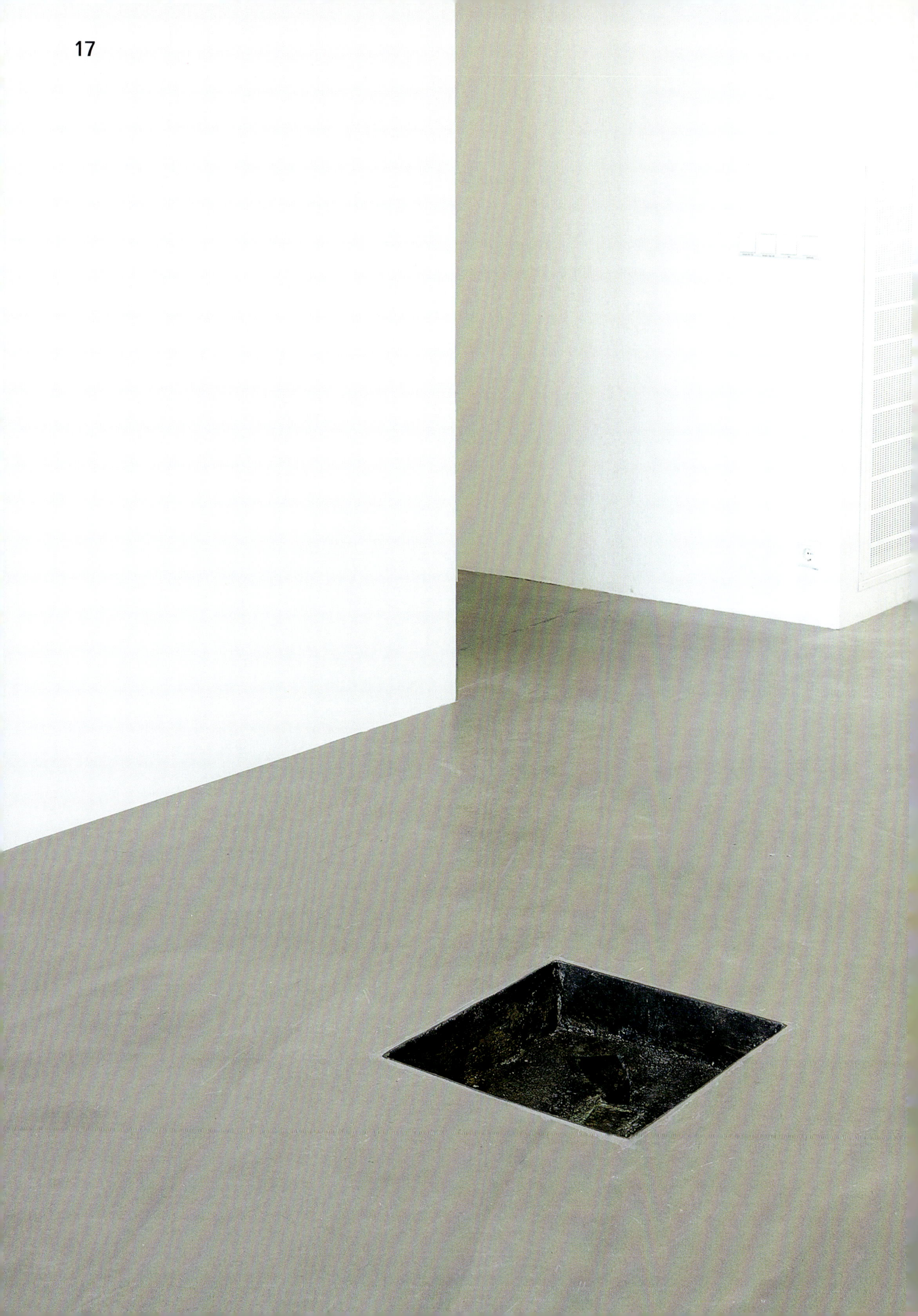

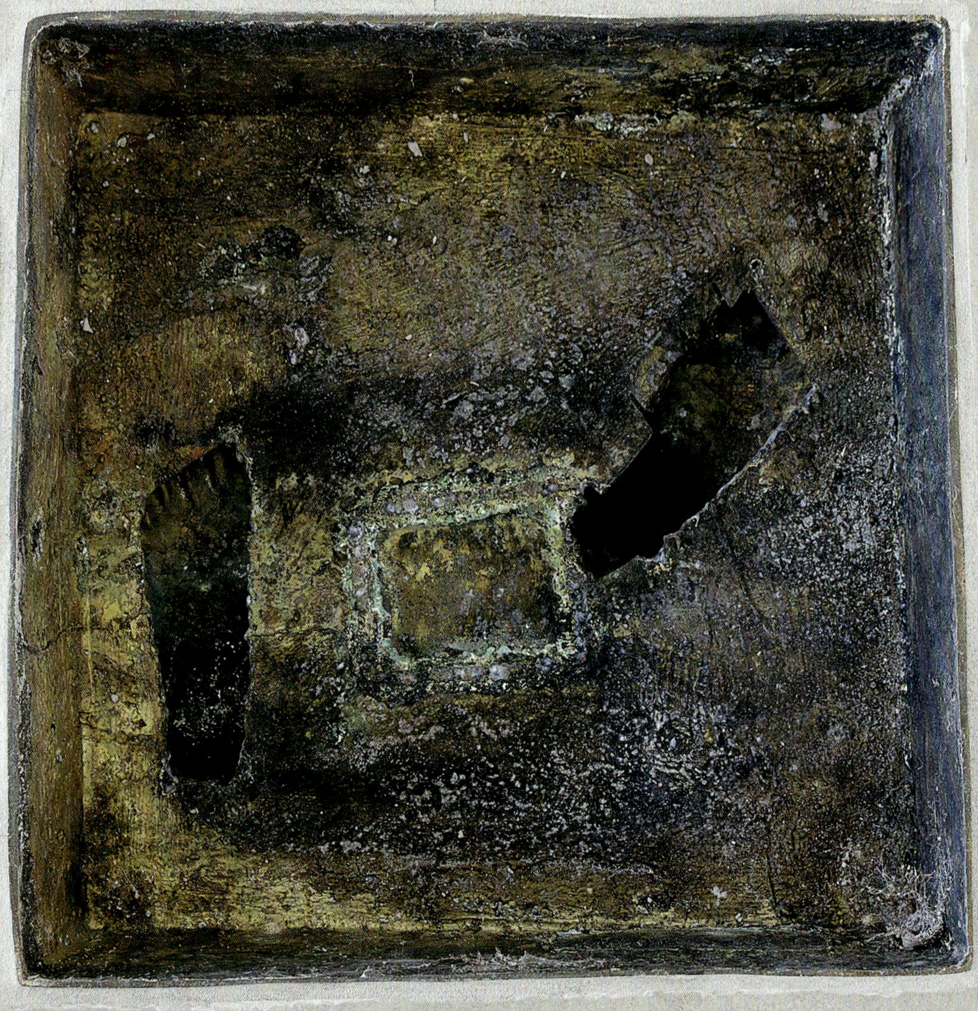

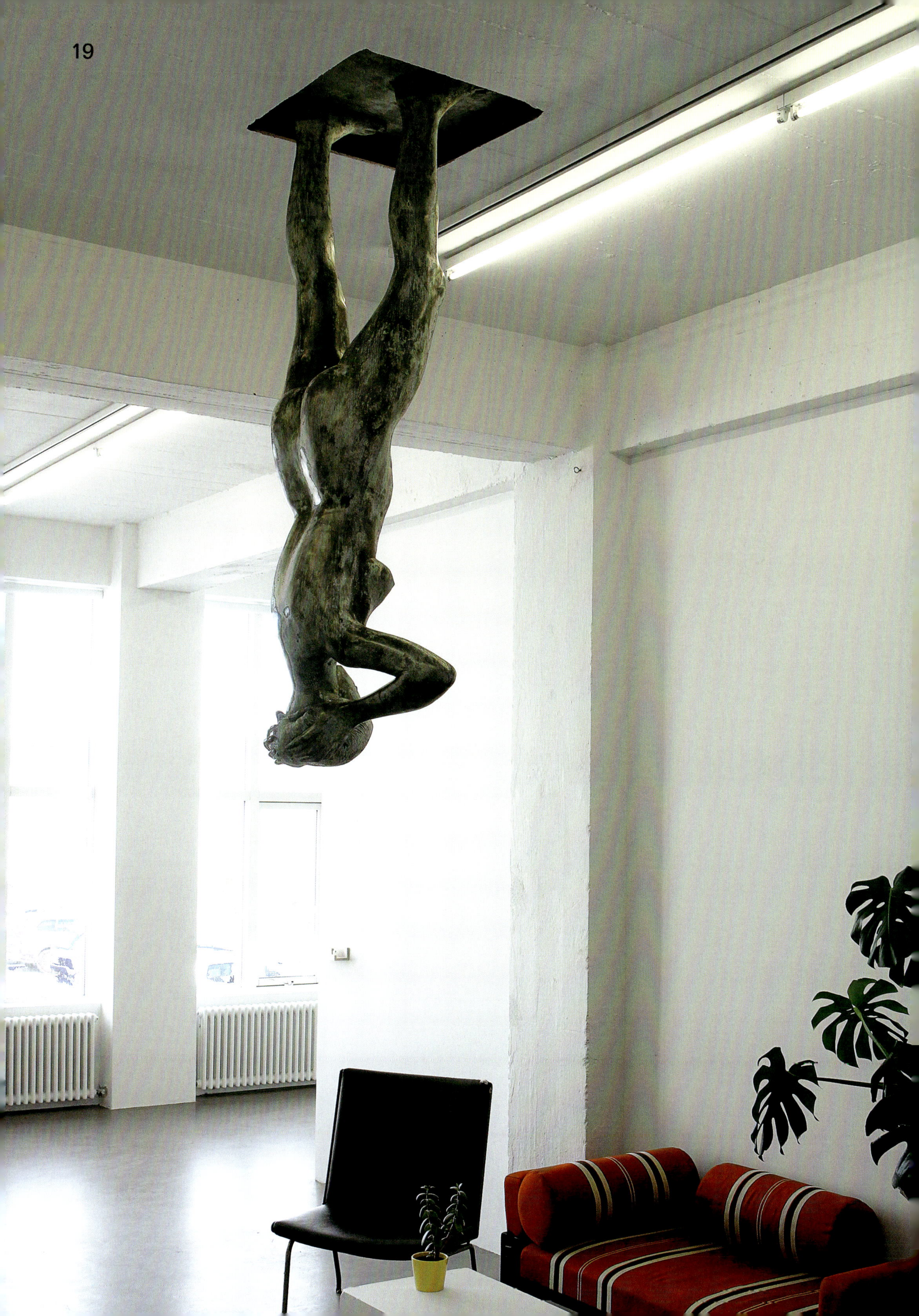

Exhibition Poster

A stack of posters on a pallet depicts the ceiling above it.

Kling & Bang, Reykjavik, Iceland, 2019

Oceans Underneath

Photographed fragments of a globe depict the undersides of the sea.

Kling & Bang, Reykjavik, Iceland, 2019

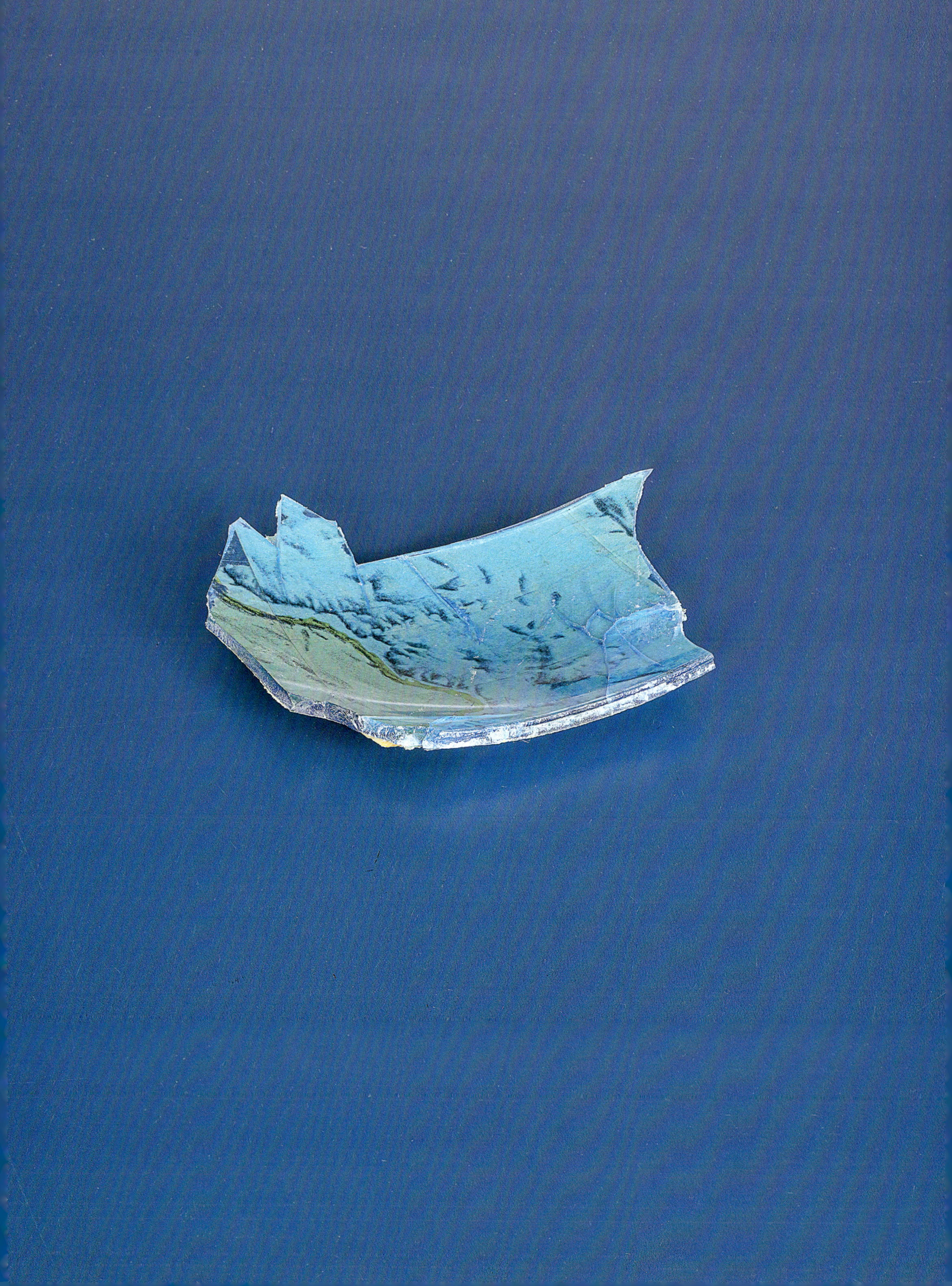

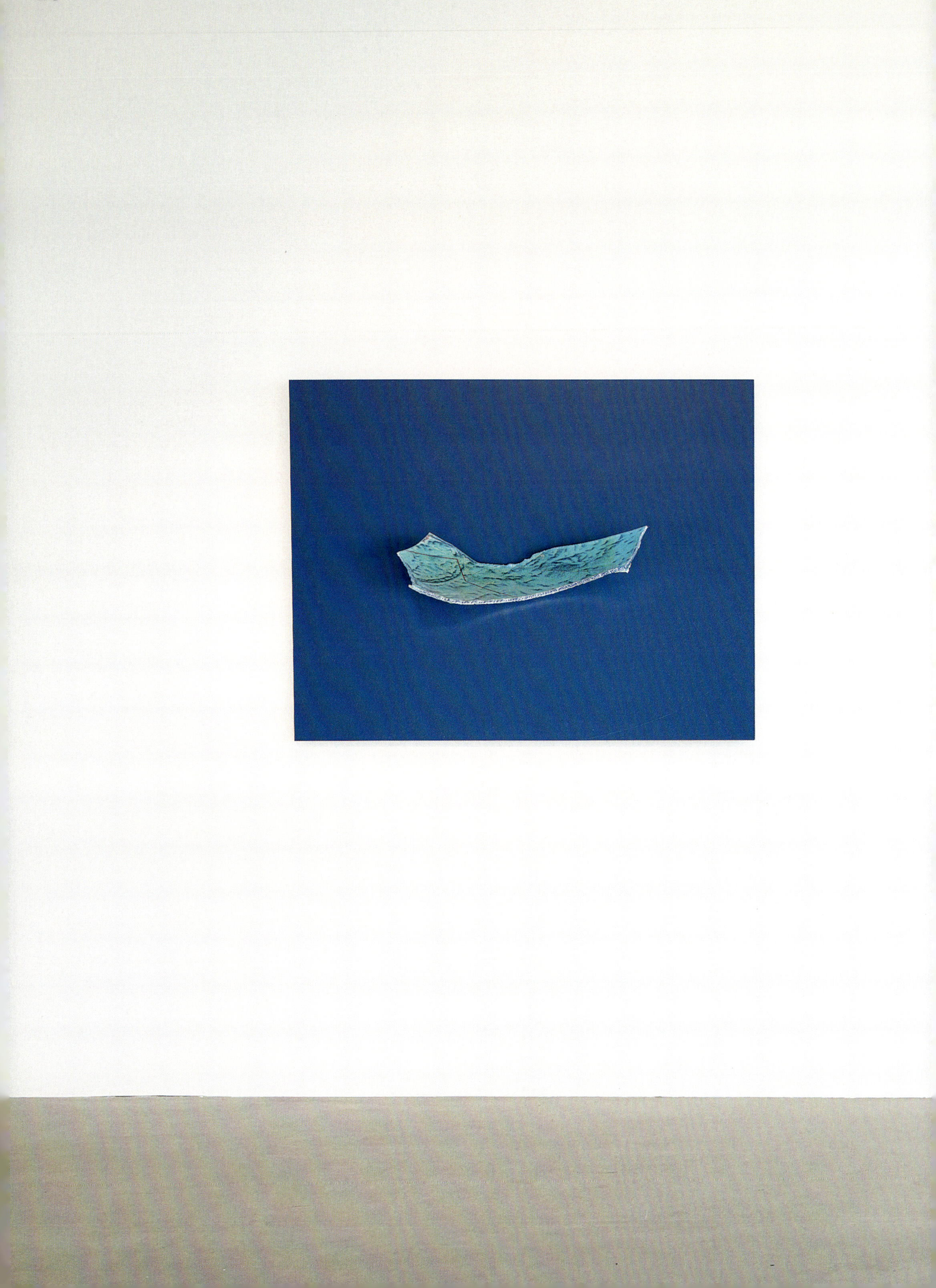

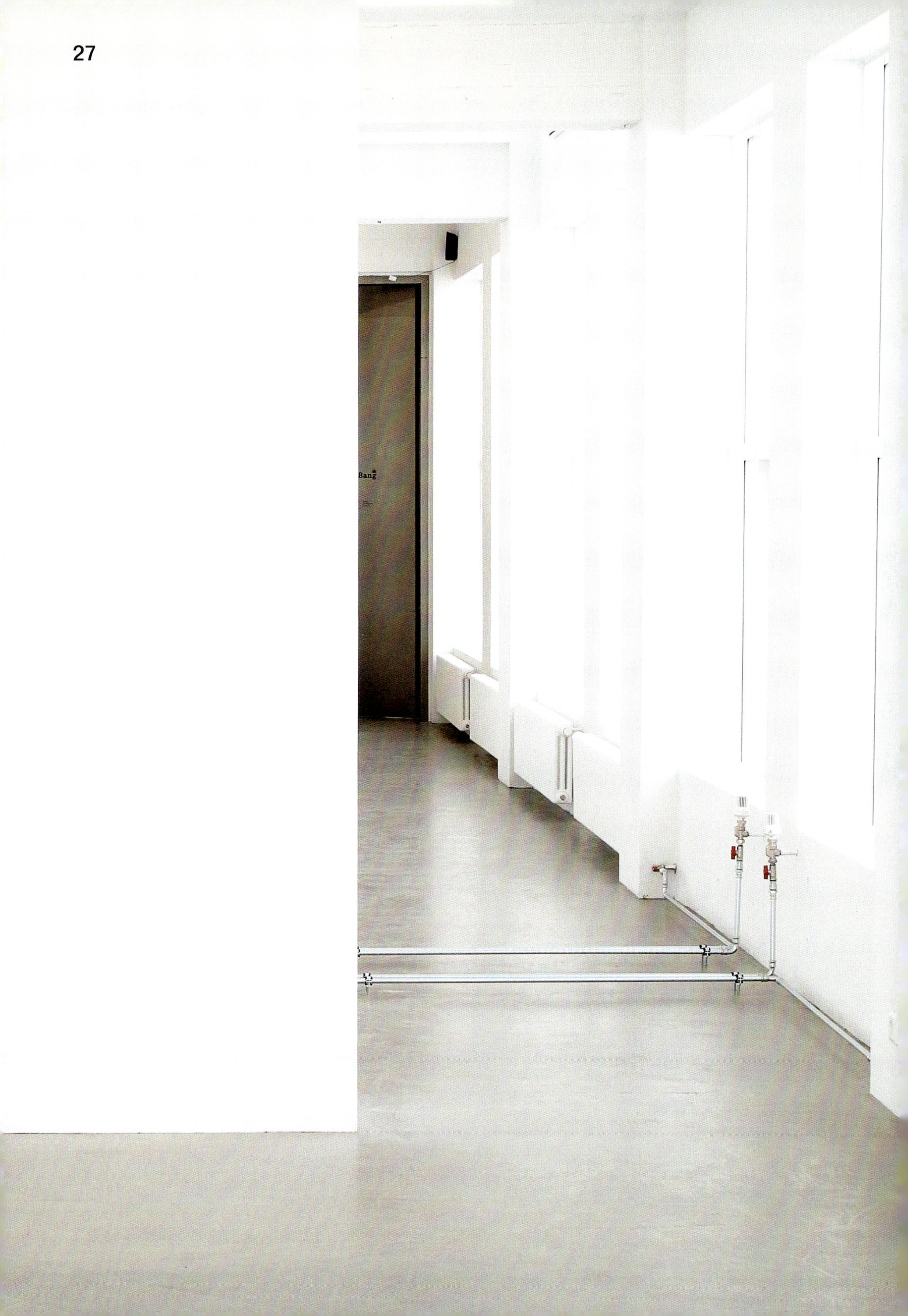

Window to the World

Six window panes are taken out of the museum's facade and replaced by plywood boards. The window panes are installed into three automatic sliding doors connected to the center. The sculpture is activated by movement.

MUSAC, León, Spain, 2009

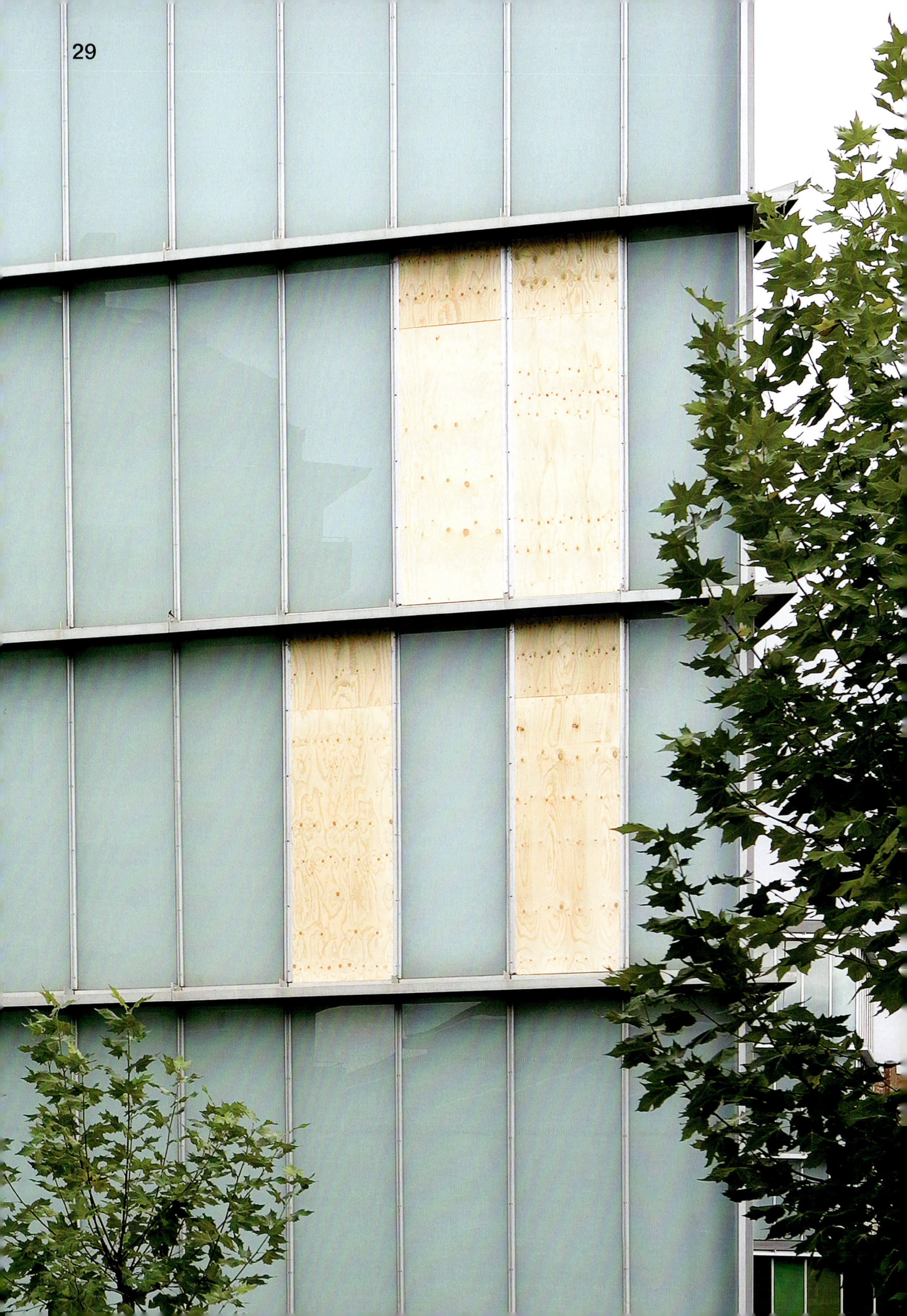

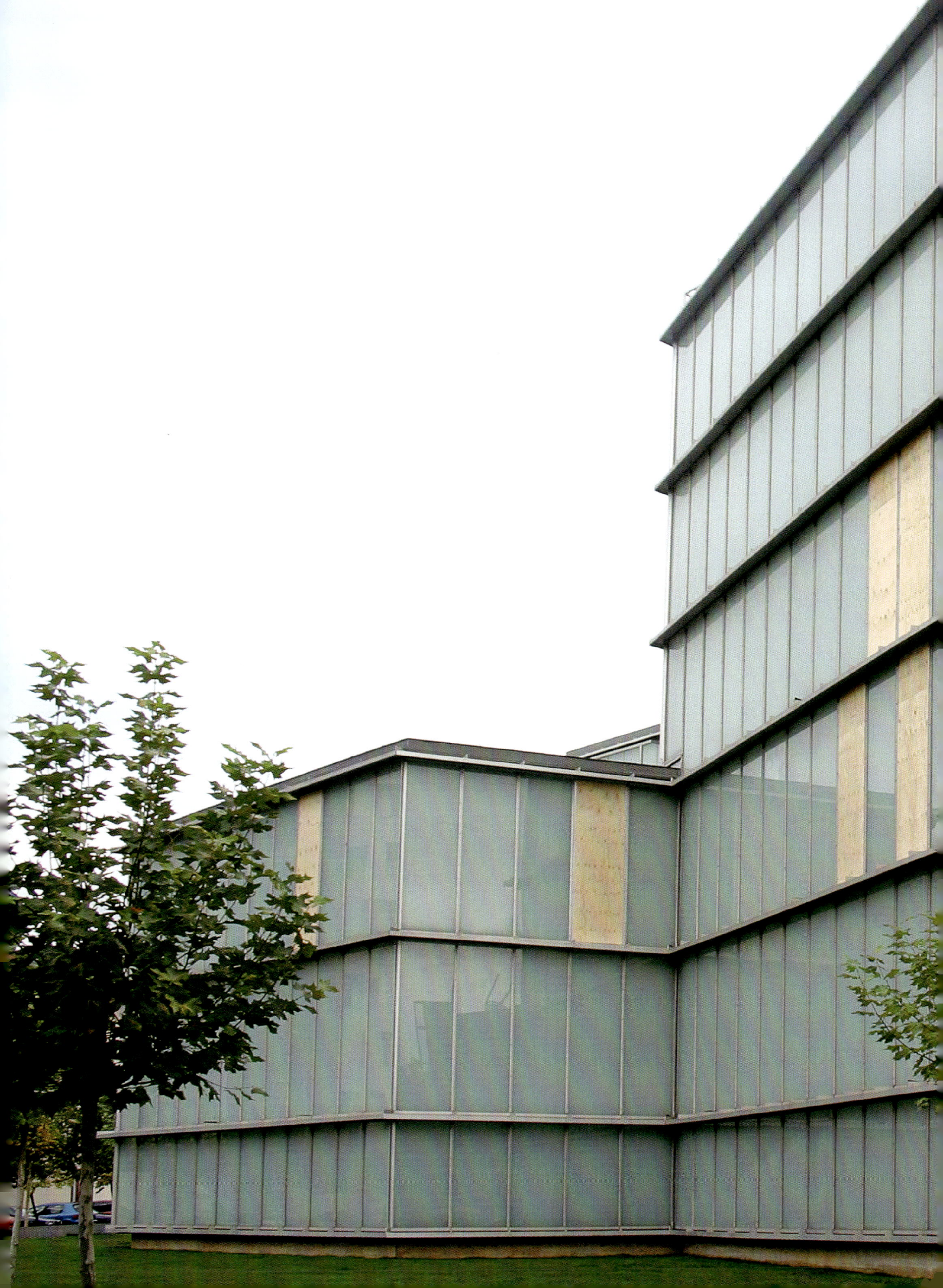

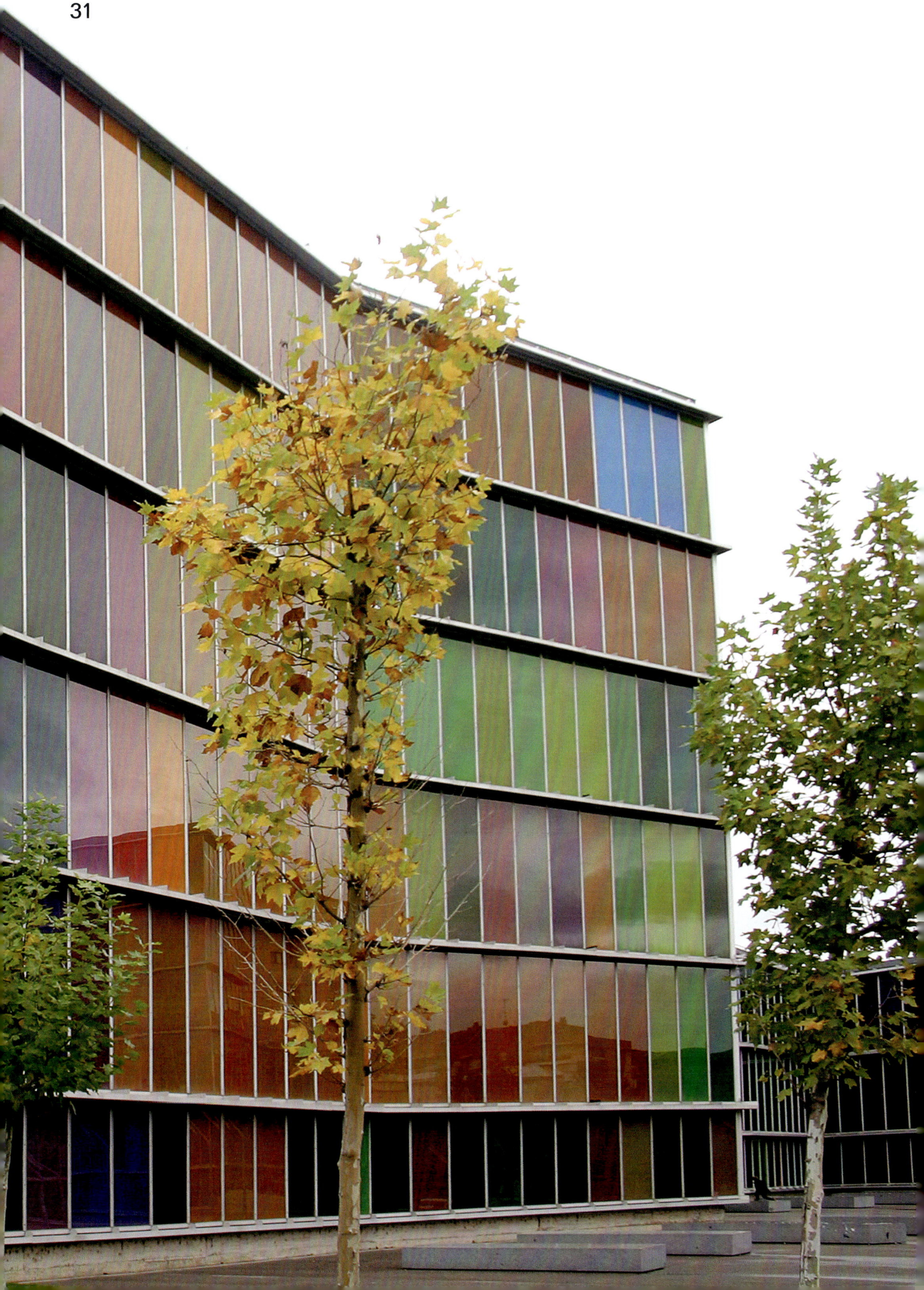

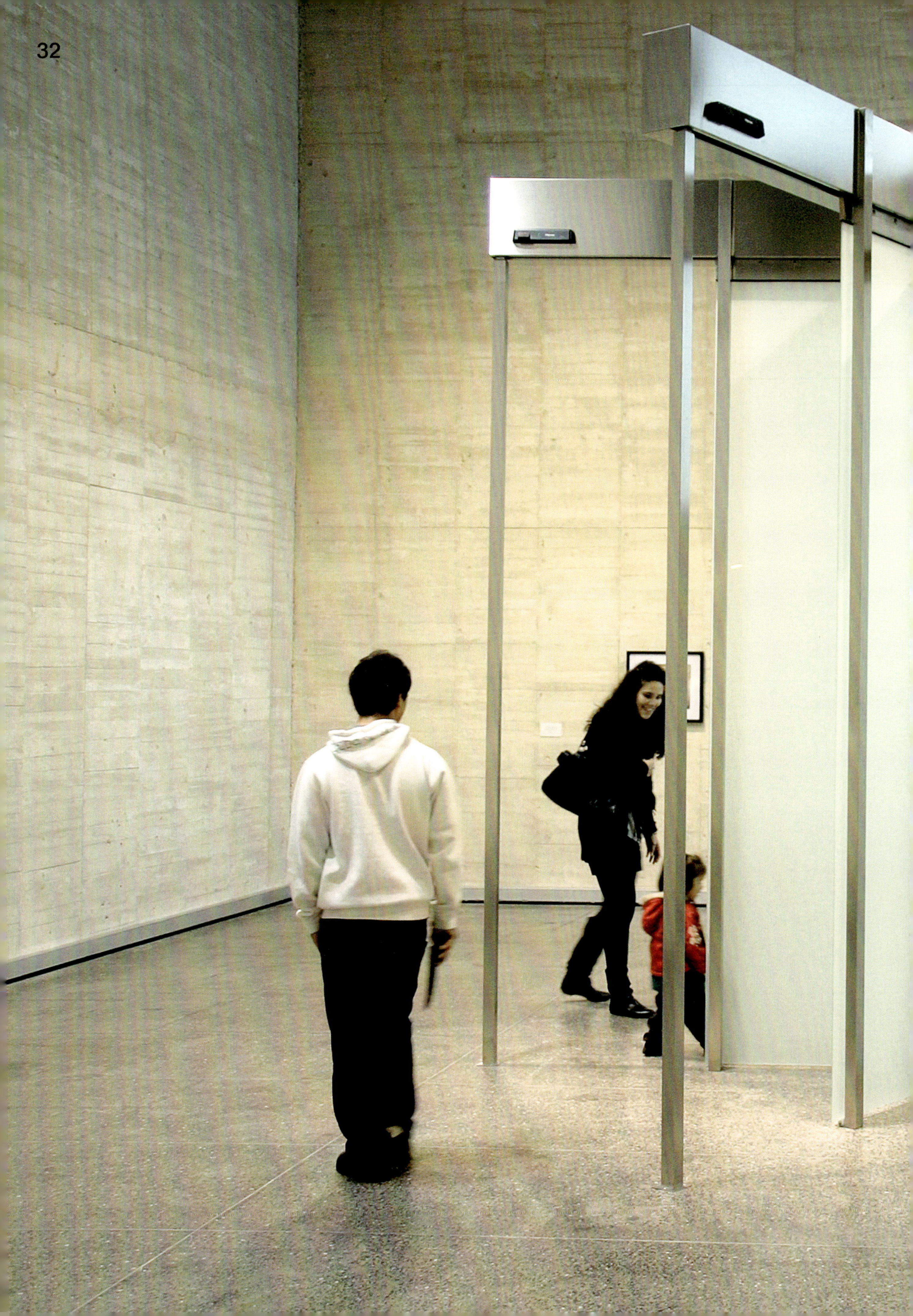

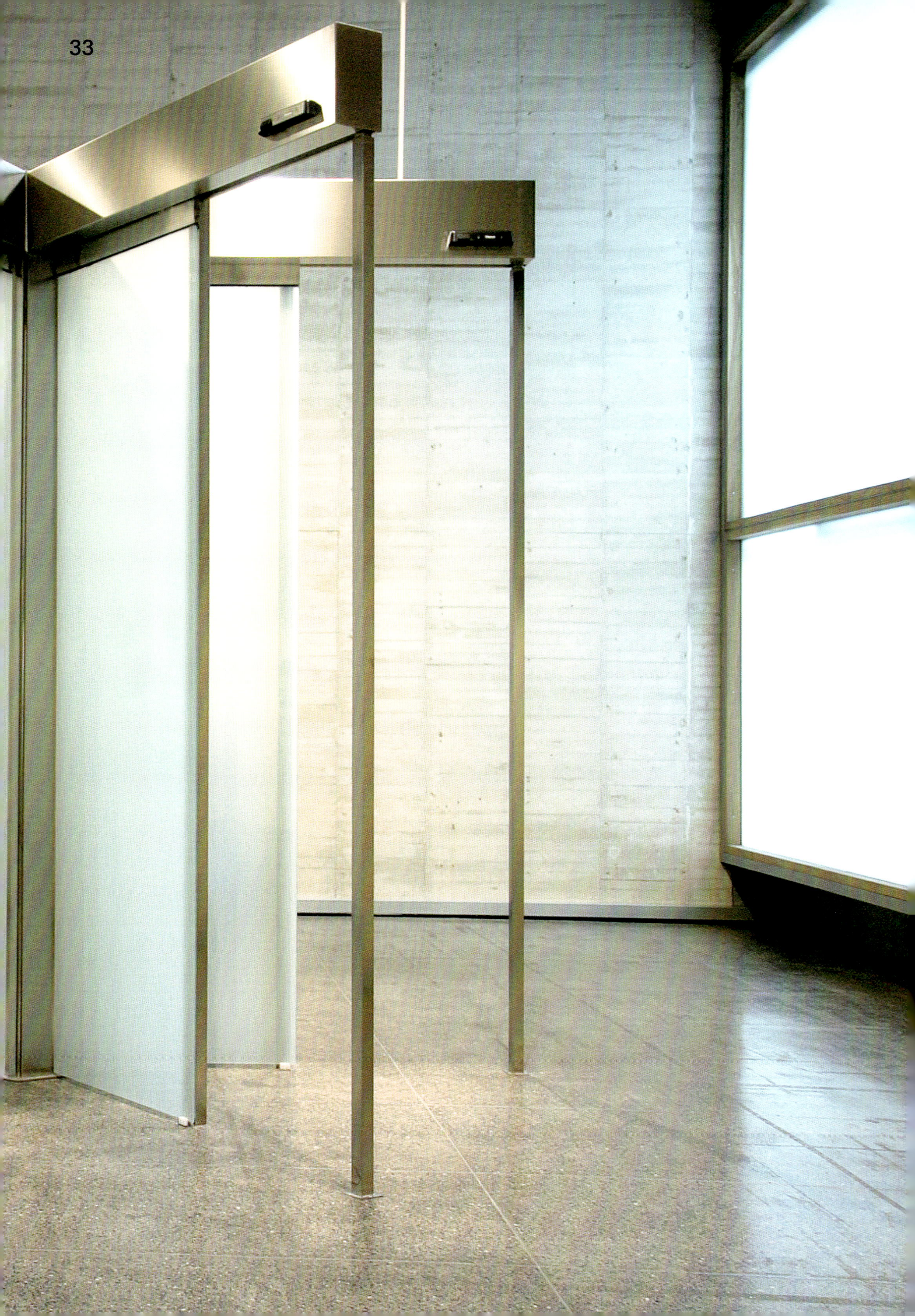

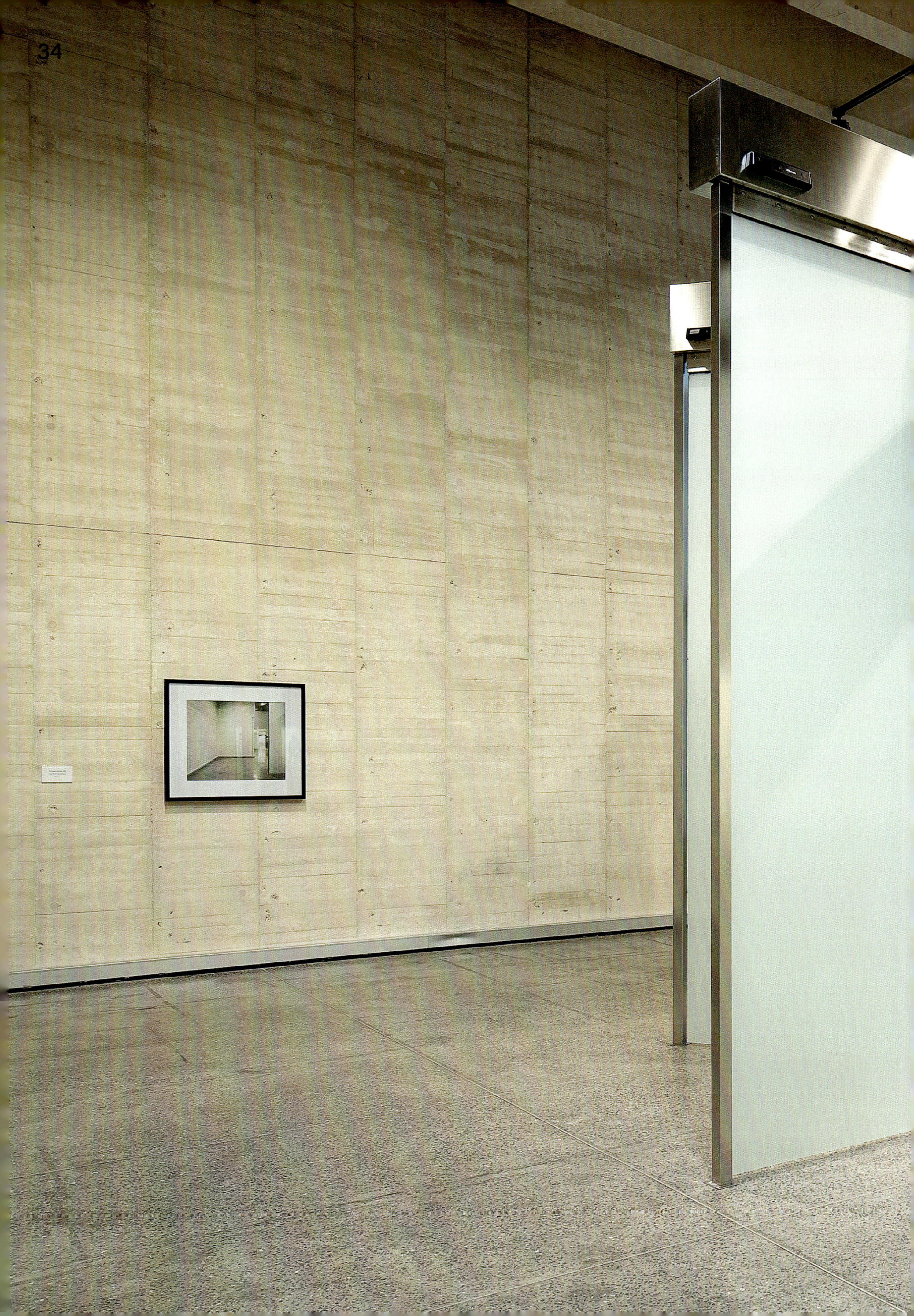

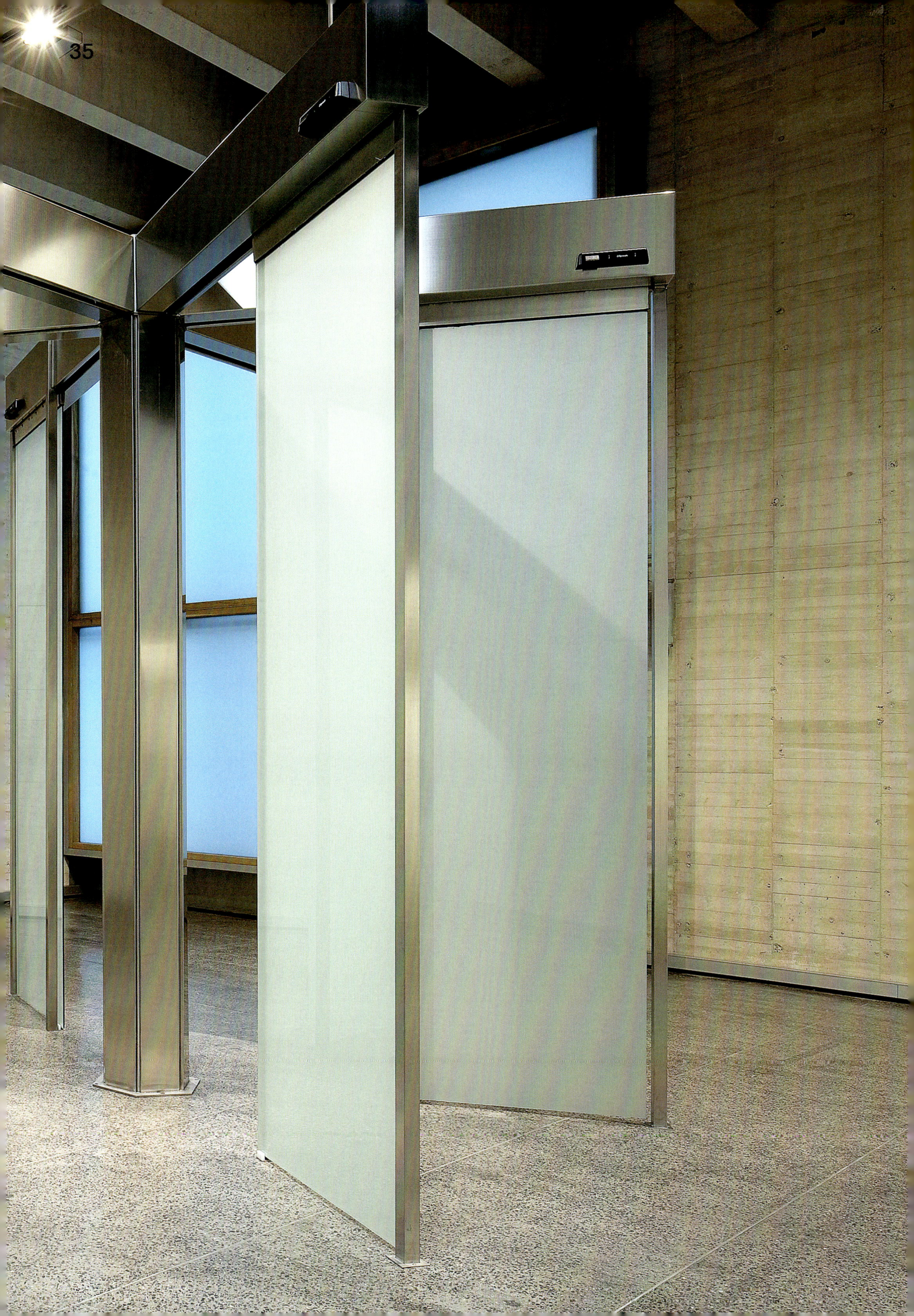

Mural

A conservator continuously exposes layers of wall color from previous exhibitions.

MUSAC, León, Spain, 2009

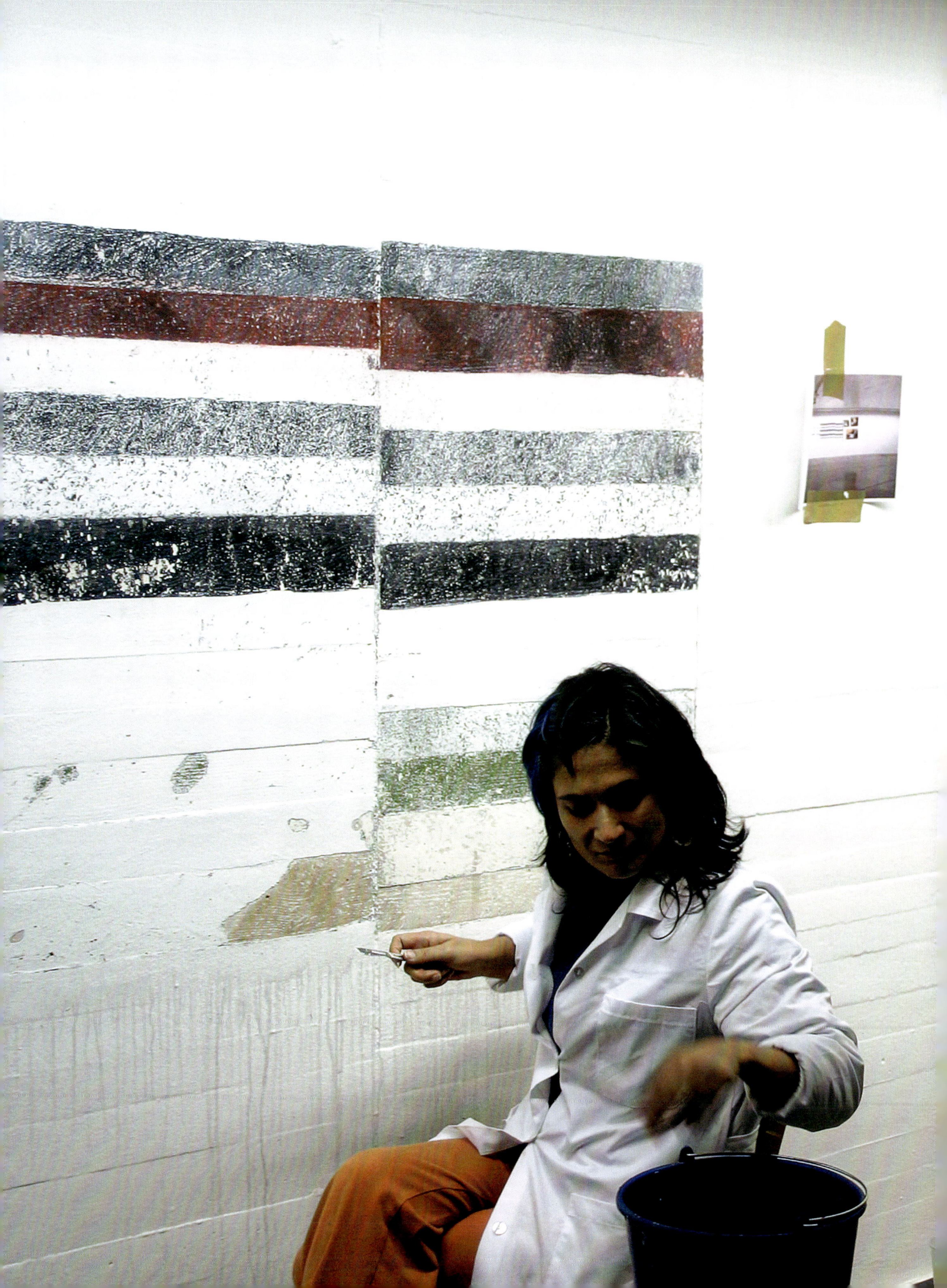

"There is no spoon"
A Kassen and the attempt to create a *glitch* in the system

Irene Campolmi

I haven't met A Kassen since recently. I have always found their work particularly fascinating for its opacity and surrealist undertones. Opacity plays a significant role in their work, and how they talk about it. Opacity is a term frequently used to address a phenomenon or an object whose way of existing in this world is not straightforward.

Its opposite term—transparency—defines a phenomenon or an object that can be easily explained or understood by how it manifests itself in the world. The contrast between "opacity" and "transparency" is undoubtedly one of the most present push-and-pull relationships within the visual arts. When one recognizes what is seen, one can identify it. To identify something as something else means to create links and patterns of recognition that explain, or at least justify, why something exists in the way it exists.

In the book *The Transparency Society*,[1] Korean philosopher Byung-chul Han warns the readers how in today's world, particularly the Western one, the word "transparency" haunts all spheres of life: politics, culture, economics, amongst others. Transparency is a feature that we expect to transform processes and structures. A transparent society is supposedly more democratic, transparent information is expected to be freer, and a transparent workplace is, in theory, more efficient. "Transparency creates trust," says Han,[2] but the more one can see through, the more one cannot see that what is seen and experienced is deceiving.

Additionally, the more one chooses to be "transparent" by sharing life moments on social media, the more one's life is subjected to control. In many ways, A Kassen's artistic practice reflects on this contradiction between opacity and transparency by revealing what seems hidden in the world and showing the complexity of what seems so straightforward.

The Martinican philosopher Édouard Glissant has defended opacity and has addressed it as the fundamental prerequisite for the constitution of the notion of "Otherness." The only way to understand what is outside of oneself is to be unable to see clearly what one's identity is not. Glissant talks about the lack of transparency as the basis for understanding differences and developing relationships between things by defining opacity.[3] To accept what one does not understand is to accept that our way of seeing and experiencing the world is not only not unique but also not as "transparent" and comprehendible as it seems to be.

The artist collective A Kassen appears to know this well. Whenever I have asked them to tell me more about their projects

---

1. Byung-chul Han, *The Transparency Society* (Stanford: Stanford University Press, 2015). Originally published in 2012 with the title *Transparenzgesellschaft* (MSB Matthes & Seitz Berlin Verlagsgesellschaft mbH, Berlin).

2. Ibid.

3. Édouard Glissant, *Poetics of Relation*, trans. Betsy Wing (Ann Arbor: University of Michigan, 2010). Originally published in French by Gallimard, 1990.

p. 28–35

The piece's title is *Window to the World* (2009); I guess insinuating what museums and art exhibitions should attempt to provide for people: creating apertures to reveal new perspectives on the world, but not from a straightforward opening. It is not a coincidence that architect Filippo Brunelleschi, while developing the concept of linear perspective in the early fifteenth century, compared its revolutionary potential to an open window to look at the world. The title of A Kassen's work seems to function as a matryoshka: once it is opened, it contains reproductions of itself that reverberate the concept, just in different shapes, forms, and colors. By selecting a window as the visualization of their research into the opacity of art and the ways museums try to make transparent the mechanisms behind the creation of an artwork, A Kassen reflects on the creation of new narratives through both artists, artworks, and the framework of the museum's operations as a cone for human vision. The work remains open to interpretation, being either a site-specific artwork, a commentary on the mission and vision of an art institution that should open a window to the world, or a critique of it. Pick the version you like the most: I feel that that is what A Kassen would suggest. However, what remains iconic is the gesture of removing intact windows to replace them with temporary plywood boards. Seen from the outside, these temporary wooden panels seem to hide troubles that the museum has undergone but cannot reveal. Therefore, this alien presence denies the original function of the building because with six wooden boards replacing the windows, the museum cannot fully be transparent as its institutional mission demands.

A Kassen's intervention disrupts the intention of the museum but also the way it should have been perceived. It creates a *glitch* in the way people experience and perceive art.

A glitch is a minor malfunction of a system caused by either an unexpected defect or other reason that develops a temporary setback: getting stuck in an elevator, experiencing a blackout, or worse, a pandemic. The term has also been in fashion since its use in the famous 1999 film *The Matrix*[5] when Neo, played by the American actor Keanu Reeves, the elected person who will save humanity from the AI manipulation of reality, at one point, has a *déjà vu*. He thinks he has seen a black cat twice through an open door of a room. Upon sharing with his mentor Morpheus, he learns that a *déjà vu* is also known to be a glitch in the matrix. I want to open a short parenthesis on the term "glitch" because it has returned with a different connotation concerning gender studies and readings of postcolonial histories in the recent history of contemporary art.

In *Feminist Glitch*,[6] Legacy Russell analyzes the term within the context of tech culture and digital lives, reading a glitch

---

5 *The Matrix* is a 1999 science fiction action film written and directed by the Wachowskis. It is the first installment in *The Matrix* film series, starring Keanu Reeves, Laurence Fishburne, Carrie-Ann Moss, Hugo Weaving, and Joe Pantoliano. It depicts a dystopian future in which humanity is unknowingly trapped inside a simulated reality, the Matrix, which intelligent machines have created to distract humans while using their bodies as an energy source. When computer programmer Thomas Anderson, under the hacker alias "Neo," uncovers the truth, he joins a rebellion against the machines along with other people who have been freed from the Matrix.

as "an error, a mistake, a failure to function," which indicates that something has gone wrong, leading to a feeling of anxiety.[7] Rather than condemning it, Russell suggests twisting the perception of the negative connotation attached to systemic alterations to celebrate glitches as a vehicle of refusal, a strategy of nonperformance within a system to which people might not want to belong. Russell looks at a glitch as a correction to the "machine" that it tries to hijack, defining a glitch as a positive thing that creates a malfunction to activate new architectures.

"To glitch," writes Russell, "is to embrace malfunction, and to embrace malfunction is in and of itself an expression that starts with 'no'."[8] In her book, Russell traces a history of the term's etymology, which finds its deep roots in the Yiddish *gletshn* (to slide, glide, slip) or the German *glitschen* (to slip). Glitch is a word that implies movement and change from the outset, and this movement, as Russell recognizes, triggers the error. The word *glitch*, as we now use and understand it, was first popularized in the 1960s as part of the rhetoric of the American space program. In 1962, astronaut John Glenn used the word in his book *Into Orbit*: "Another term we adopted to describe some of our problems was " glitch.' Literally, a glitch [...] is such a minute change in voltage that no fuse could protect against it."[9] Later, in 1971, "glitches" appeared in an article in the *Miami News* about Apollo 14's failure to perform when a glitch had nearly botched a landing on the moon. Traversing through these origins, we can also understand glitch as a mode of nonperformance: the "failure to perform," an outright refusal, a "nope" in its own right, expertly executed by the machine.[10]

Herein lies a paradox: a glitch moves but also prevents. It incites movement while simultaneously creating an obstacle. Thus, a glitch extends beyond the most literal technological mechanics: it helps us celebrate failure as a generative force, a new way to take on the world.[11]

In the Danish translation (*fejl*), glitch is more like a mistake. But as Russell suggests, when systems fail to respond or return to their function, maybe it is worth considering this "malfunction" as an opportunity to reflect on and change the structure through which the system operates. In many ways, the ruptures that a glitch generates open up a landscape of possibilities that could be followed from the more to the less predictable. Bringing in the notion of a glitch to talk about A Kassen is useful to explain how their work—from the art

6. Legacy Russell, *Glitch Feminism. A Manifesto* (New York: Verso, 2020).

7. Ibid.

8. Ibid., 17.

9. Ibid., 28.

10. Ibid.

11. Russell explains the concept thoroughly in the book at p. 18–37.

installations in public spaces, museums, art galleries, and festivals to their more conceptual artworks—could be understood as a gesture that undermines the construction of sense which is an aspect so embedded in the Western notion of "making art."

Once one begins to look at their interventions as ways to question the imposed role that Western society assigns to art, which is—among other things—to make sense of the chaotic neoliberal and consumerist lives we live by opening up perspectives on new ways of being, experiencing, and living, A Kassen's work makes more sense than ever. Rather than loudly questioning the system, their work subverts the meaning of this great construct on which the industry relies, also called "the art world."

p. 146–149

Under this light, art installations such as *Pigeon's Portal* (2008), a rectangular steel structure passing through the room of the upper floor exhibition space of Nikolaj Kunsthal, Copenhagen, make a different kind of sense. In its effort to not be useful, it defies the meaning-creation system of the art world. A Kassen has constructed other works through the same logic,

p. 46–53

for example, *Inverted Lamppost* (2016) at the Sorø Kunst-museum, where lampposts were installed inverted between two floors of the museum, presenting to the visitors entering the museum a steel post with a concrete block on top, as if the lampposts had just been unearthed from the nearby corner, and placed upside down into the museum. Suddenly, the lampposts were used to light the exhibition space instead of the public space. But isn't the art museum also a public space?

There are numerous examples in which A Kassen's work has shown its opacity and porosity to subvert the "transparency" of reality ironically. In 2017, the group was invited by CC – Copenhagen Contemporary to participate in a group show in one of the large halls of the institution. The story goes that while the artists were discussing possible solutions and ideas for the show, someone from the collective spilled a splash of coffee onto the floor plan of CC's exhibition hall, sparking the idea of converting those coffee stains into an artwork. The result of that process was that A Kassen realized large-scale ponds of coffee displayed in the exhibition halls of CC.

p. 134–137

Another public art installation, *Swap* (2016/17), challenges the art world's desire to unpack the opacity of an artwork. First realized as a temporary installation in 2016 for the Danish music and art festival called *Heartland*, an event that takes place every summer in the park of the Danish Castle of Egeskov, the work was re-proposed again in 2017 in Lund, Sweden, as a permanent work for the Spyken High School. *Swap* is an artwork that consists of swapping existing patterns or portions of an area of the city into another area. In the case of *Heartland*, a circular area from the 300 years old garden of the Egeskov Castle was exchanged with a circular area in the nearby city of Odense. In the case of Spyken High School, instead, two outdoor circular areas of paving stones, respectively from the new and the old part of the high school, were cut out and exchanged.

Since Western society condemns error and malfunction as a threat to the system that creates normative ways of living and understanding the world, propositions that rethink this approach, such as A Kassen's, are to be treated not just as an artwork but as a strategy to challenge established systems of thinking. The work of A Kassen creates a "glitch," a temporary interruption that could be understood as a malfunction in a social and economic system like the global art world, which has already been disturbed by its orchestrated desire to exist in society to create a sense of the nonsense neoliberal capitalistic structures oriented to money and exploitation of resources of all kinds. The glitch that their work creates is a correction to the "machine" and, maybe, the start of a new beginning. People who have experienced or will experience their work might question whether their work makes sense of its existence. Still, A Kassen's practice disrupts the Western art world and market, even following its logic.

Some might question the purpose of converting coffee stains on a piece of paper into an art installation or swapping urban elements of a city from one area into another one. My response would be that there is no reason, just as there is no reason not to do just that. The presence of a glitch that interrupts and prevents a system from functioning is just another way the system could function.

In the film *The Matrix*, when Neo manages to overrule the normative ways in which the reality created by the matrix functions, he realizes that what in the matrix was identified as an error, a mistake, a malfunction was instead an opportunity for change itself. Maybe there is no error, no malfunction, and mistake, and we need to use our imagination to accept the absurd and nonsense presences in our daily lives. An error does not exist as a problem, but, as the etymology of the word addresses, it exists as a deviation (from the Latin *errare*— to wander) from the accustomed path. There is no error, and maybe, there is no need to make sense of everything. "There is no spoon" is the iconic sentence uttered by Neo in *The Matrix* when he understands the potential of the glitch. There is no barrier to impede our imagination in its plight to change the system we live in.

Inverted Lamppost

Five lampposts are installed upside down and go through the floor. The lamp heads are visible from the museum's basement, while the foundations stick out in the ground floor and the outdoor space.

Sorø Kunstmuseum, Sorø, Denmark, 2016

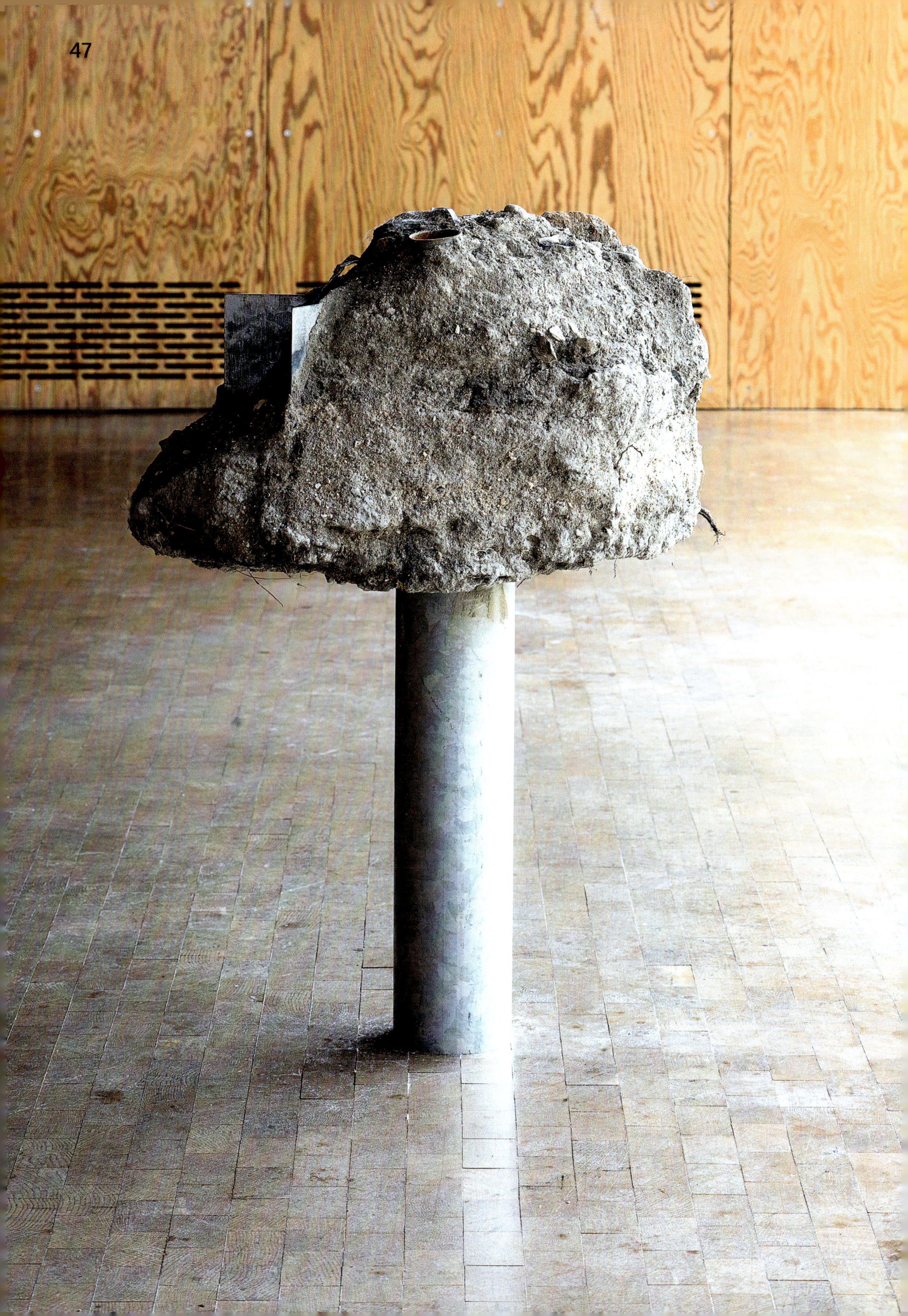

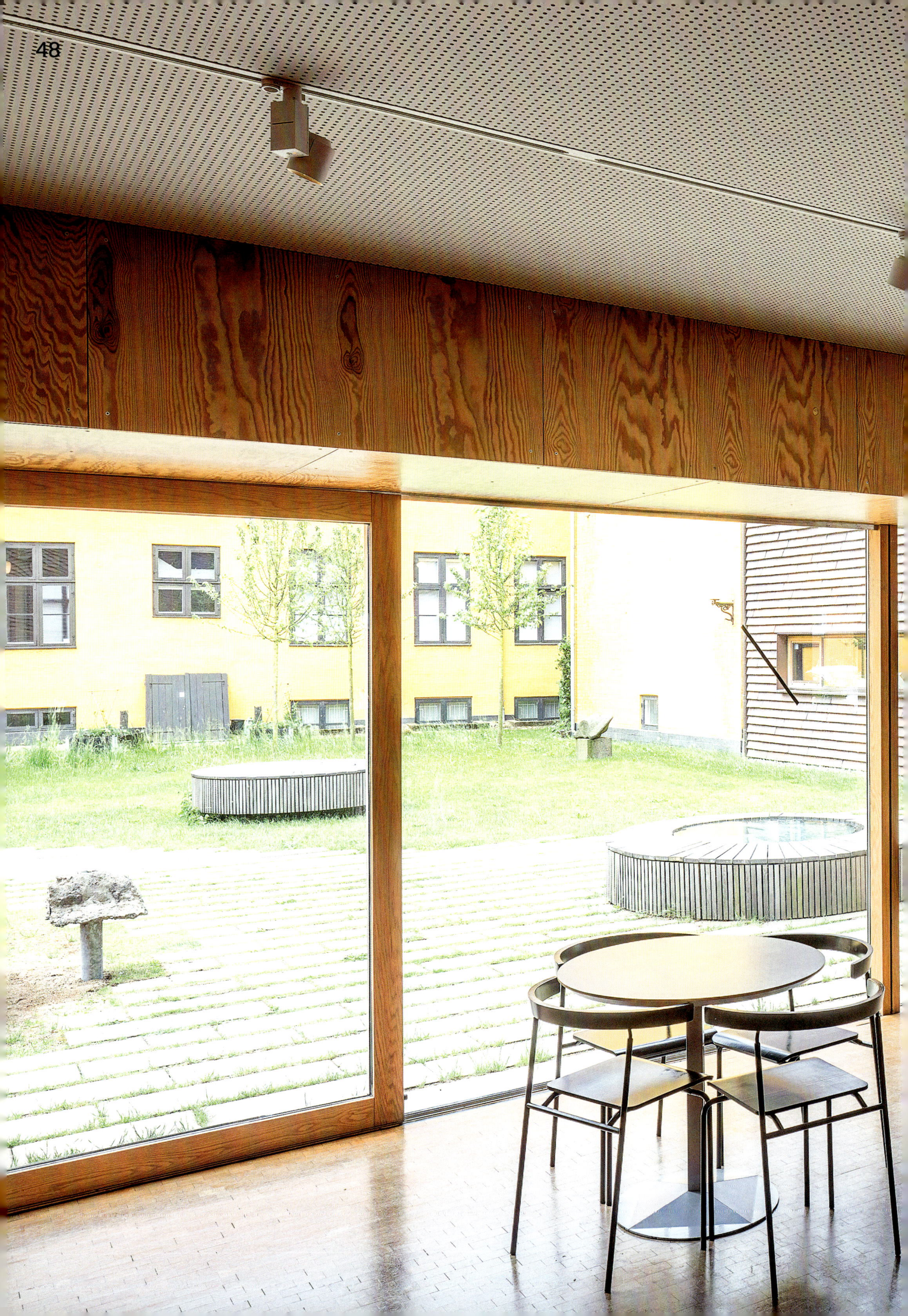

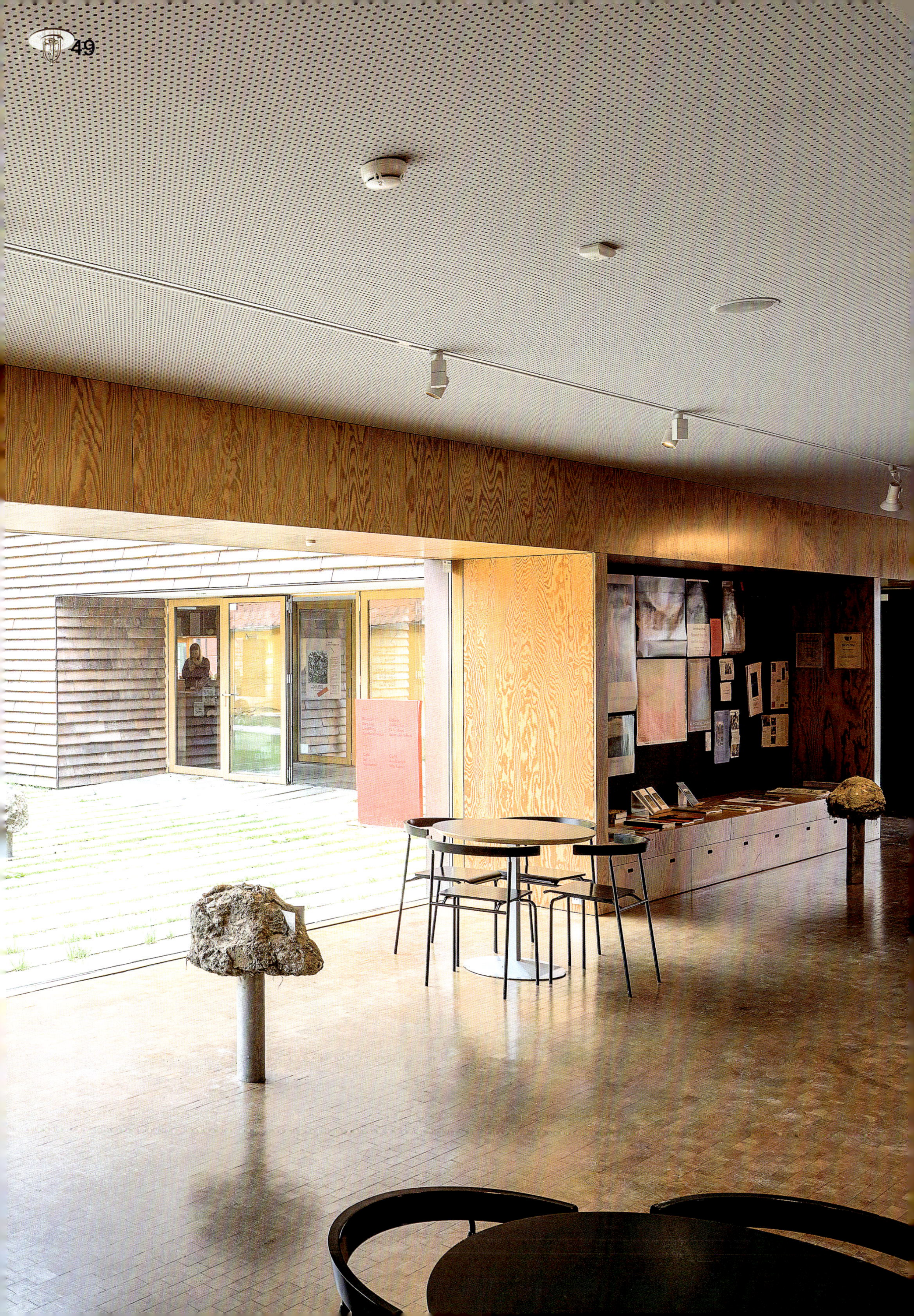

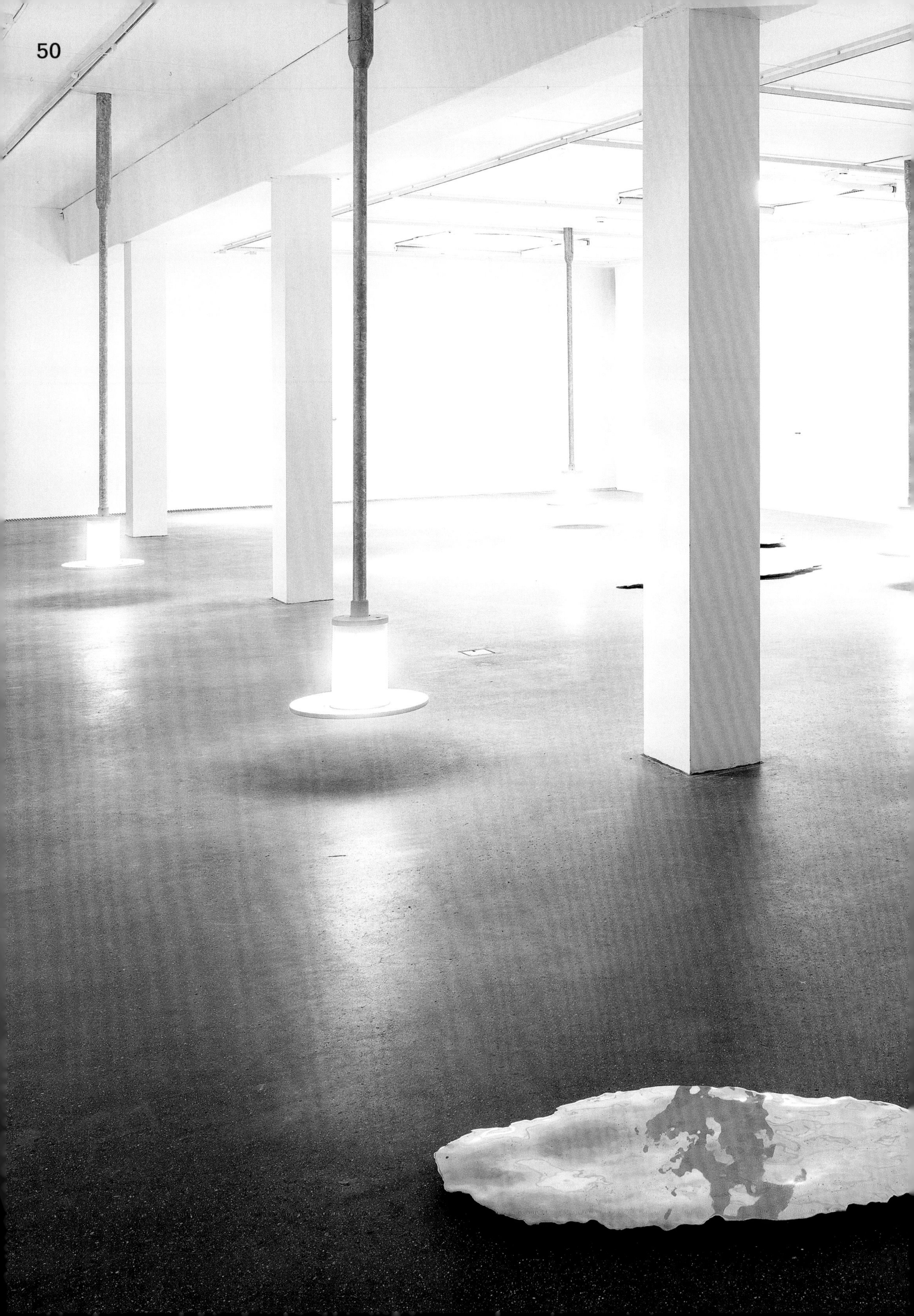

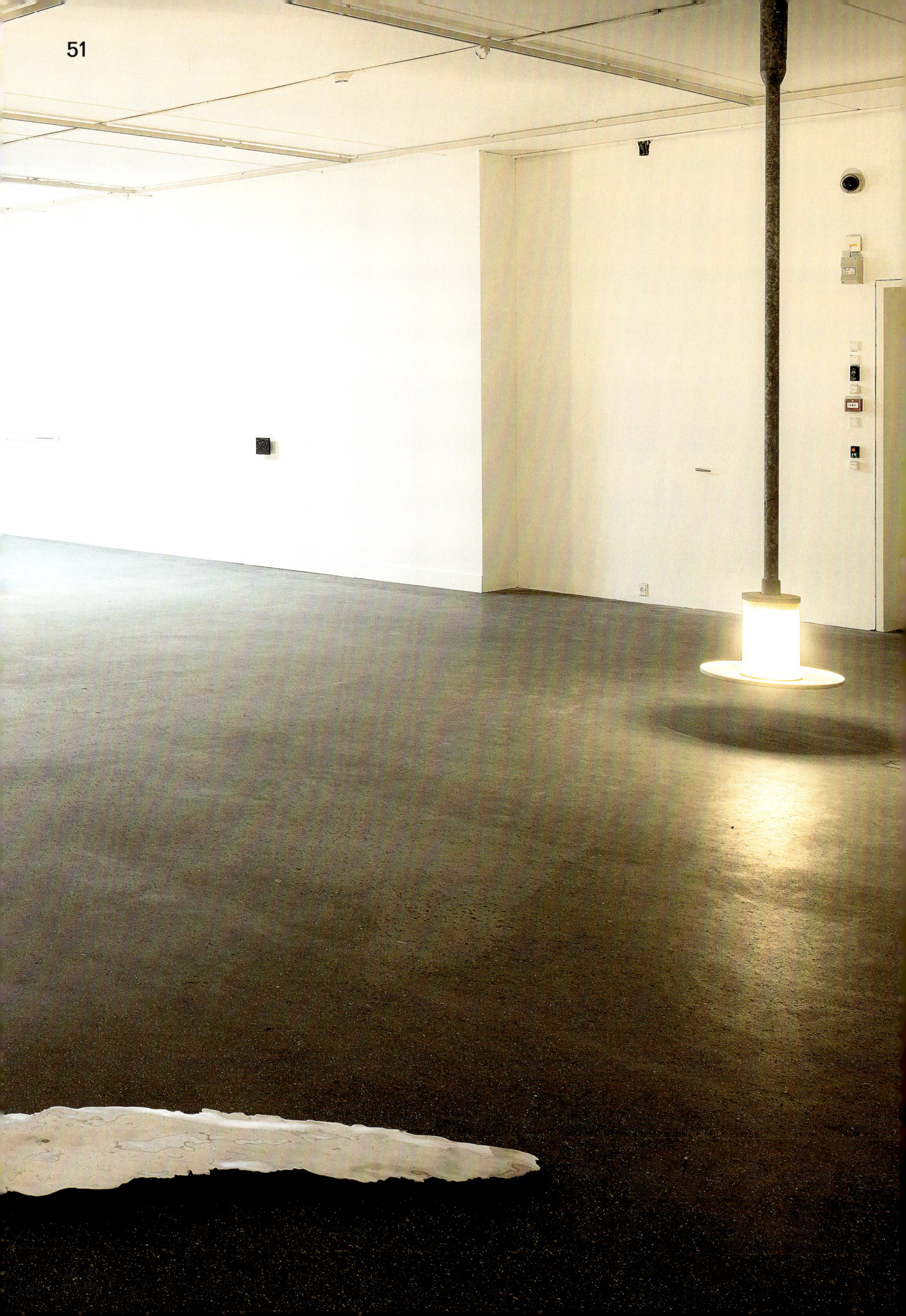

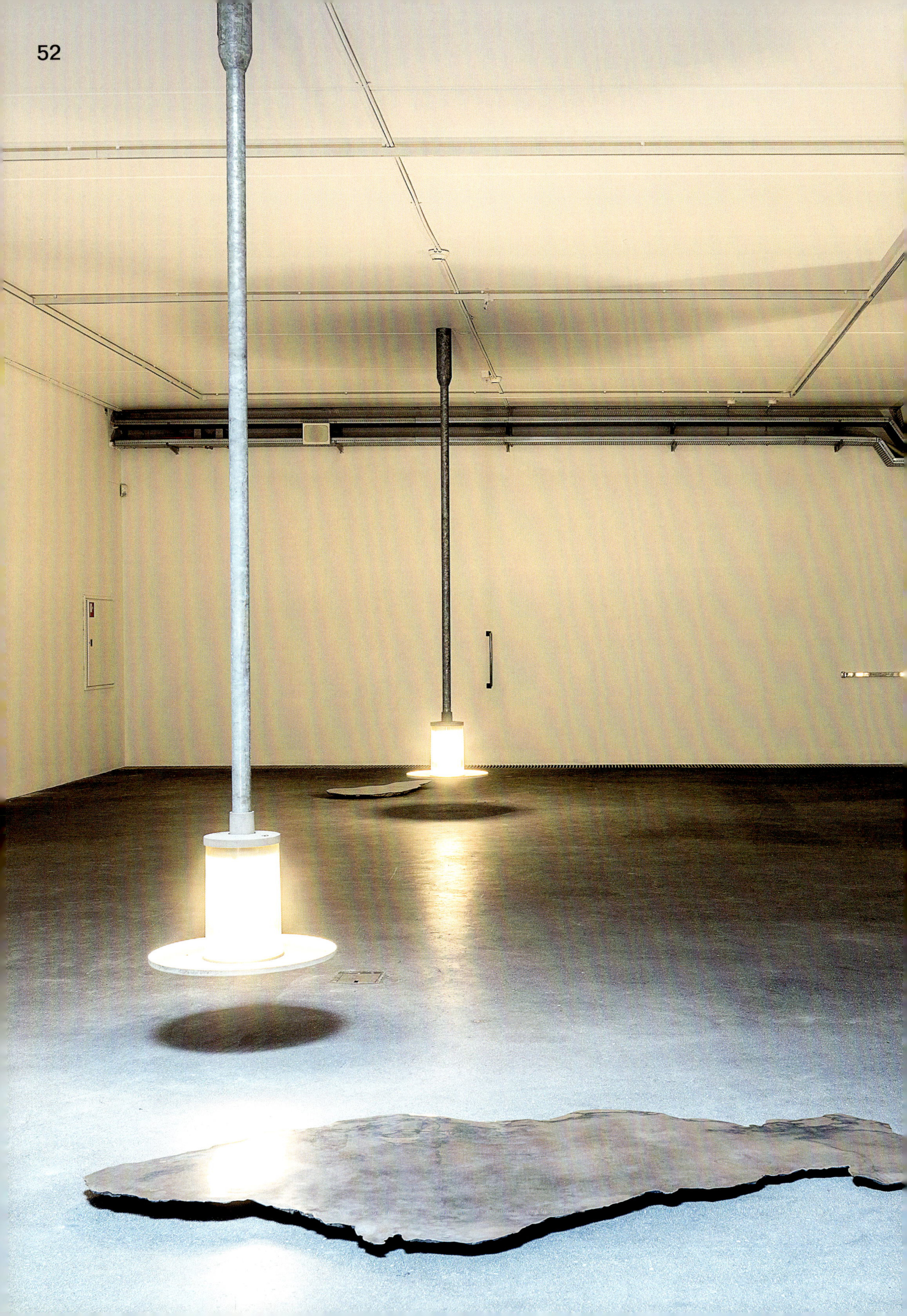

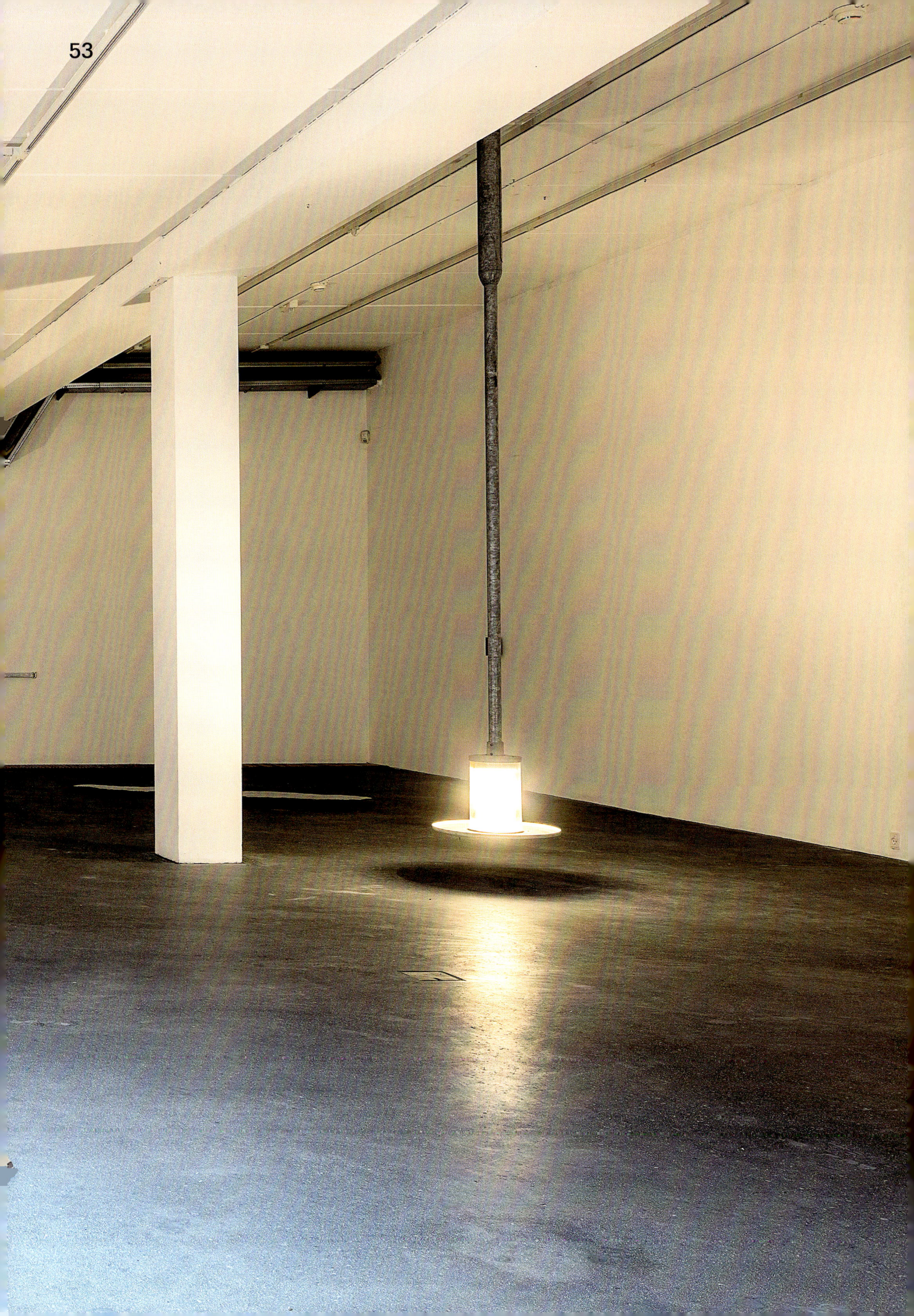

Puddle

A plaster mold of a puddle is made and reproduced in aluminium.

Galleri Nicolai Wallner, Copenhagen, Denmark, 2015

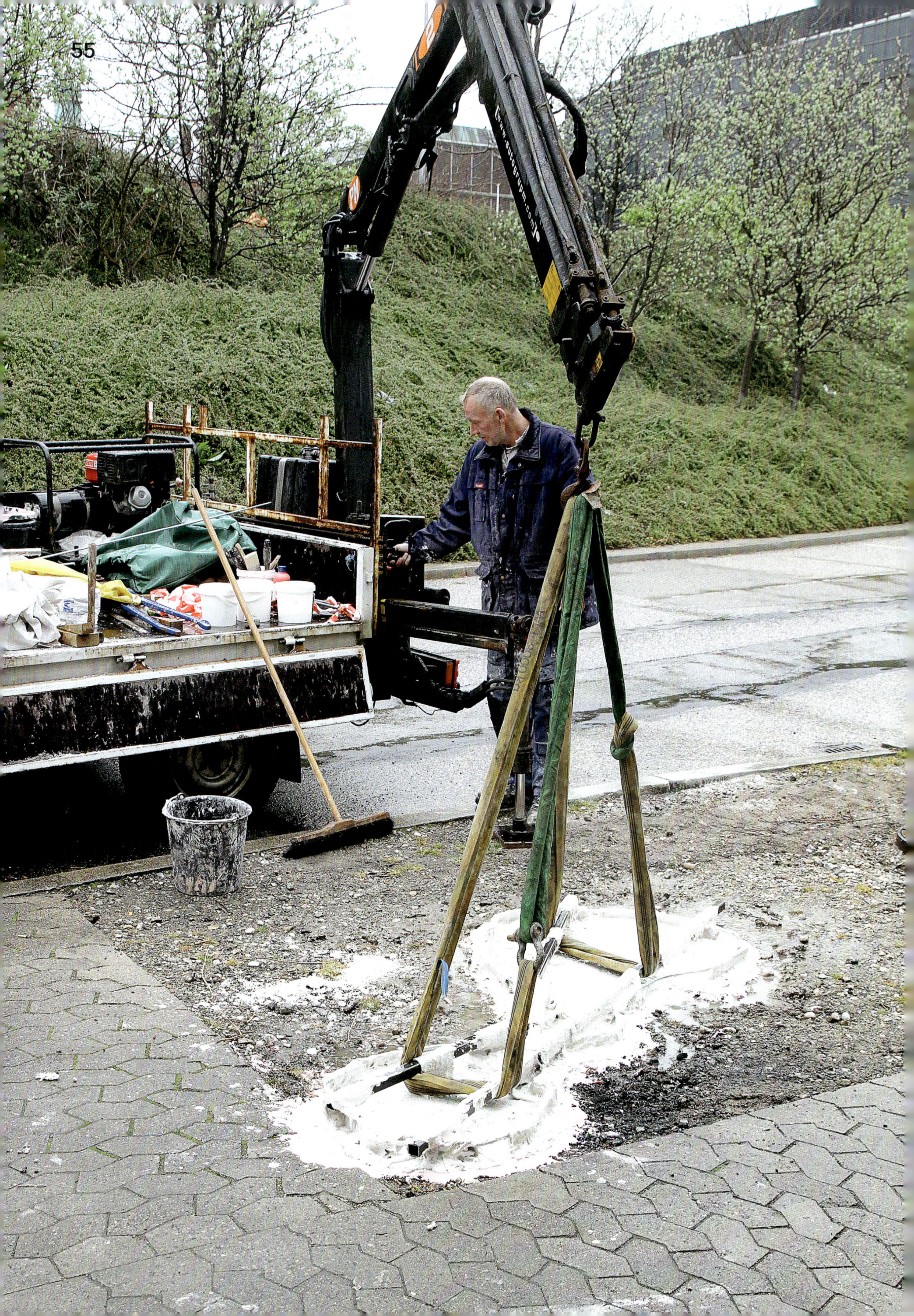

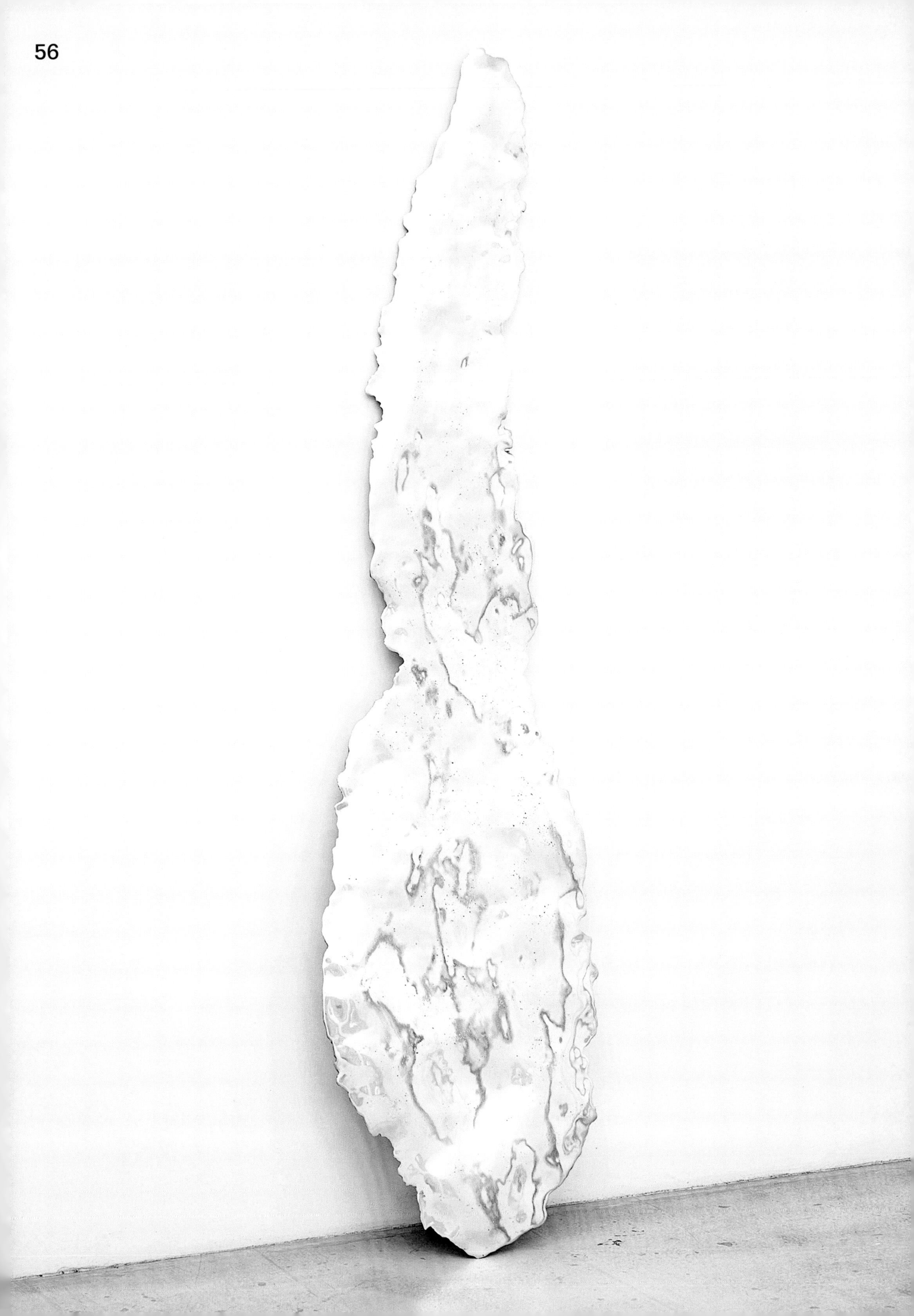

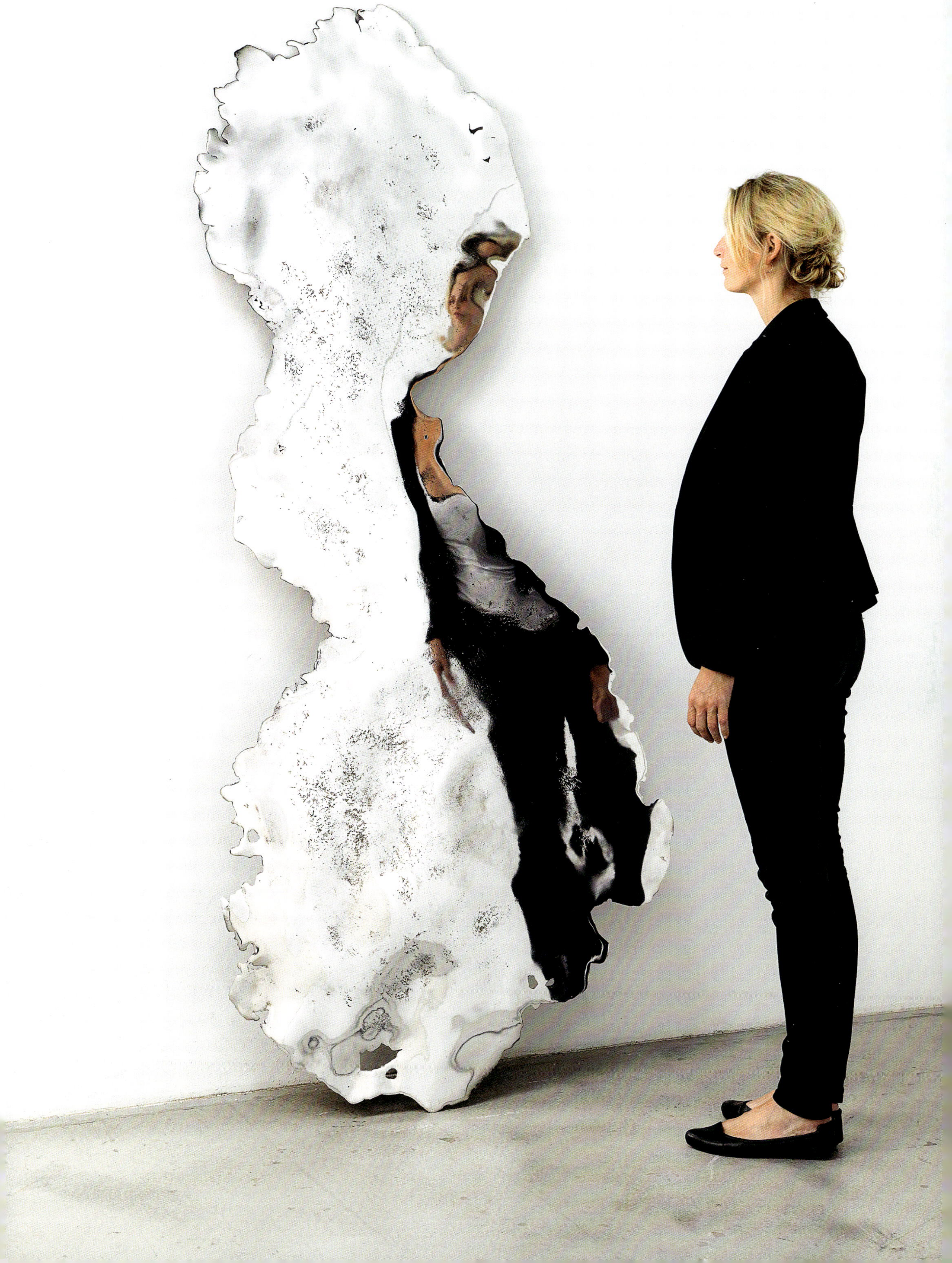

Handles

Door handles are borrowed from the local area and mounted on the walls of the exhibition space.

Sorø Kunstmuseum, Sorø, Denmark, 2016

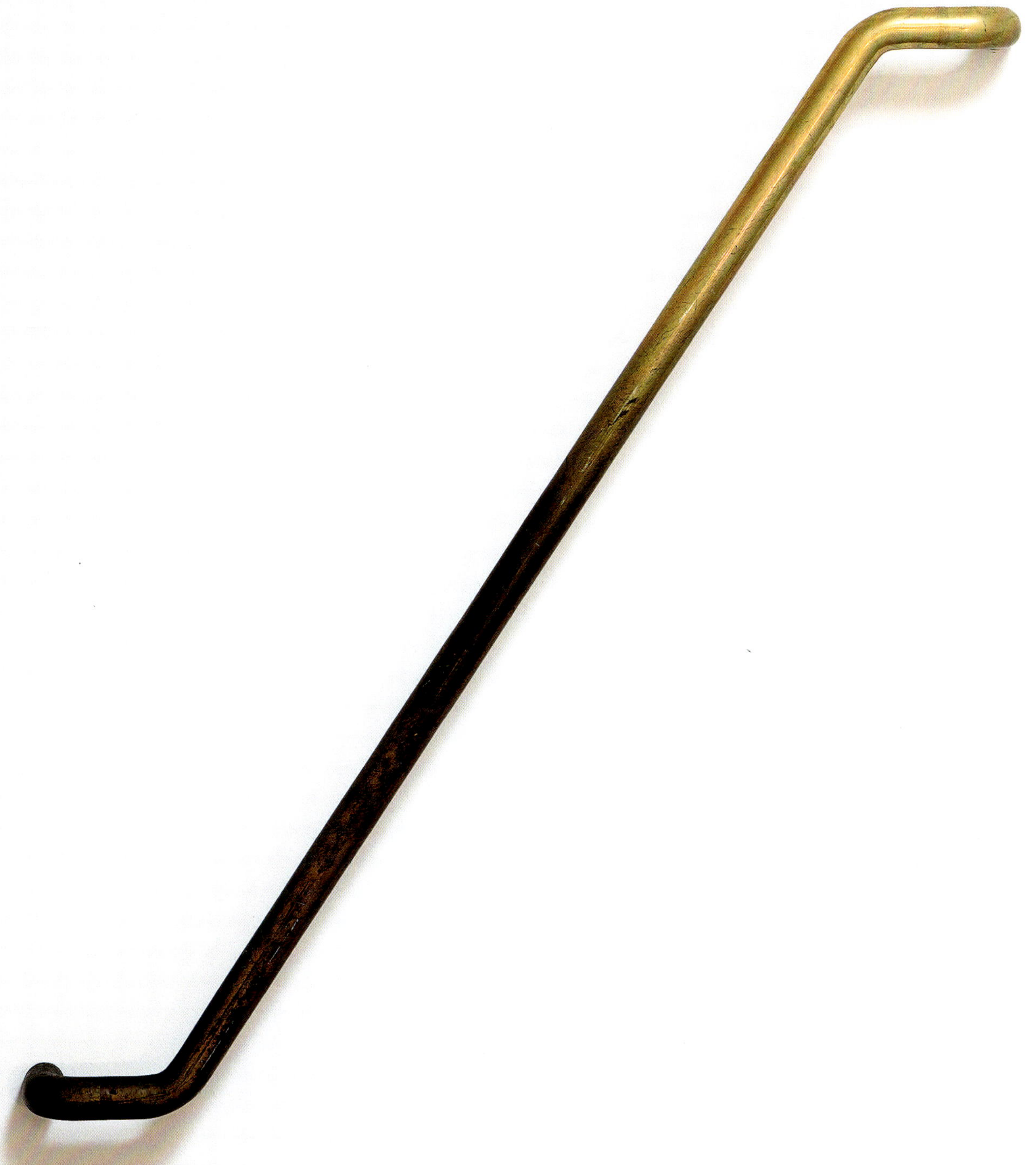

Encirclement

A photograph is framed using materials from the photograph itself.

Maisterravalbuena Gallery, Madrid, Spain, 2012

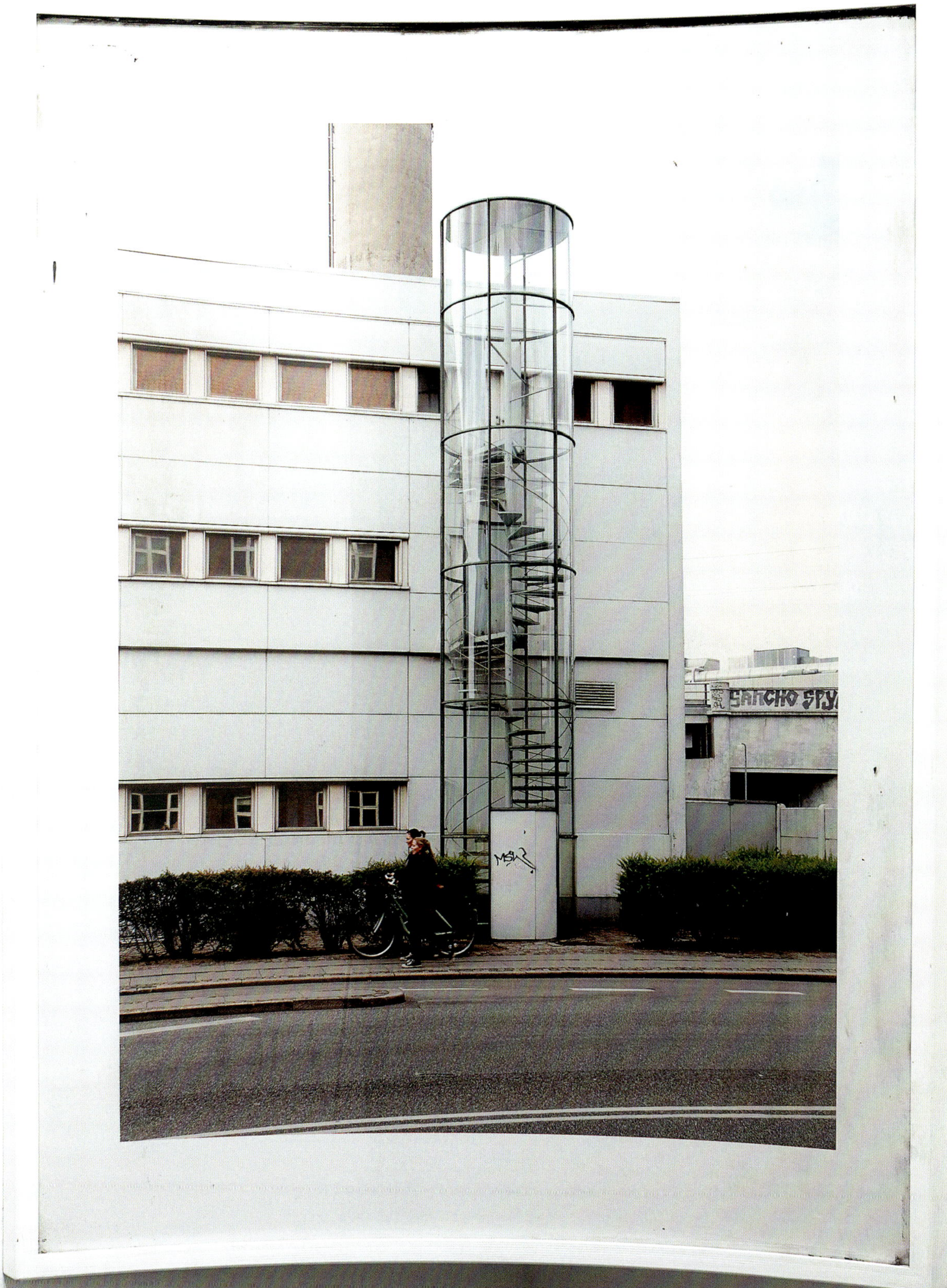

Atlas

A statue of Atlas is cut up into units corresponding with the dimensions of cobblestones.

Fondation CAB, Brussels, Belgium, 2016

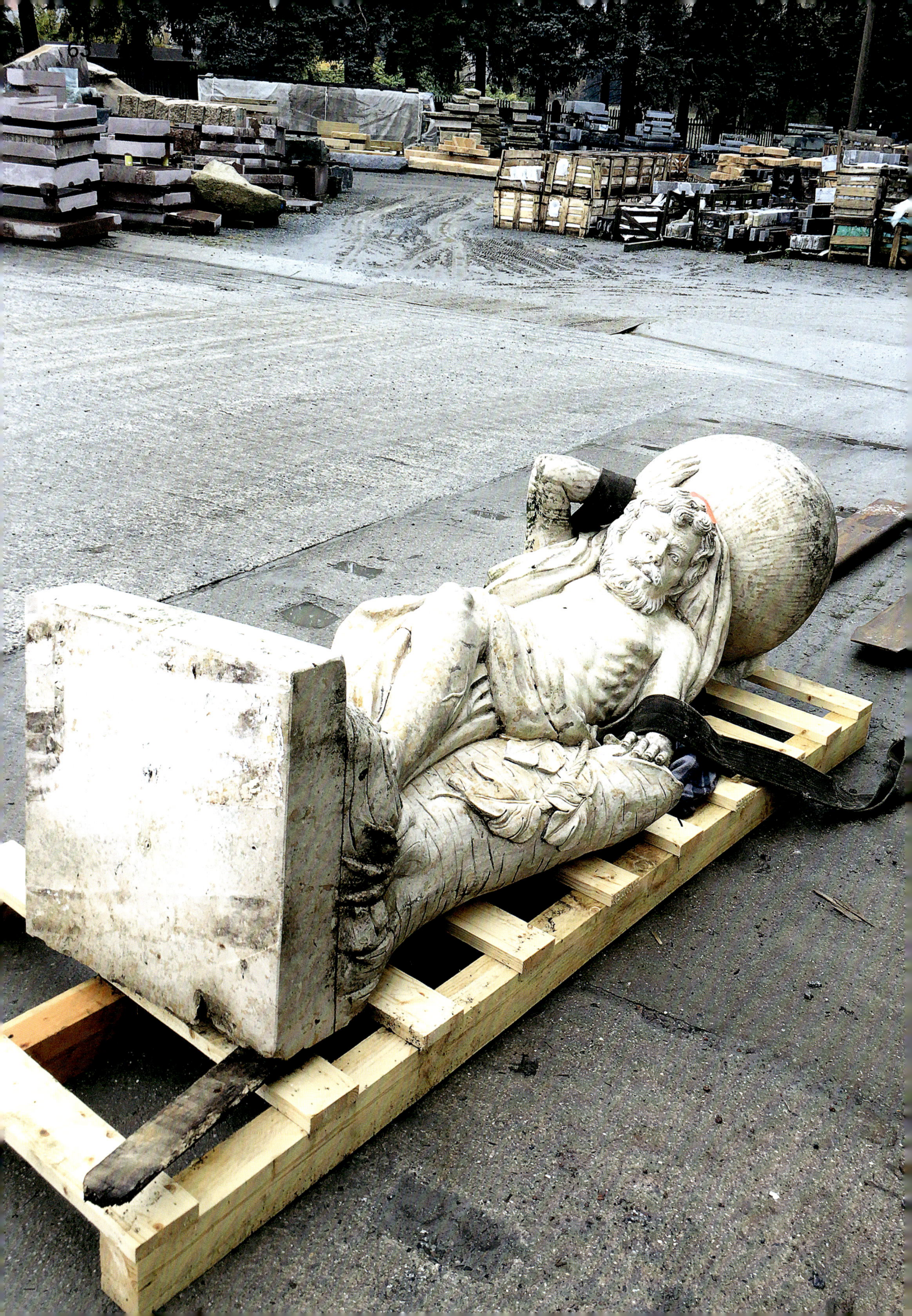

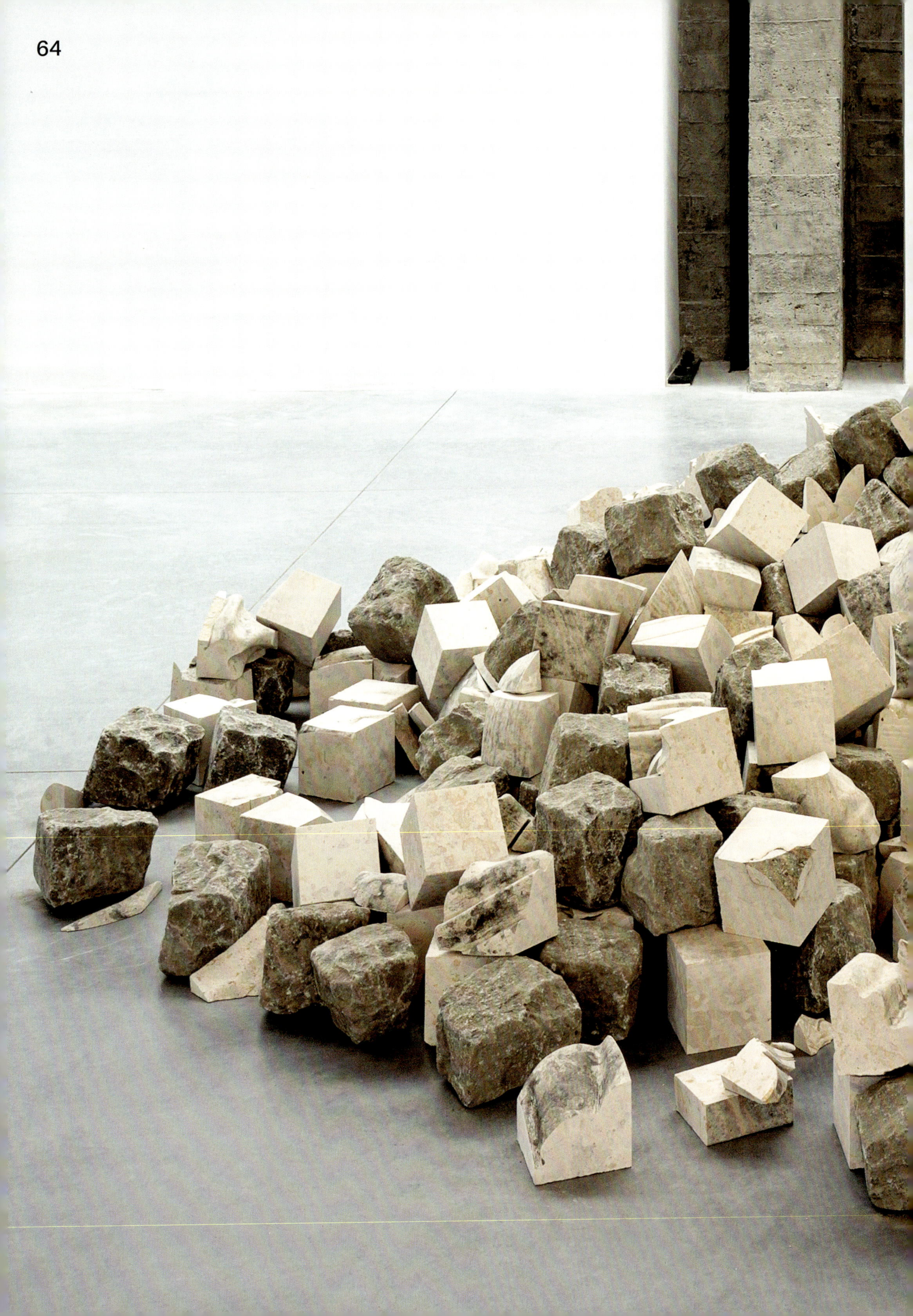

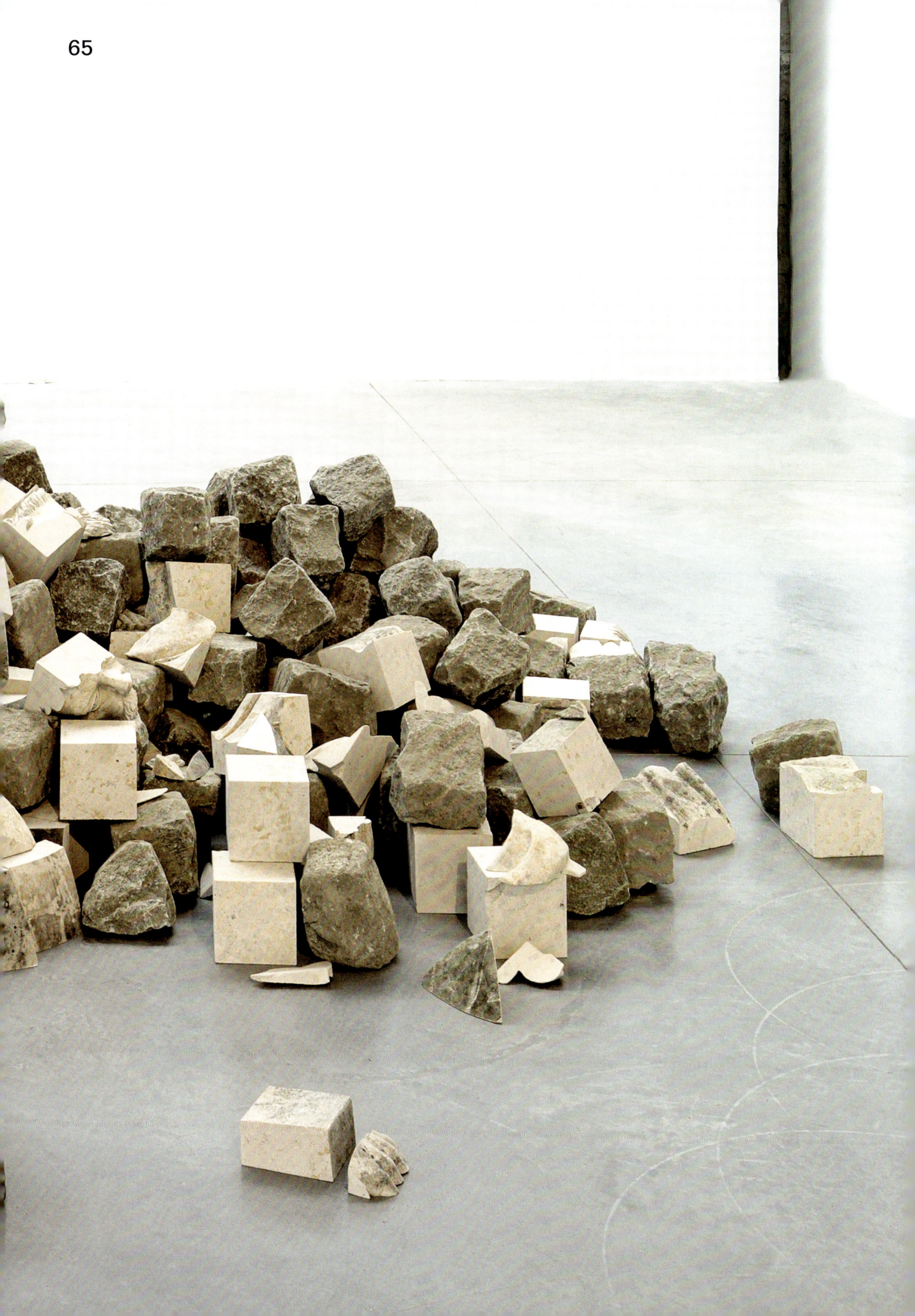

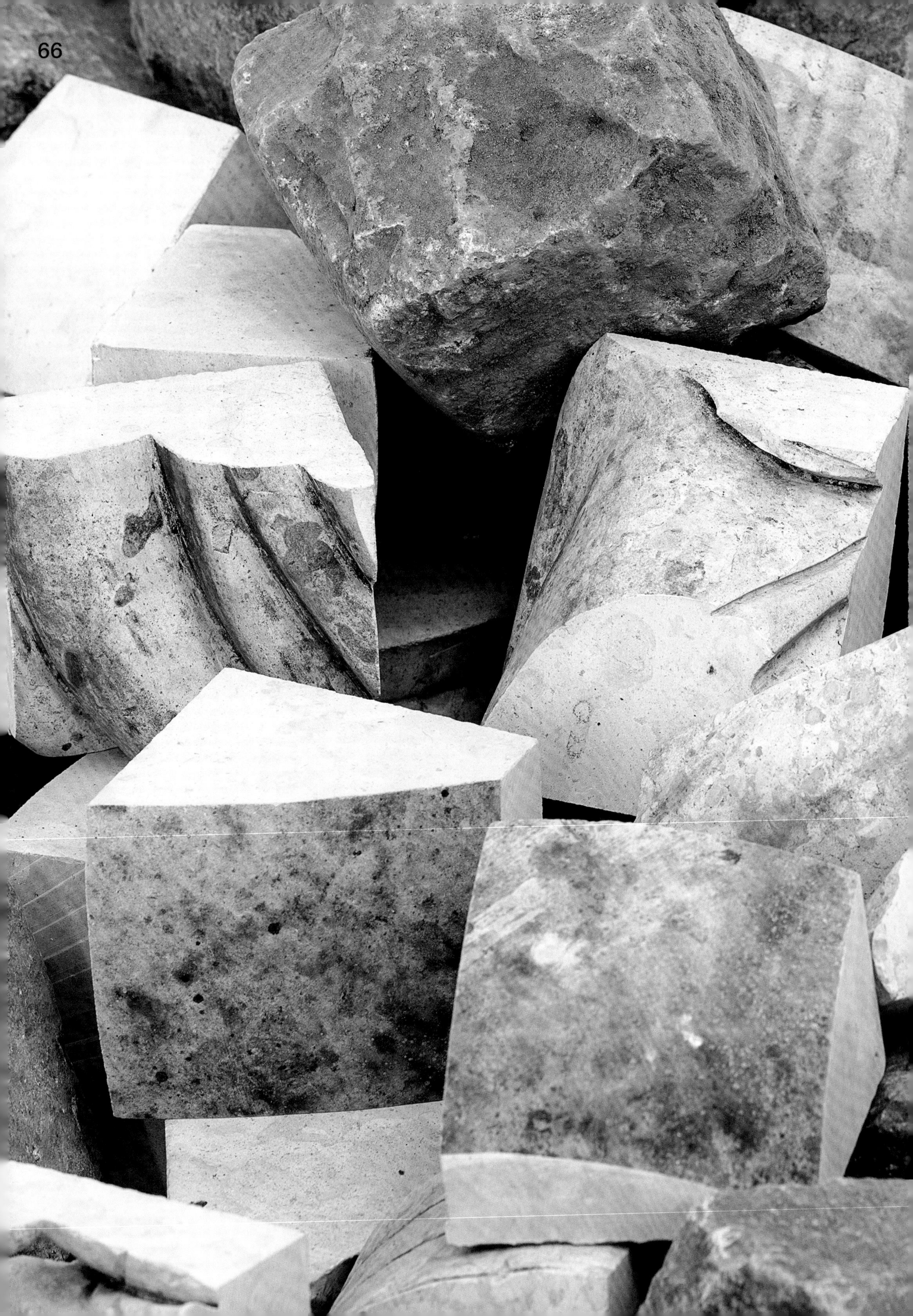

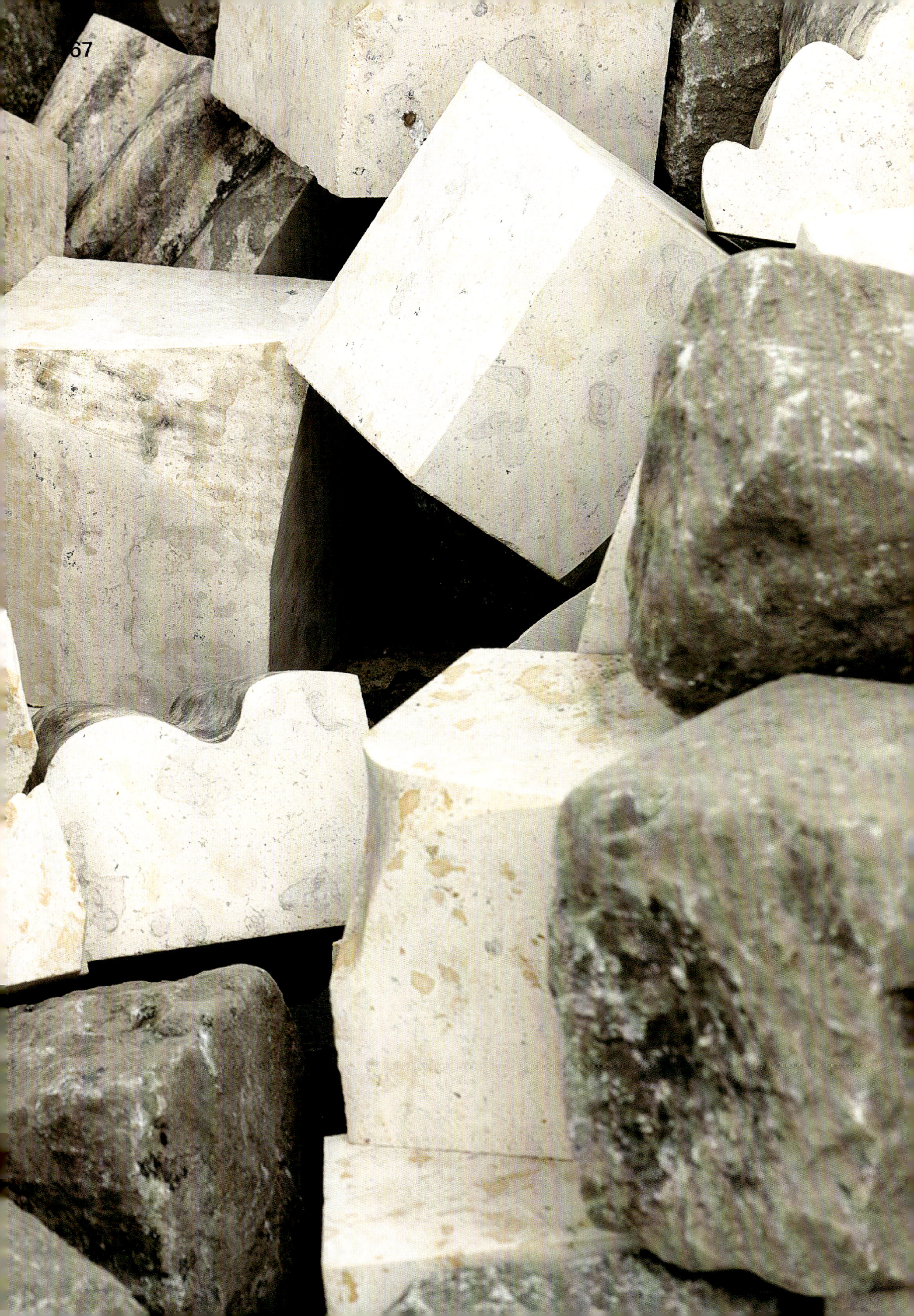

Drawer

A drawer is installed in the gallery wall allowing the audience to look into the gallery storage room.

Galleri Nicolai Wallner, Copenhagen, Denmark, 2006

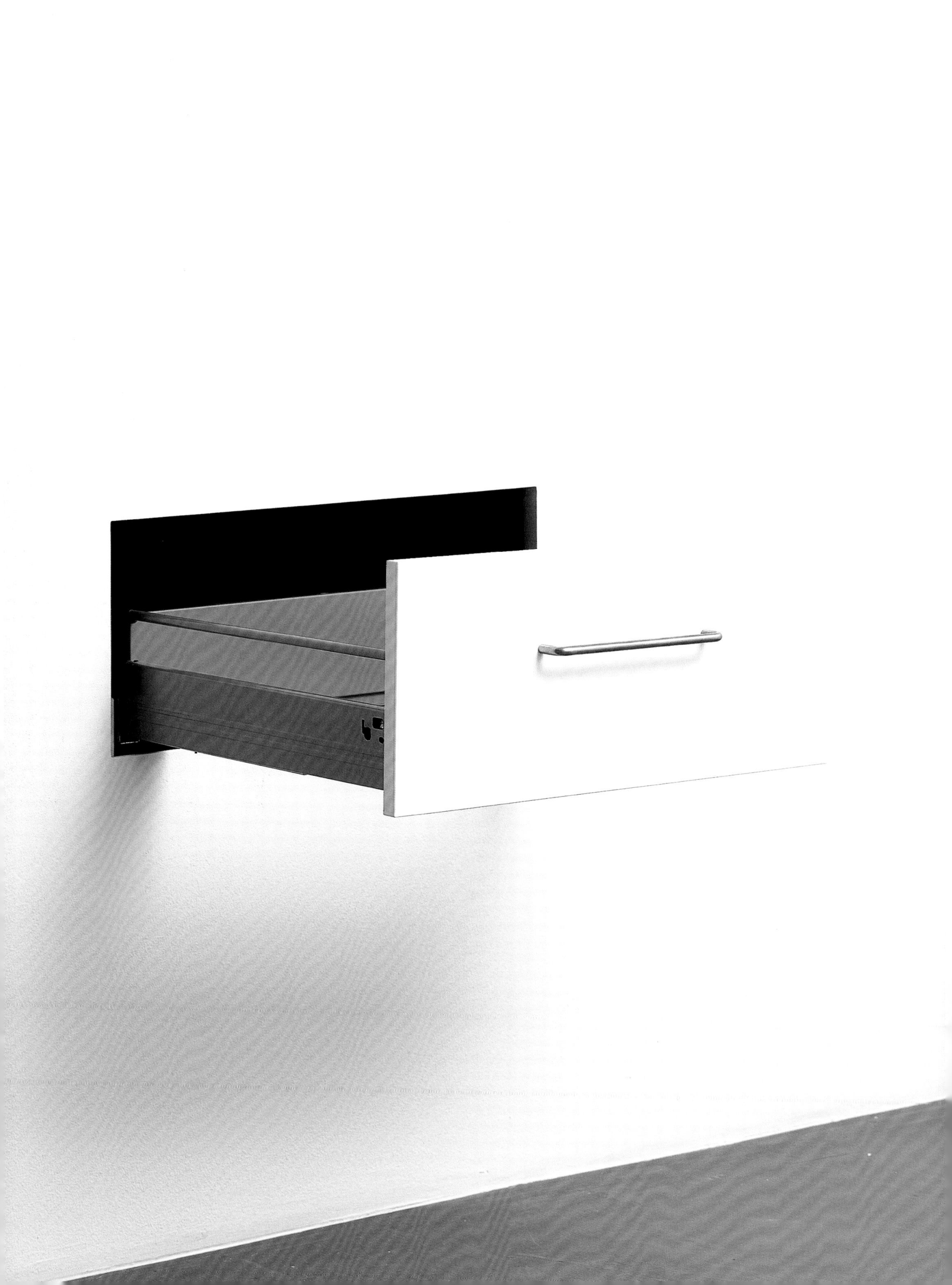

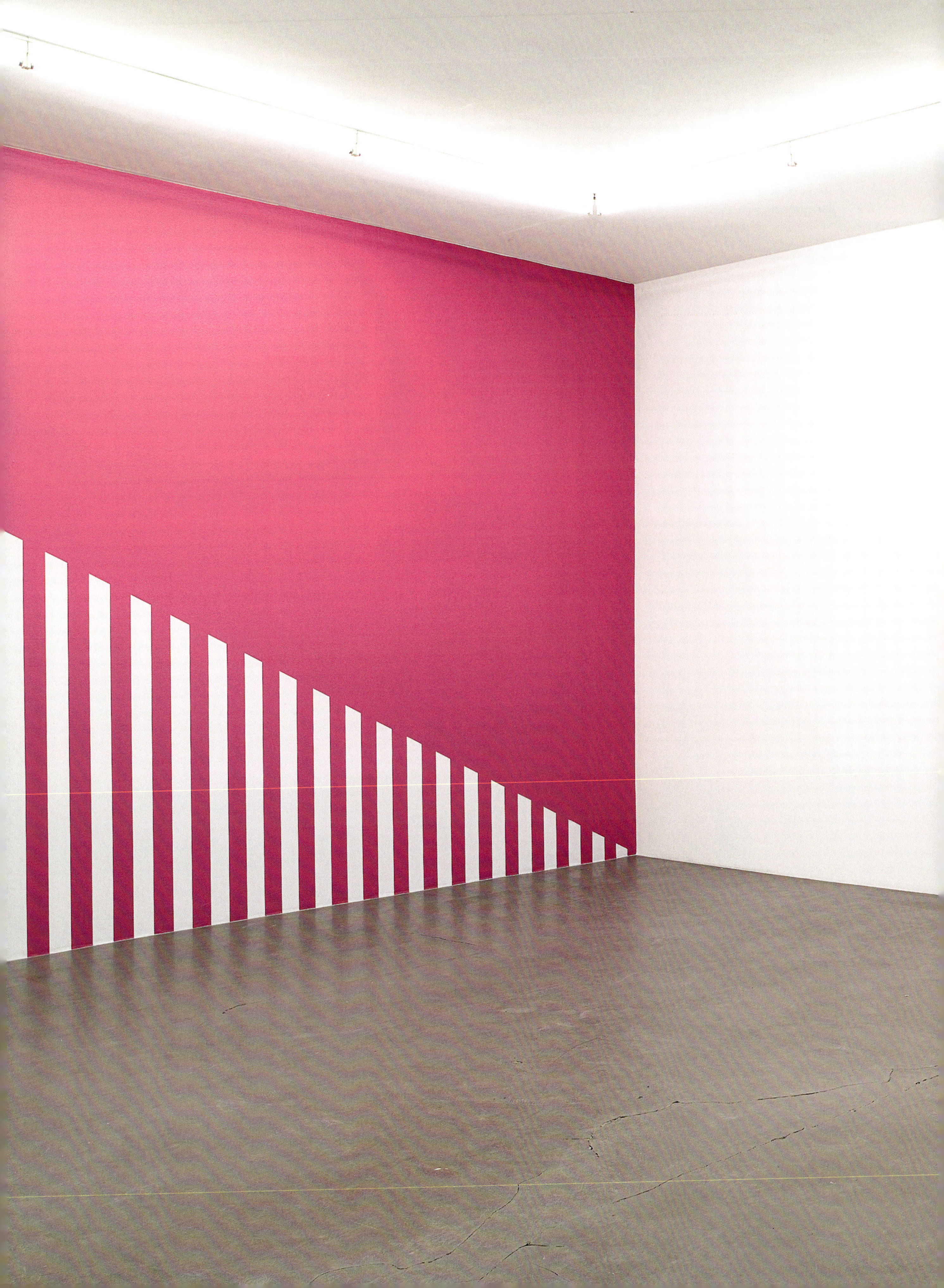

Drip

White wine drips from the ceiling of the gallery. A stand-in with a wine glass catches the drops.

Galleri Nicolai Wallner, Copenhagen, Denmark, 2006

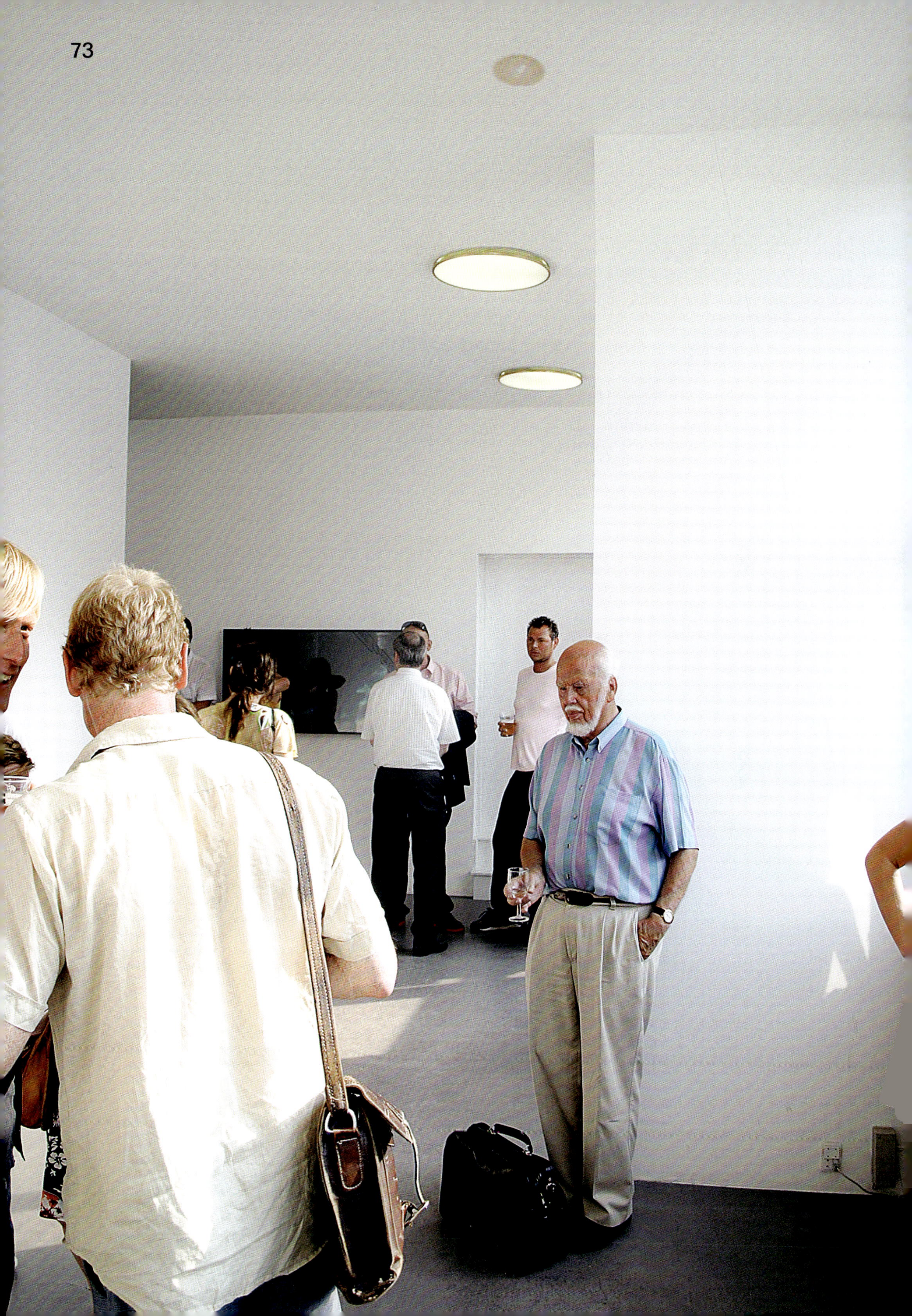

Mirror

Scans of antique mirrors up for auction are taken from Sotheby's catalogue, printed at actual size, framed, and auctioned again at Sotheby's.

New Galerie, New York, US, 2012

75

437

A KASSEN

Est. 2004

Mirror #4

signed on a label affixed to the reverse
digital c-print on Dibond
75 by 45 in. 190 by 114 cm.
Executed in 2013.

PROVENANCE

New Galerie, New York

$ 4,000-6,000

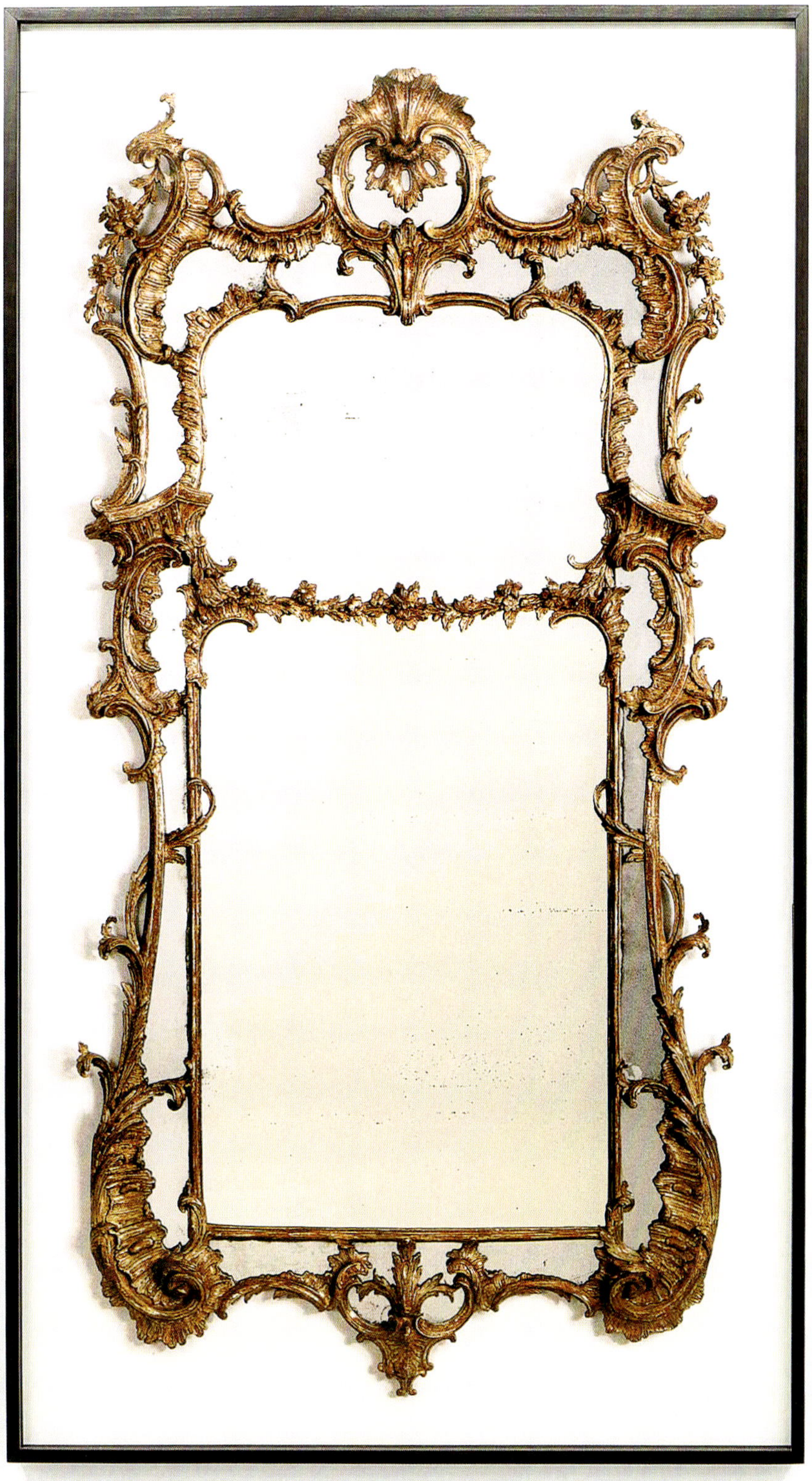

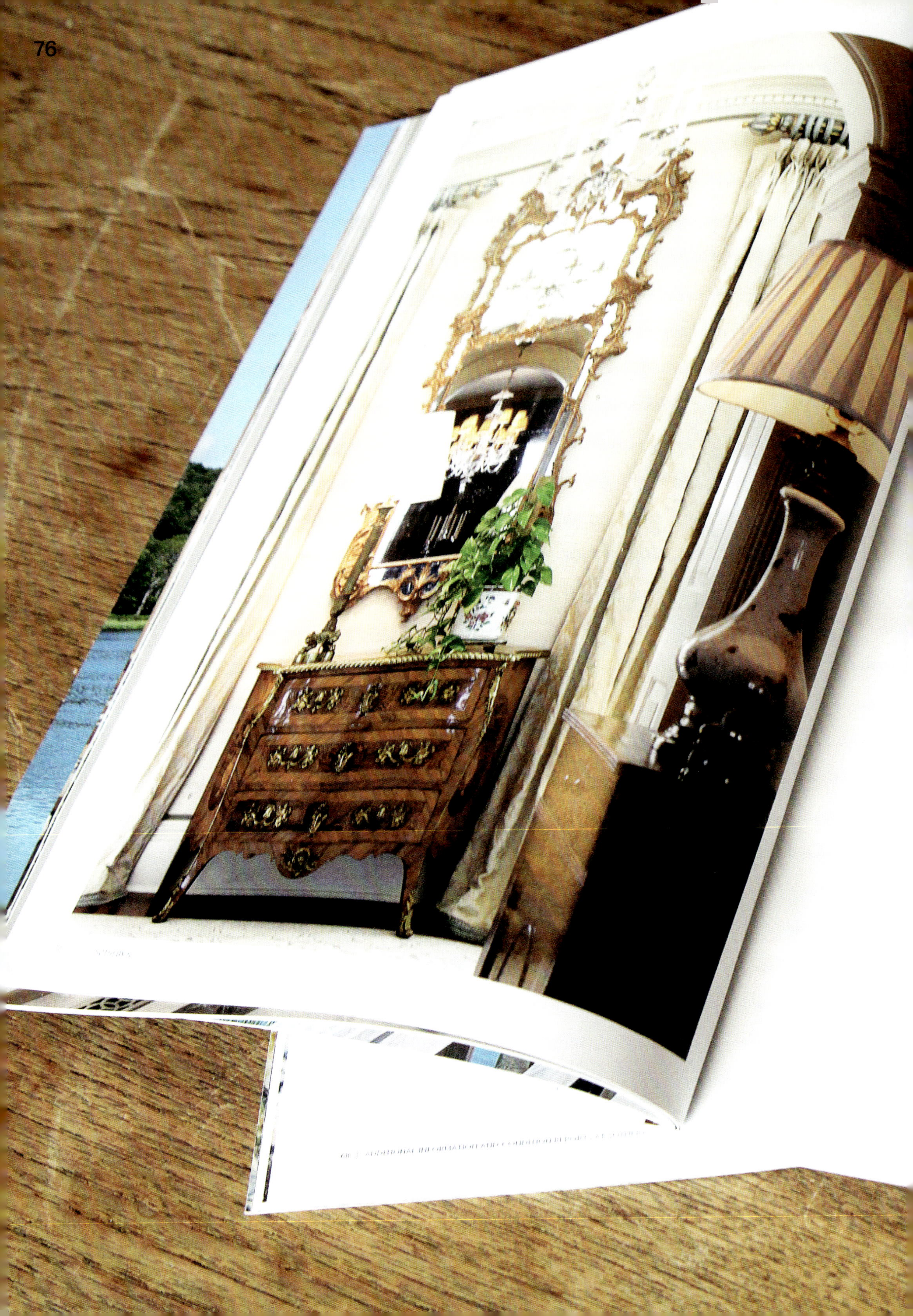

8

A fine George III giltwood pier mirror
circa 1760

PROVENANCE

Apter Fredericks, London, 2001

$ 40,000 60,000

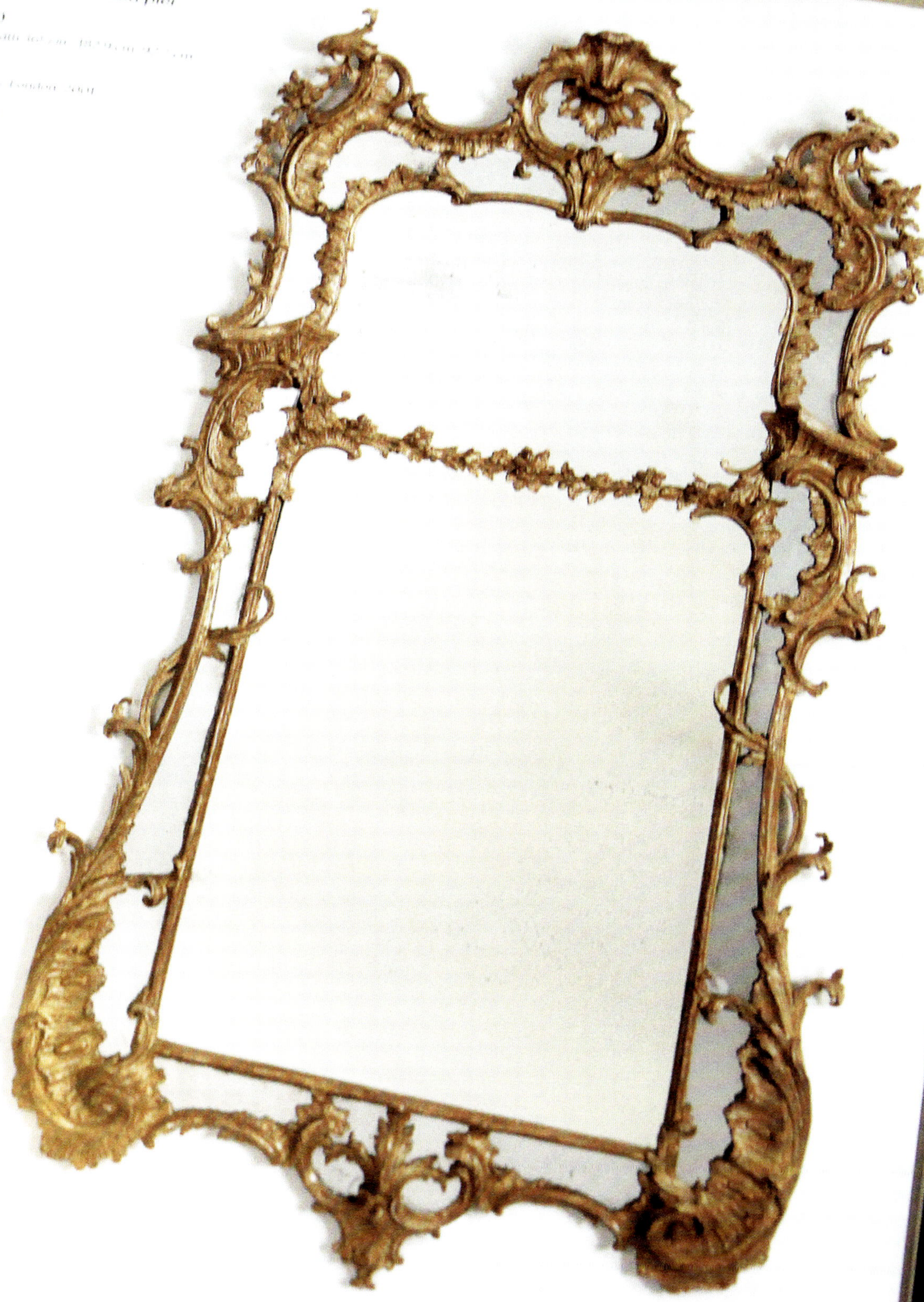

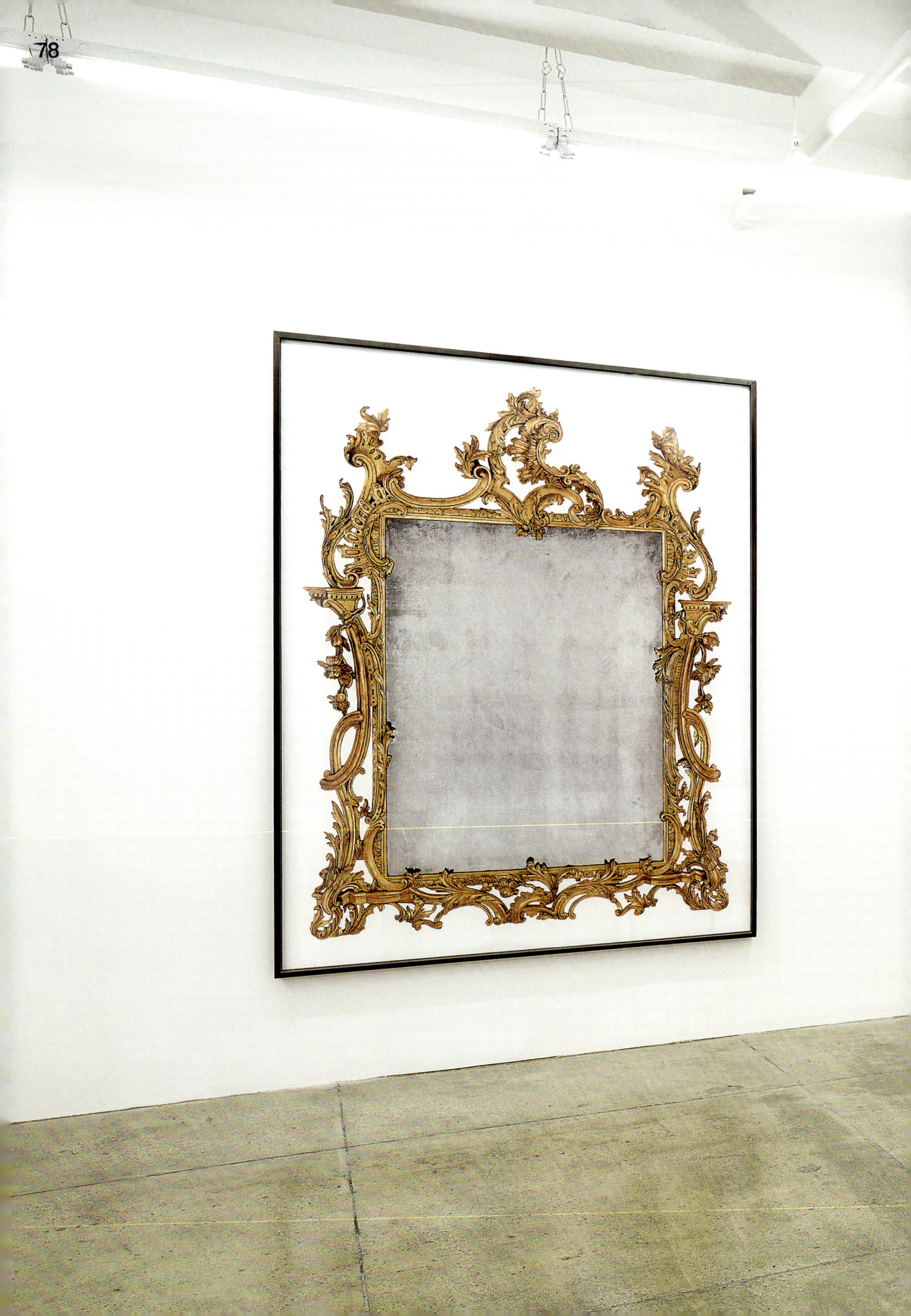

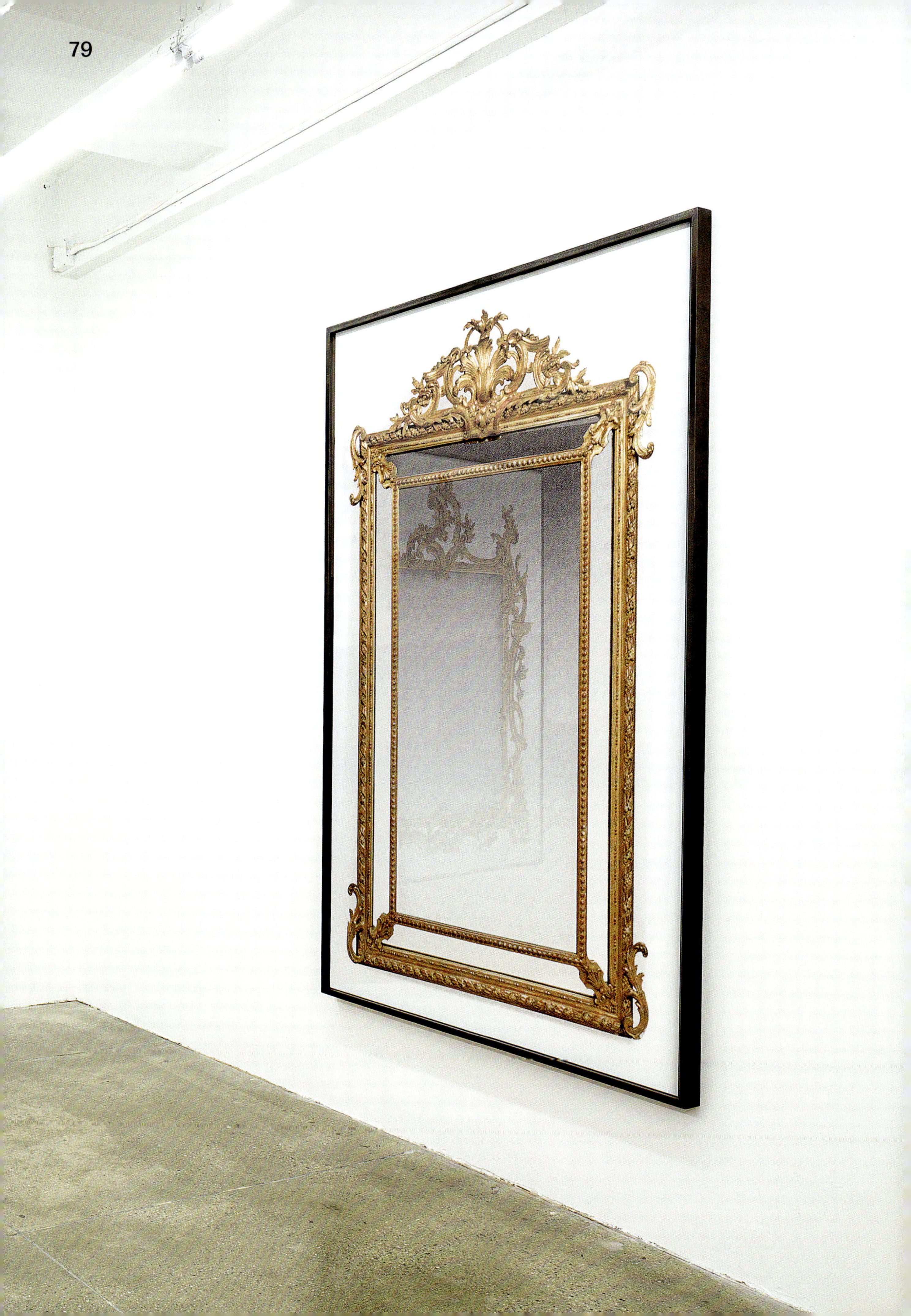

Necklace

Over time, stones have been thrown to vandalize the gallery windows. The stones are collected from the canal below the windows and made into necklaces worn by the gallery staff.

Nettie Horn Gallery, London, UK, 2012

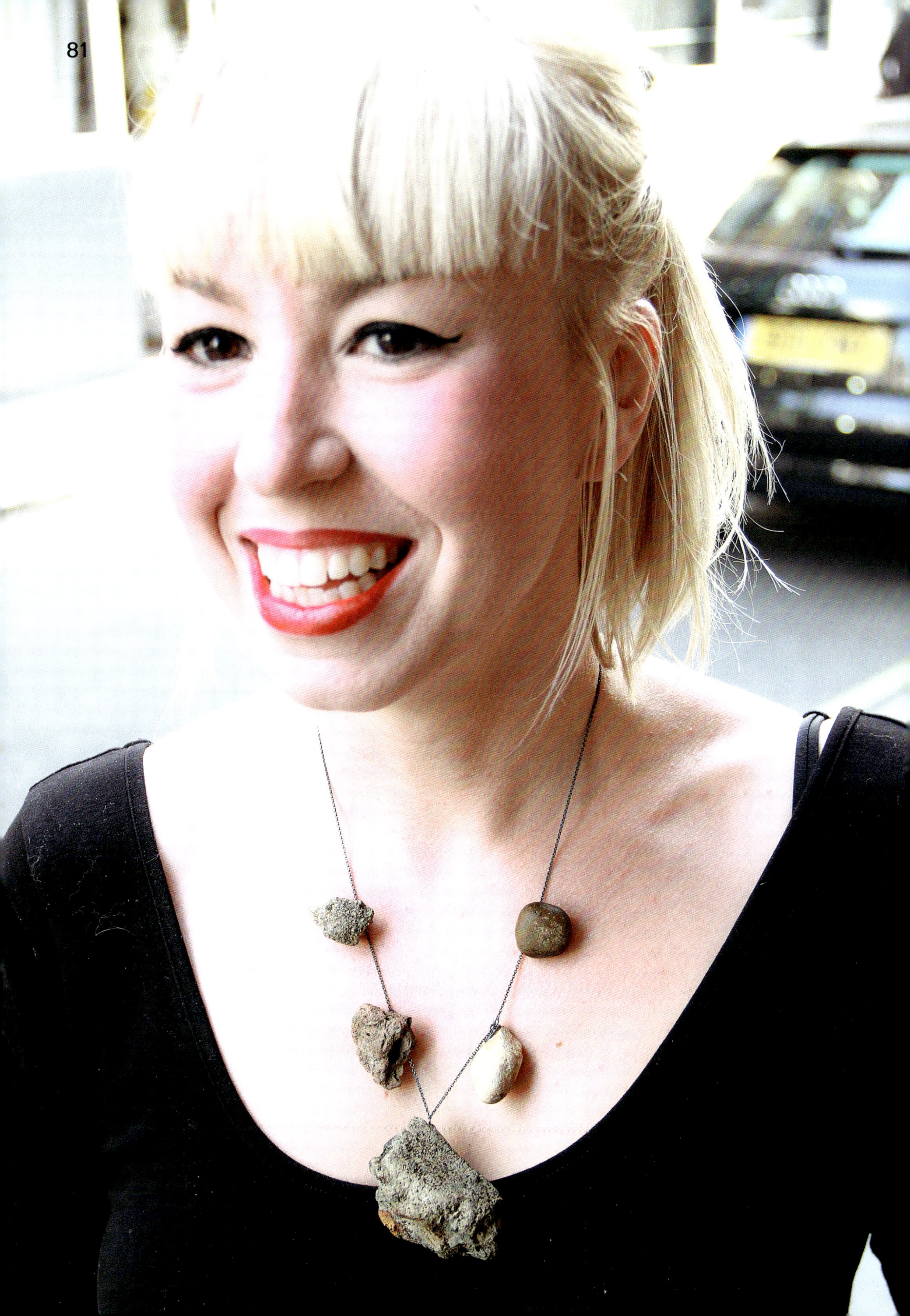

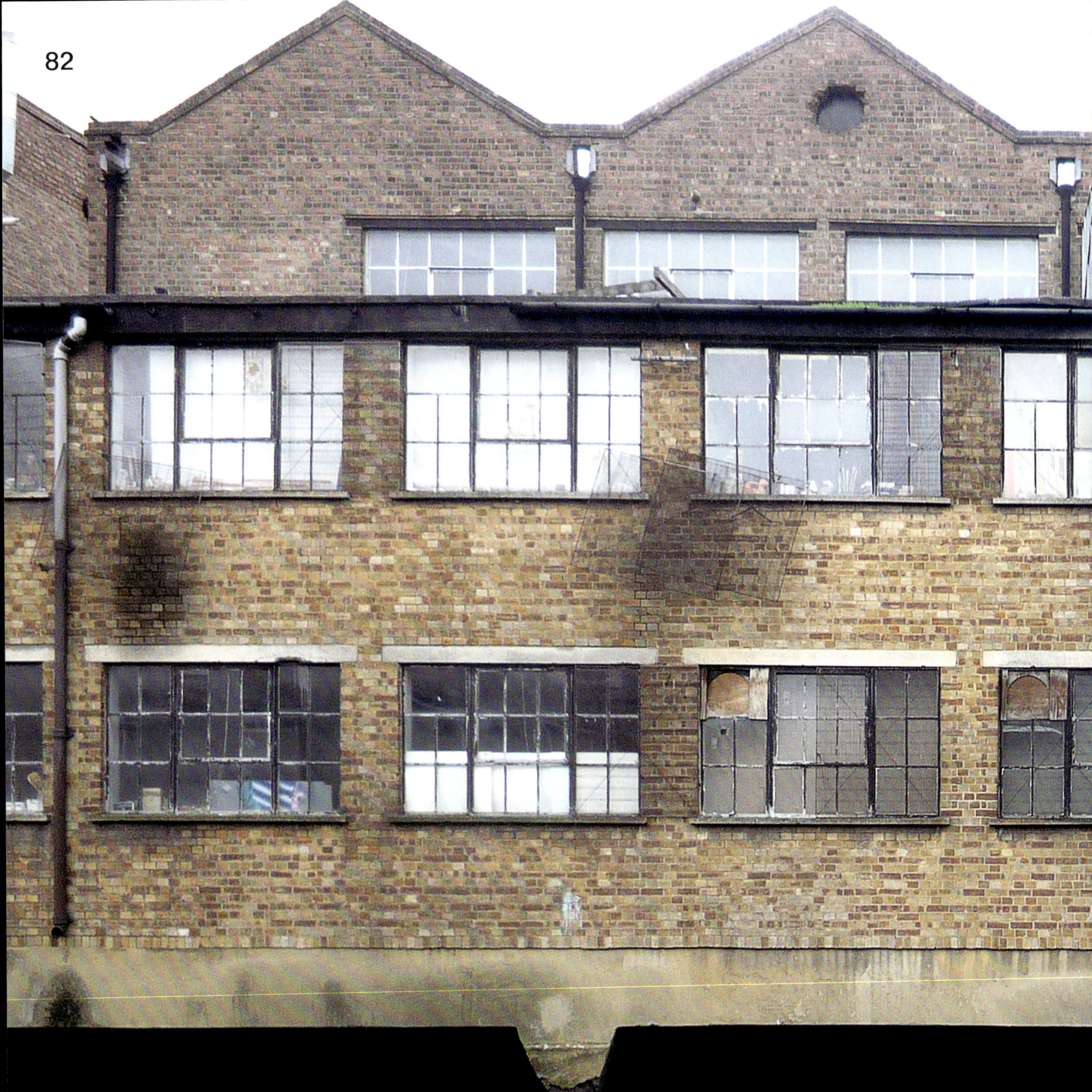

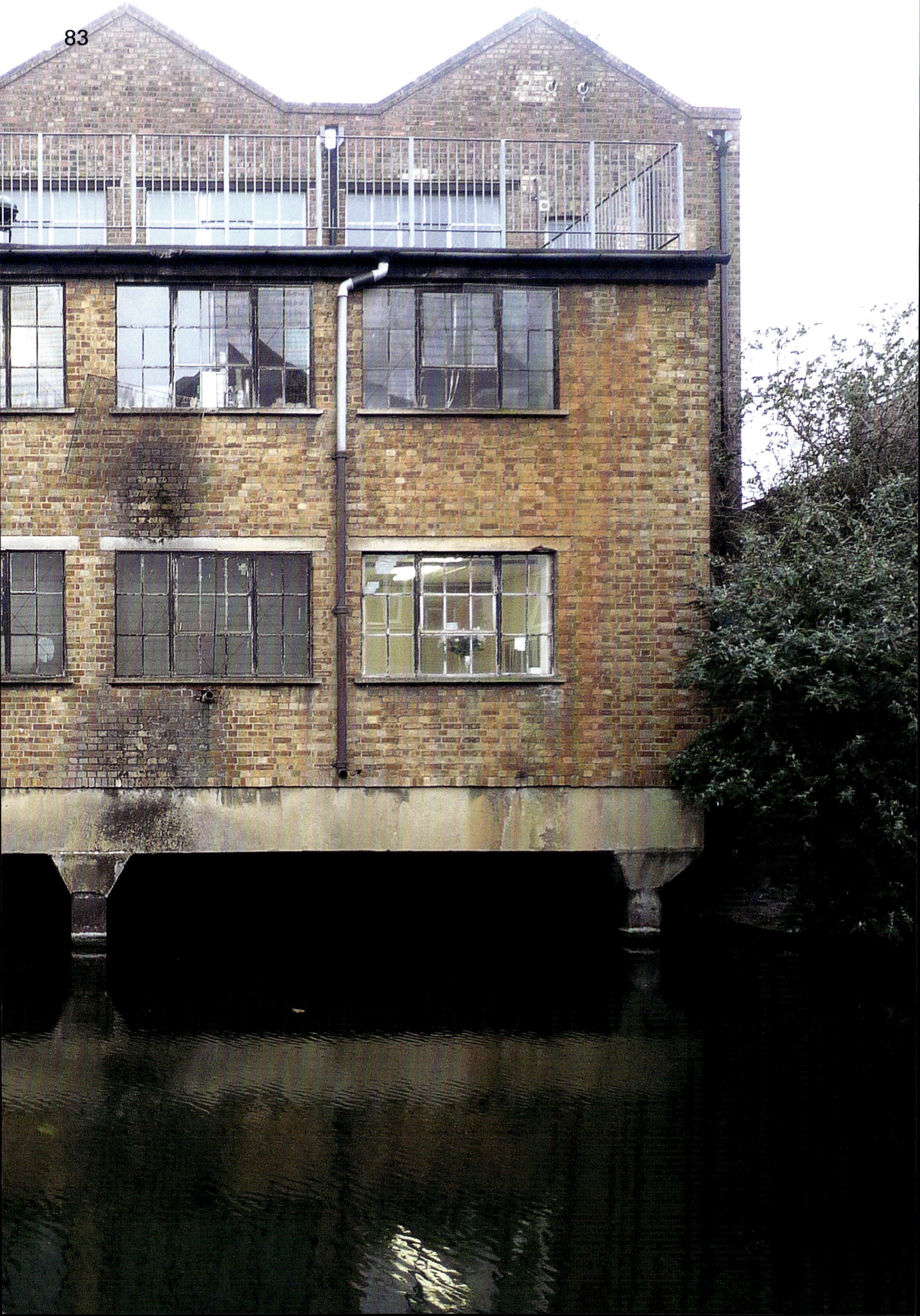

Minus Roof

Part of the roof of the Wysing Arts Centre is temporarily removed. Visitors are invited to board a small plane at a nearby airfield and fly over the building, creating a visual connection between the visitors in the plane and the ones in the exhibition space.

Wysing Arts Centre, Cambridge, UK, 2009

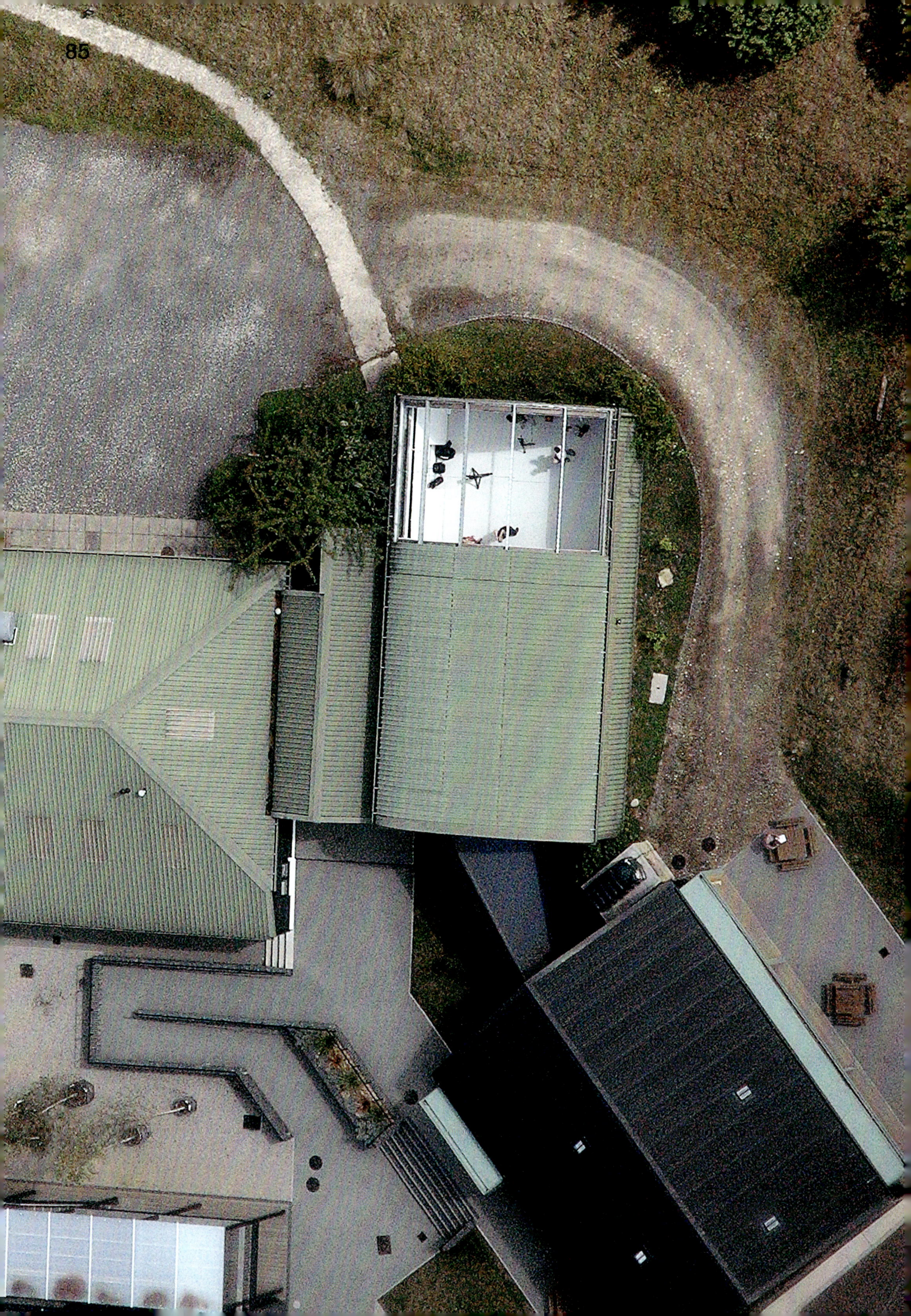

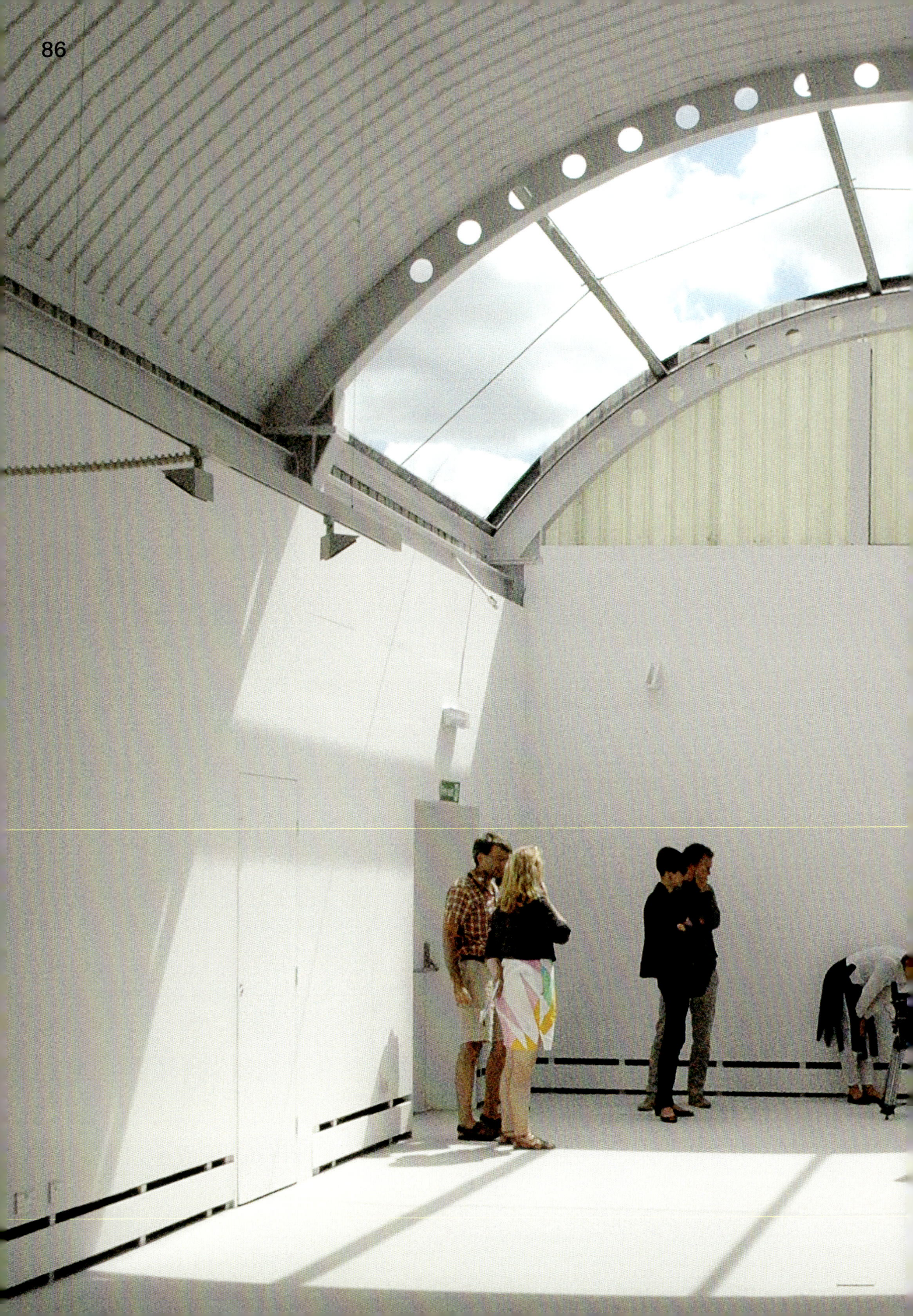

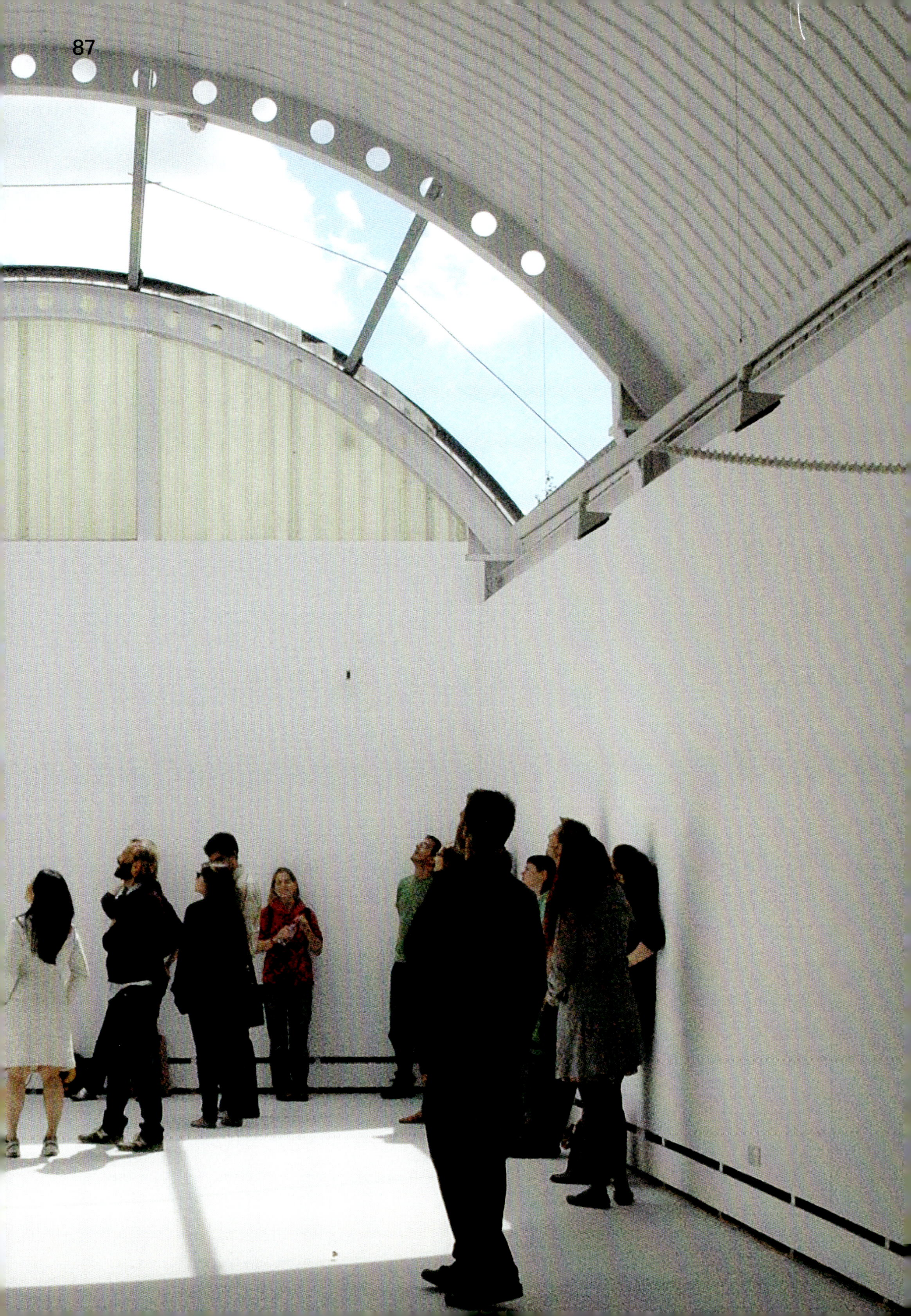

Endless Hour

Customized hourglass.

Bærum Kunsthall, Oslo, Norway, 2021

Ponds

Coffee spilled on to the floor plan of the exhibition space. Coffee ponds are made in the exhibition space in the same position, size, and shape as the stains on the floor plan.

CC – Copenhagen Contemporary, Copenhagen, Denmark, 2017

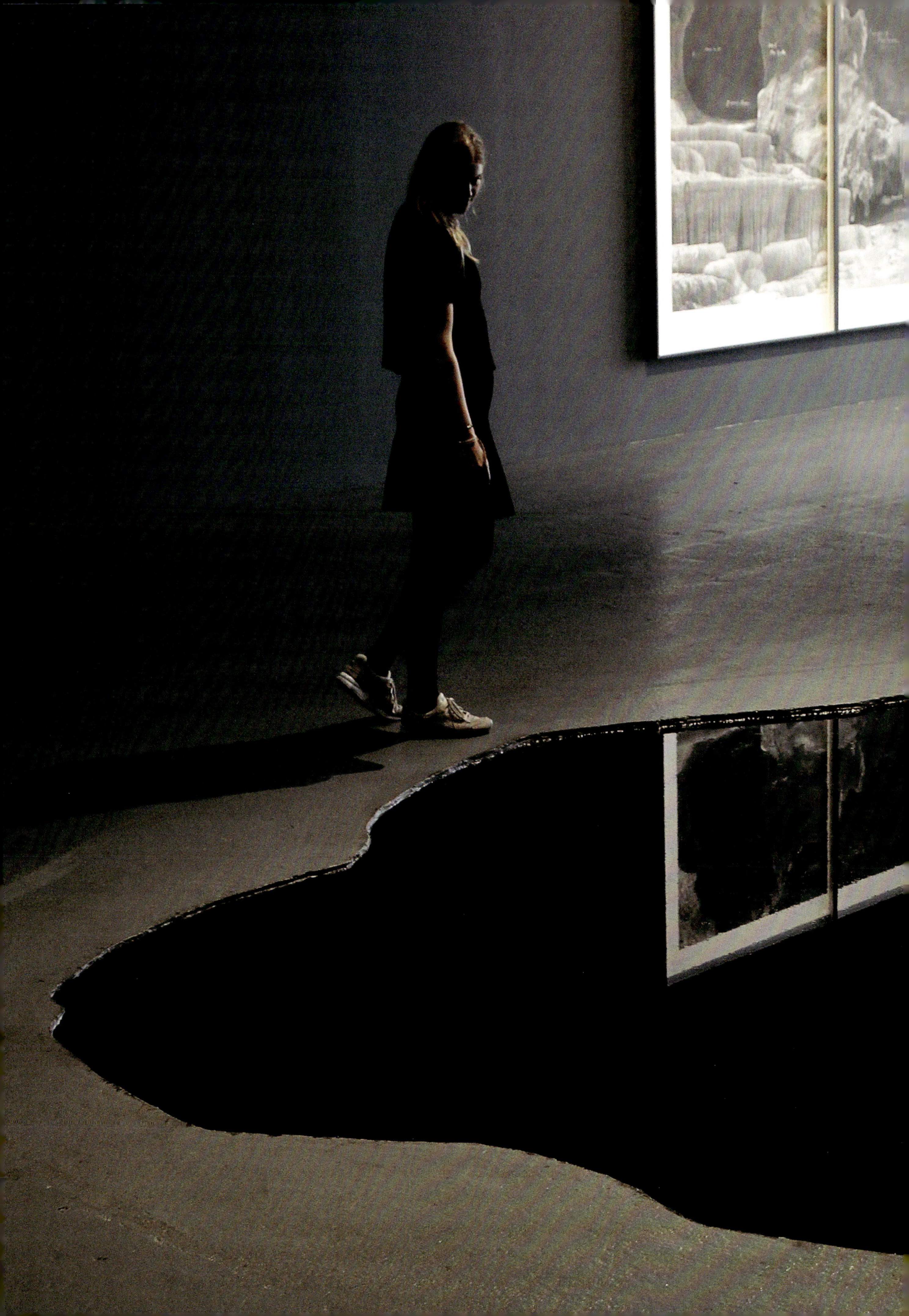

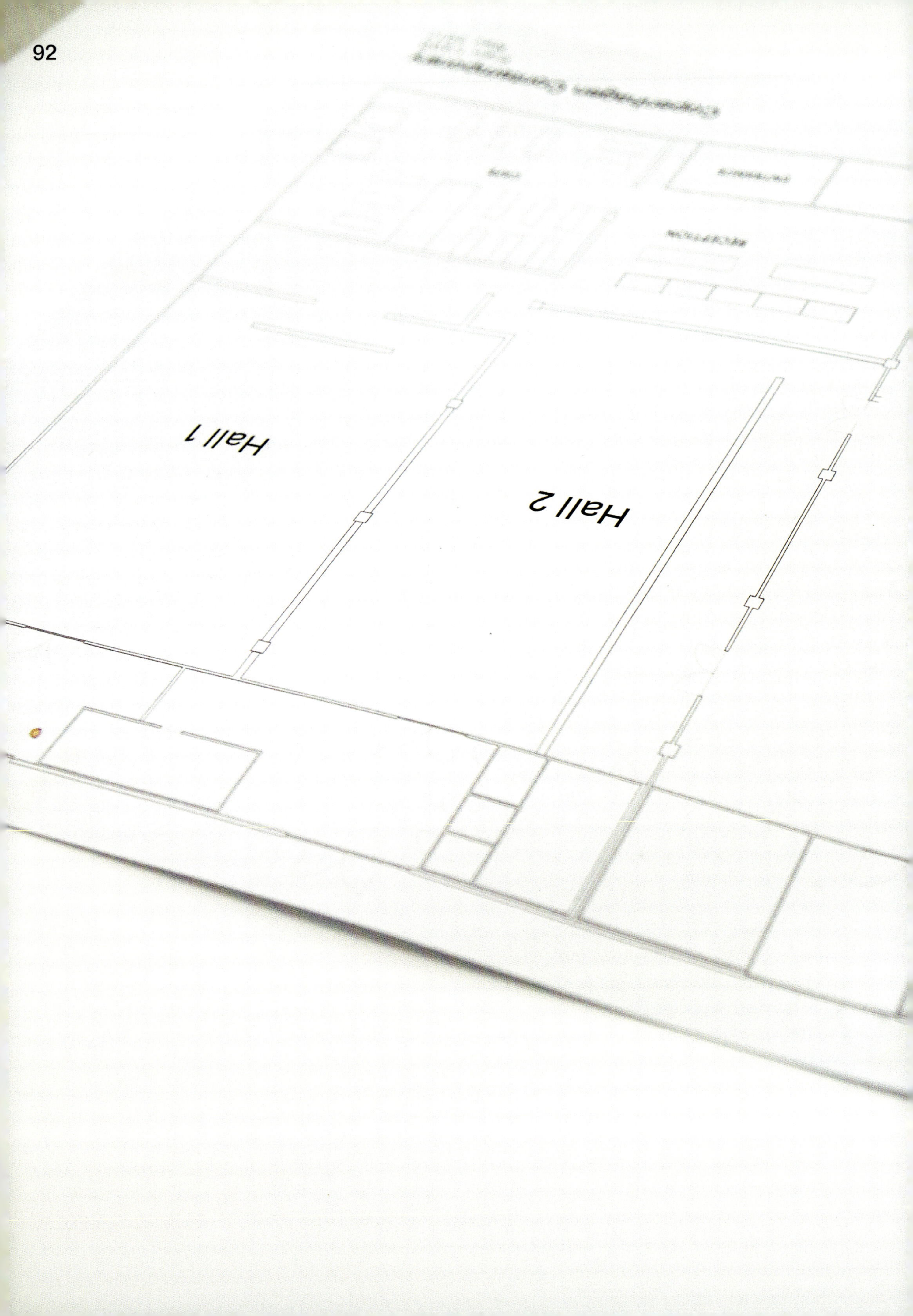
Hall 1
Hall 2

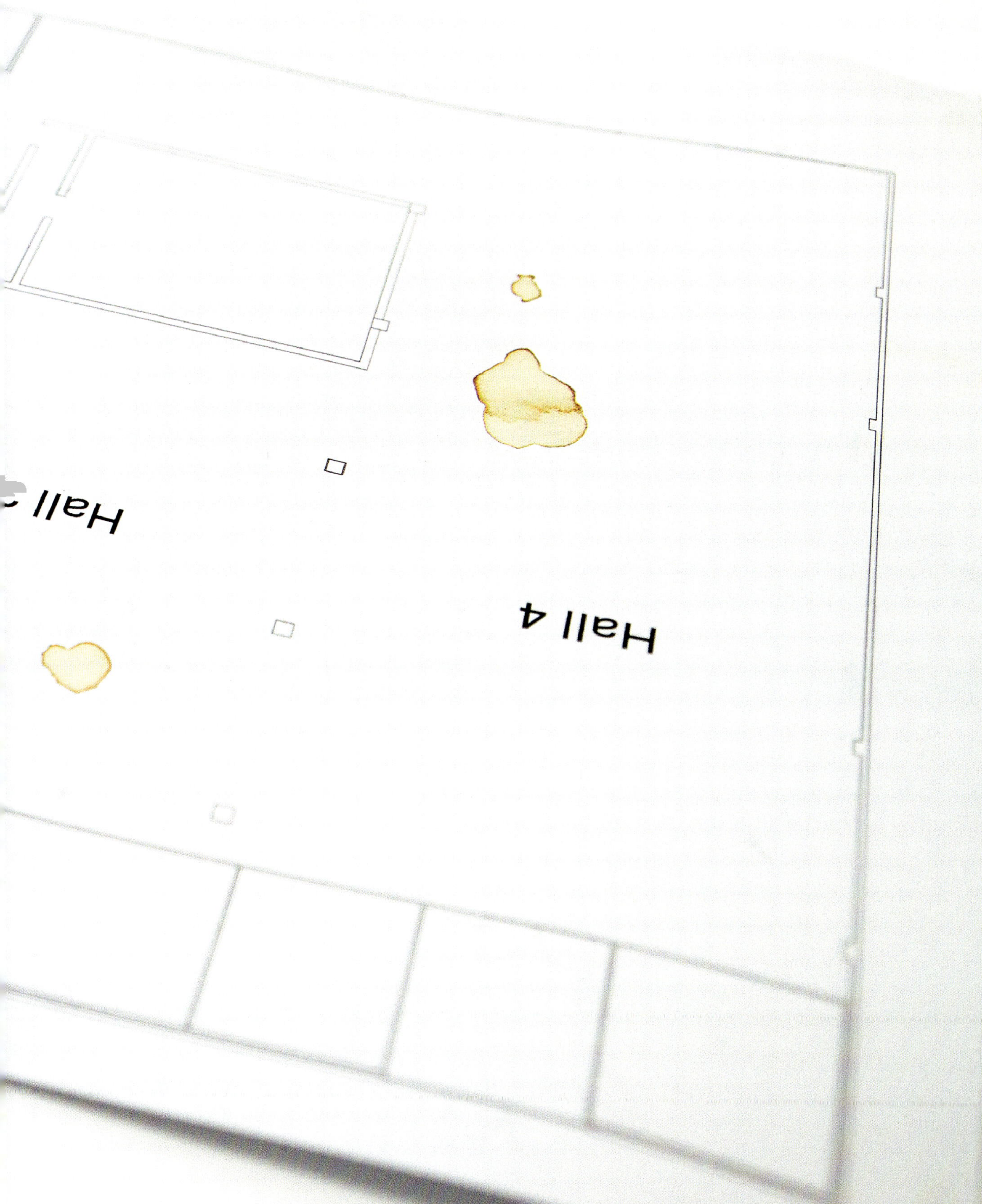
Hall
Hall 4

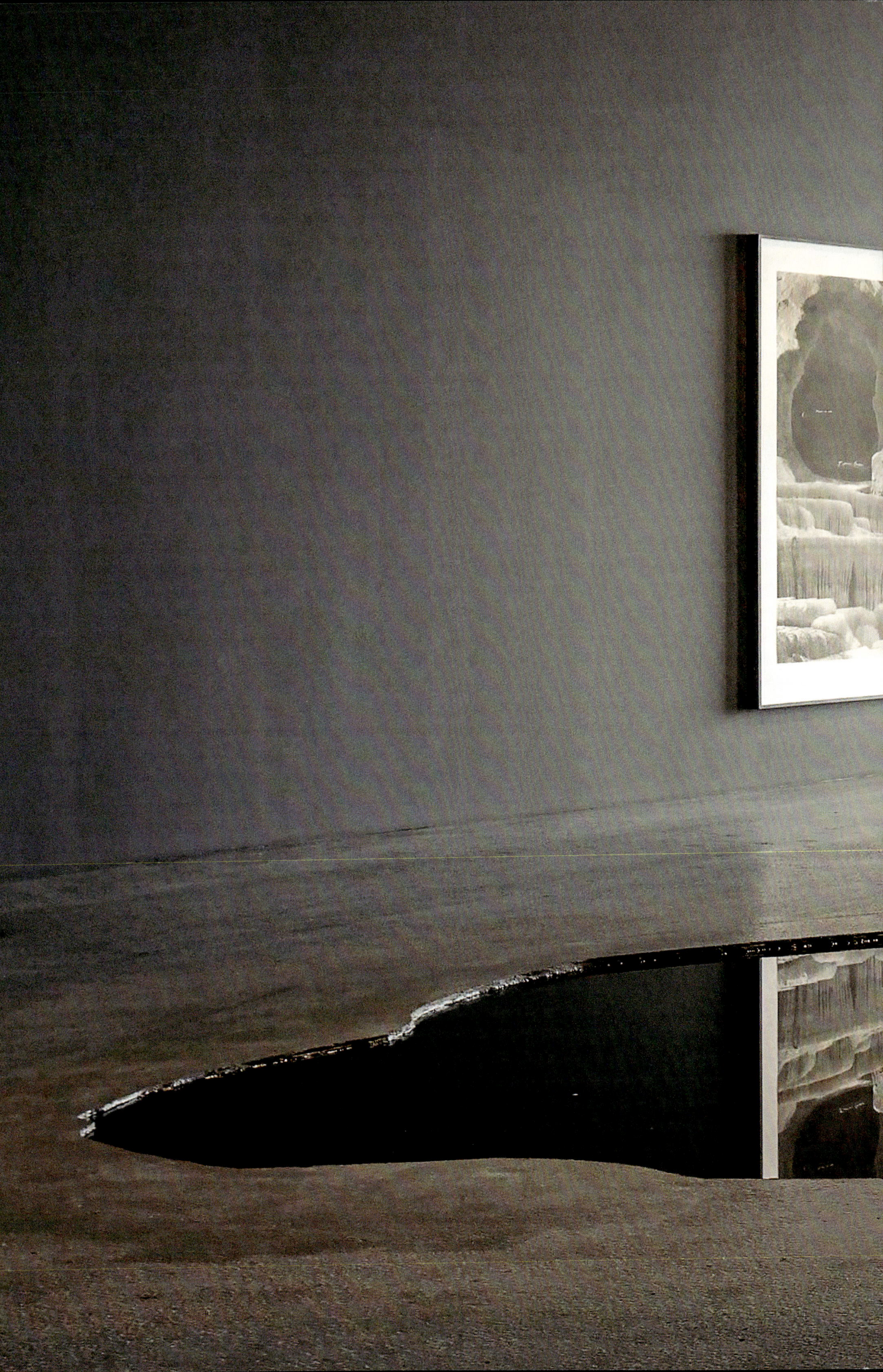

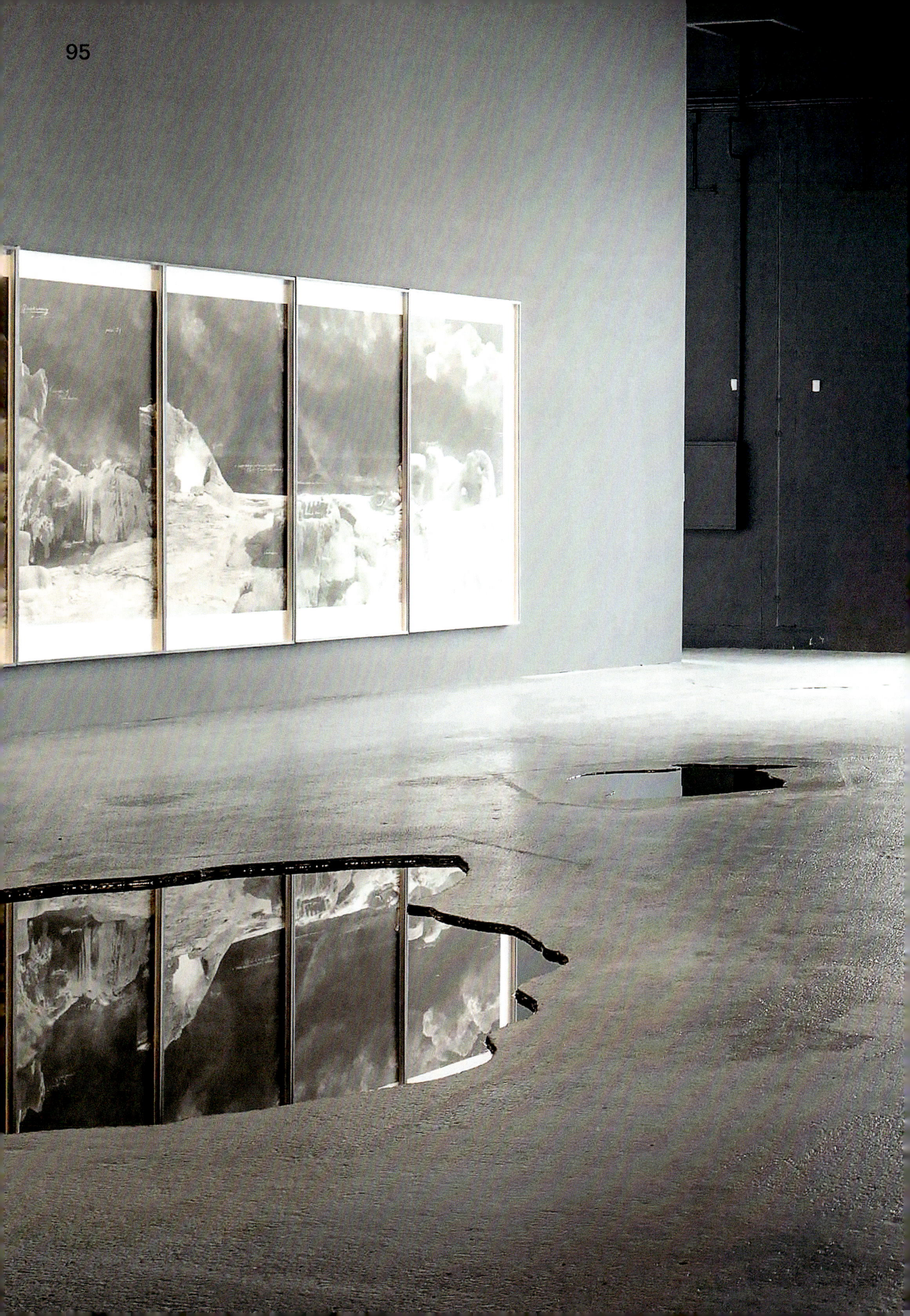

The Color of Things

Objects are photographed before being pulverized. Their dusts are mixed with a binding liquid and applied to the wall as pigments.

Galleri Nicolai Wallner, Copenhagen, Denmark, 2018 (p. 97)
KUNSTEN Museum of Modern Art, Aalborg, Denmark, 2022 (p. 98–99)

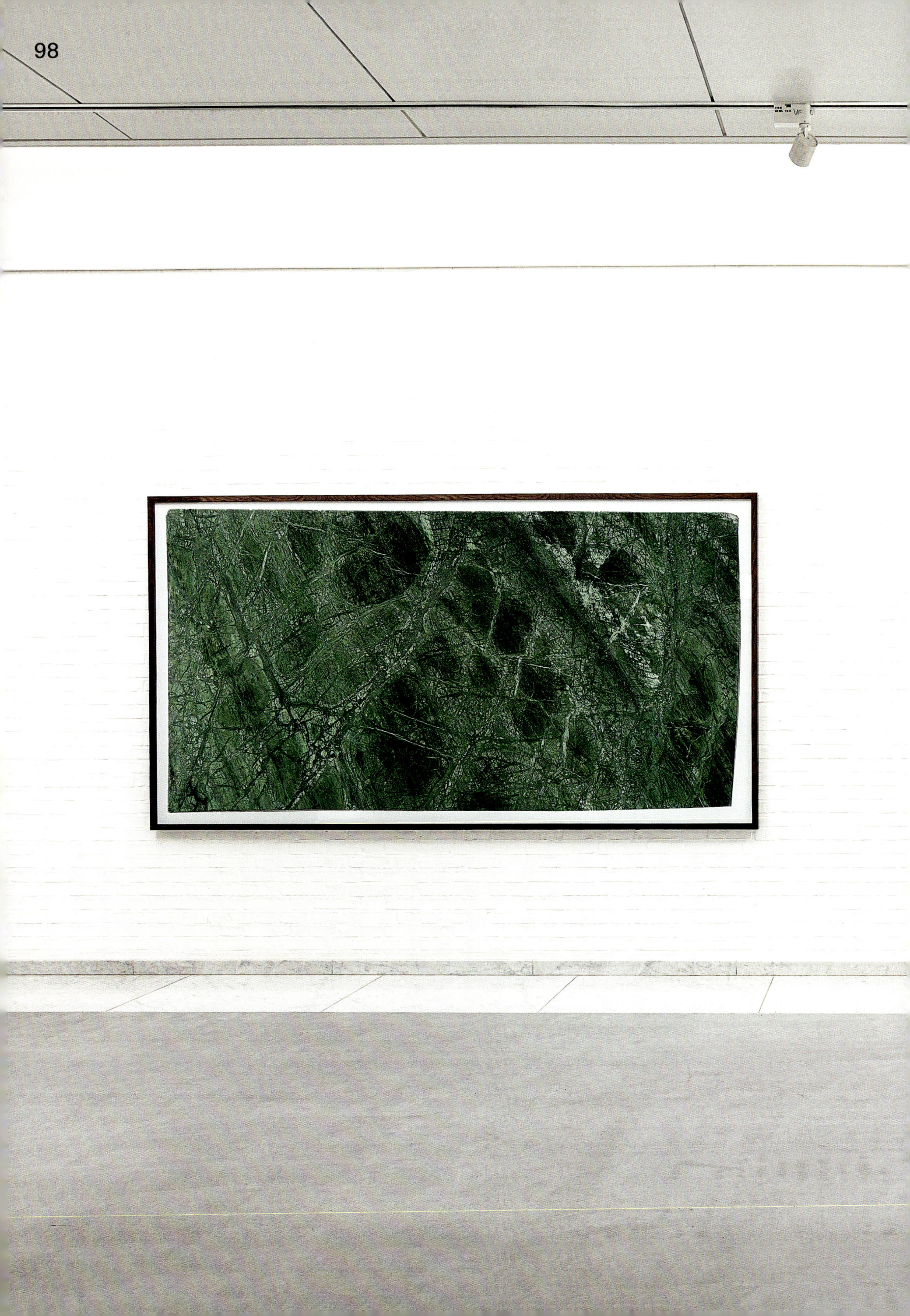

Naked Photographer

Artists are instructed to undress and photograph their clothes.

Invited artists: Anna Molska, Att Poomtangon, Elina Brotherus, Elmgreen & Dragset, Ignasi Aballí, Jacob Aue Sobol, Jonathan Monk (p. 101), Jordi Colomer, Julian Charrière, Kirsten Justesen, Lasse Schmidt Hansen, Marcius Galan, Maria Loboda

---

Maisterravalbuena Gallery, Madrid, Spain, 2015

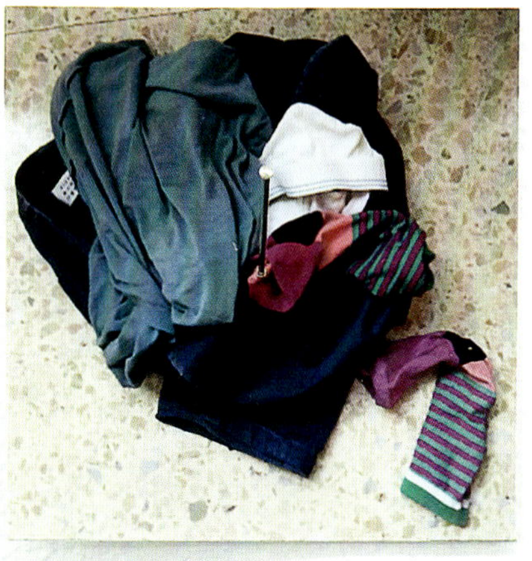

Stone

Residents of Brück are photographed behind the stone at the entrance of the town.

Brück, Germany, 2011

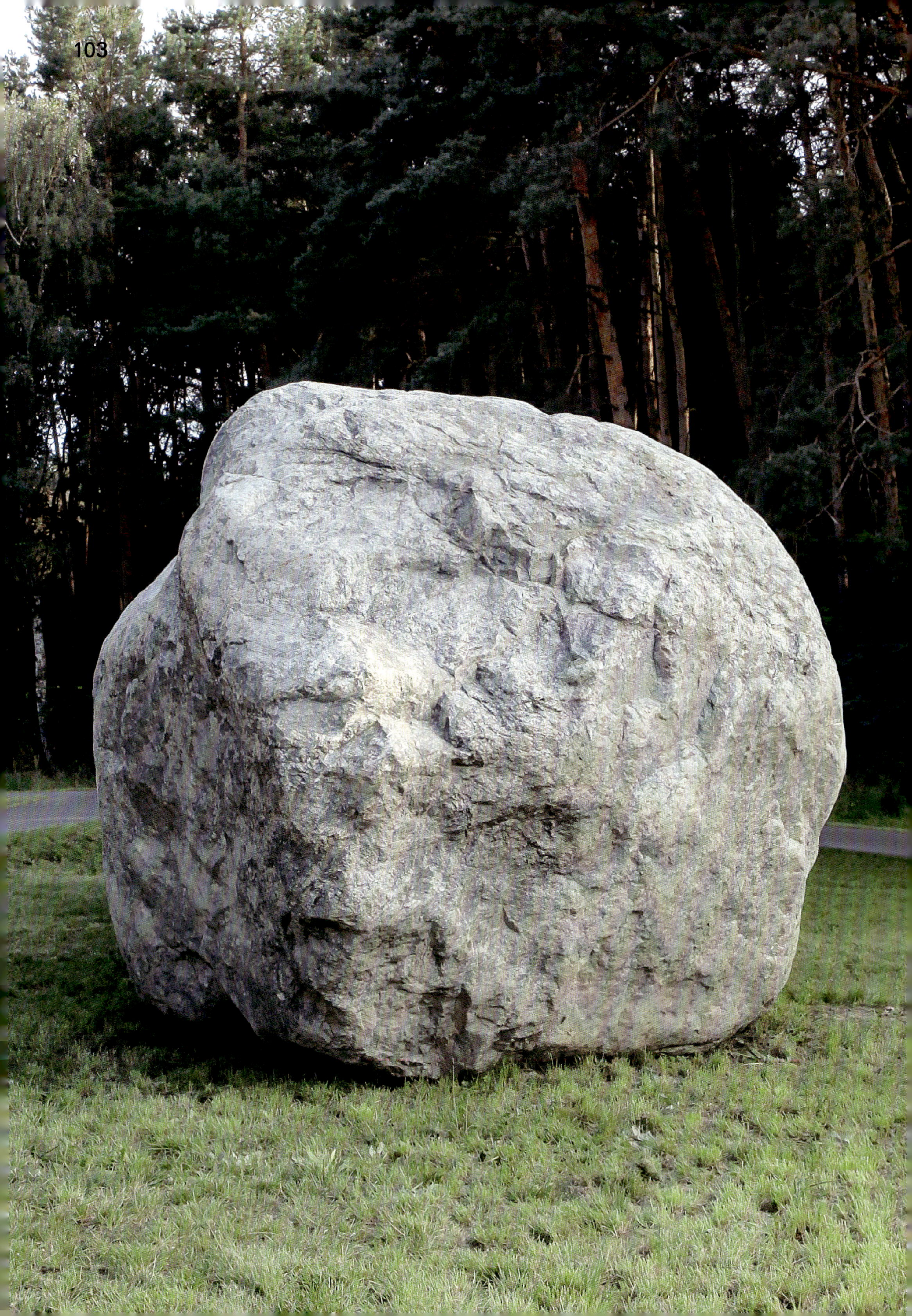

Bronze Pour

Liquid bronze is poured into the river of Kistefos and collected in a net. Three resulting shapes are 3D scanned, enlarged, and casted in bronze.

Kistefos, Jevnaker, Norway, 2016

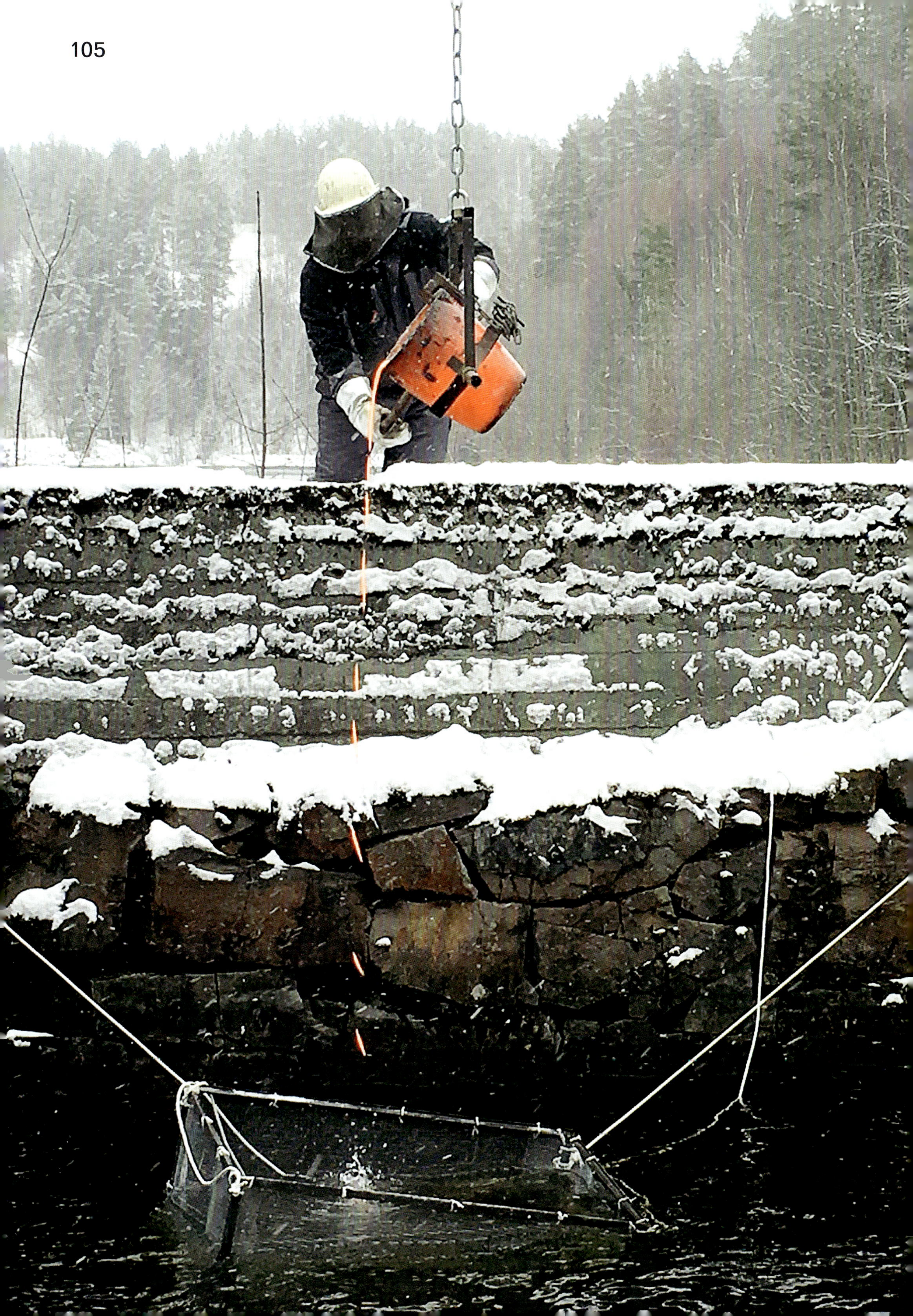

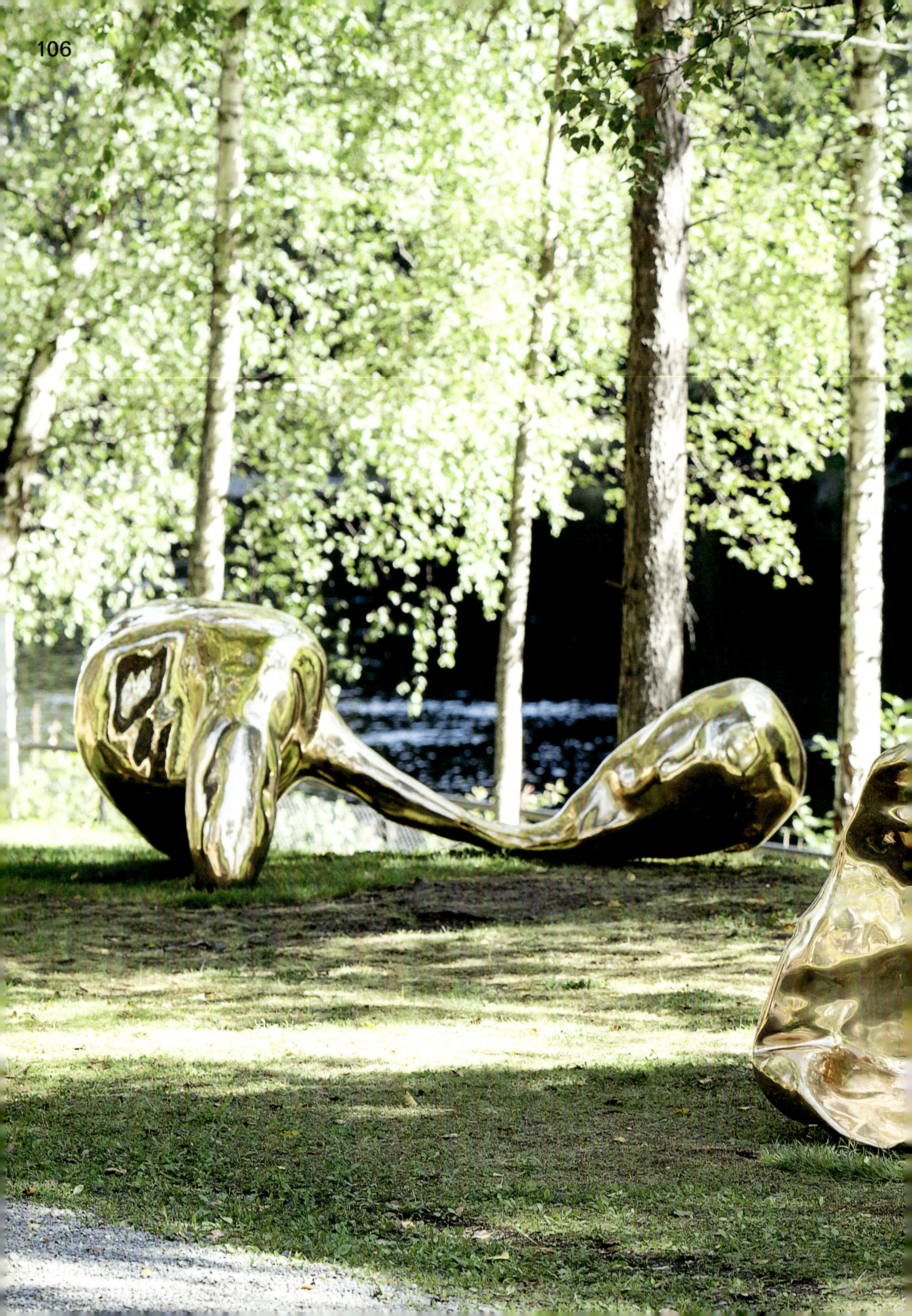

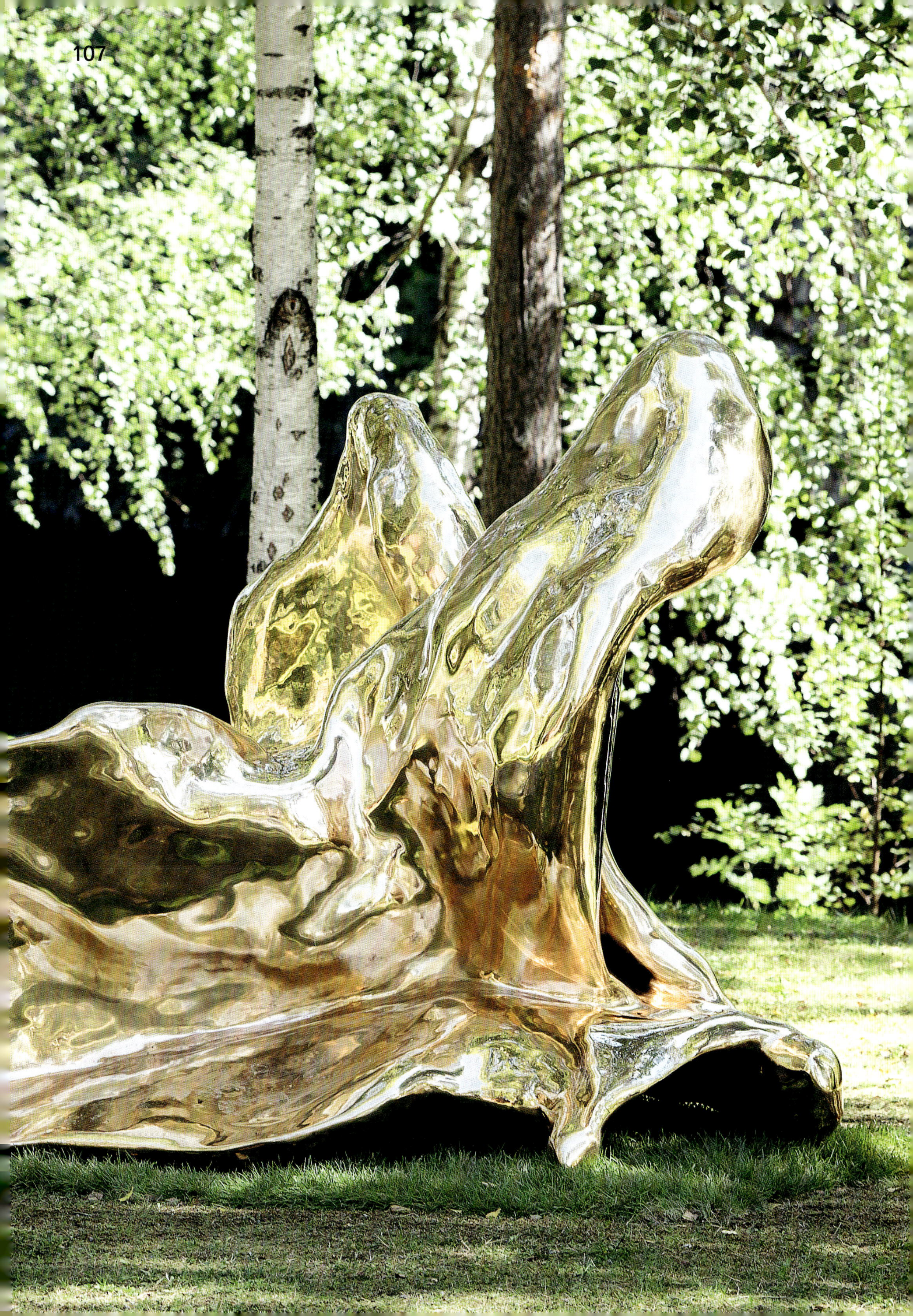

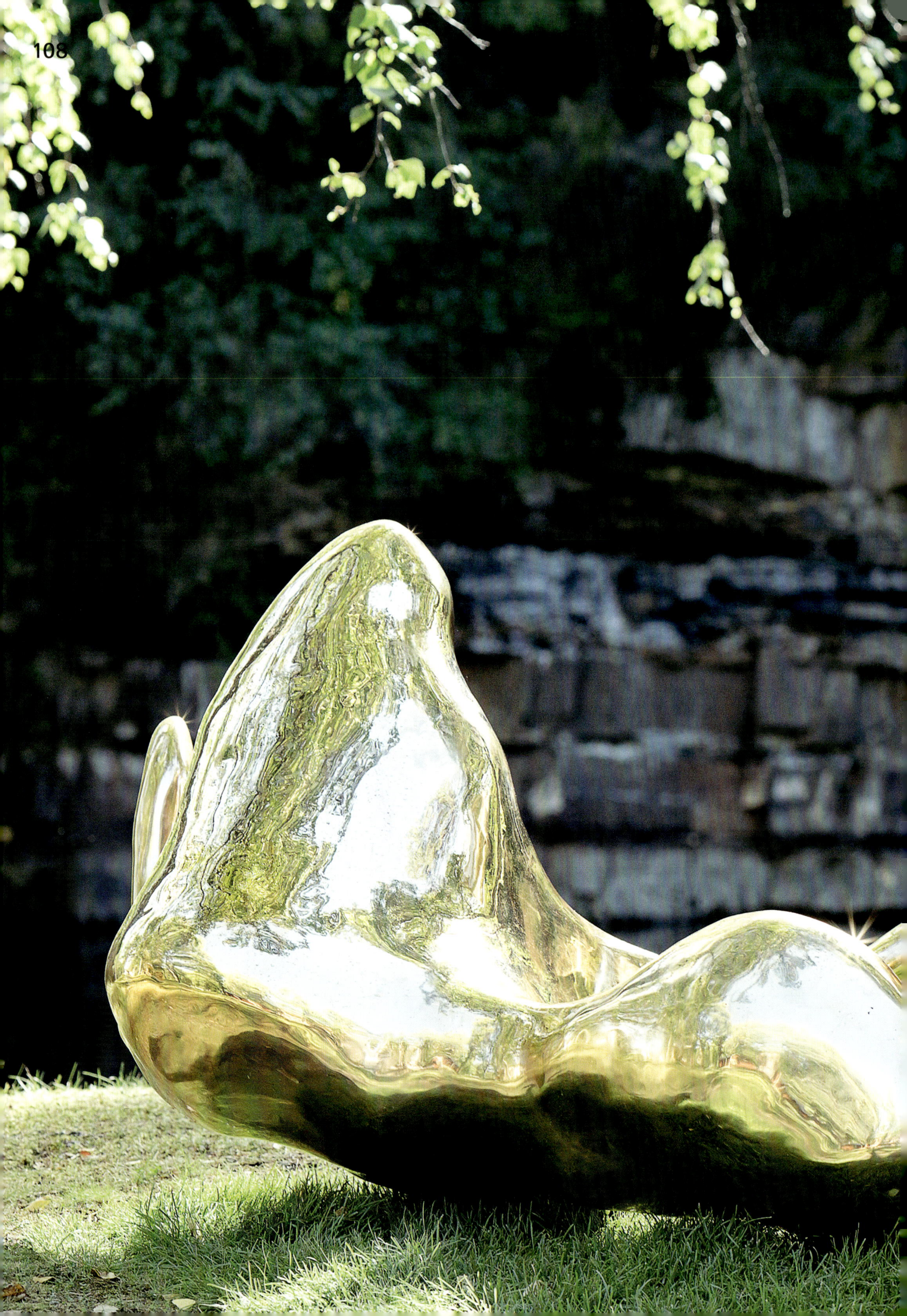

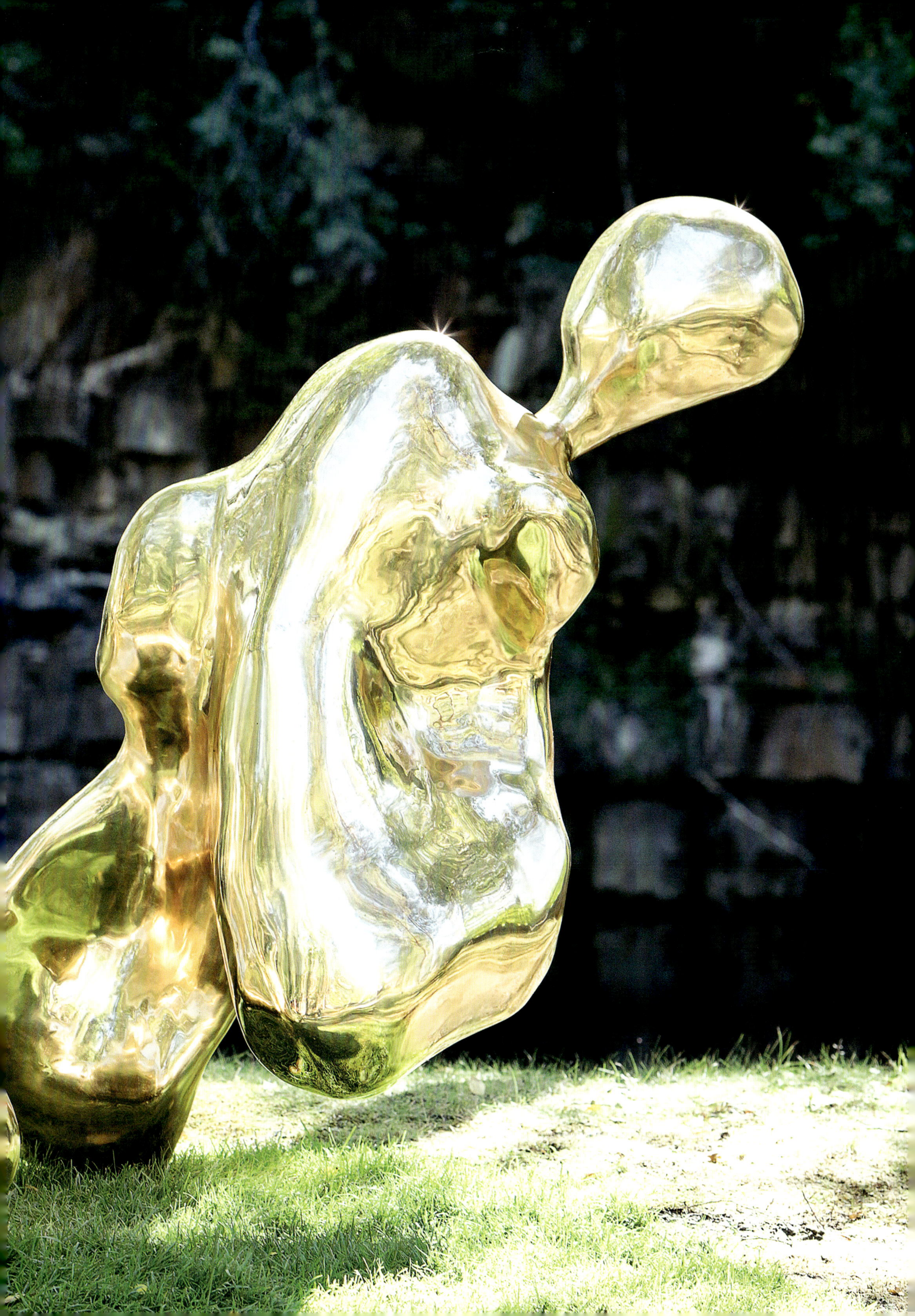

Permanent Reflection

Two photographs depict the reflections of their own framing glass.

Lund konsthall, Lund, Sweden, 2015

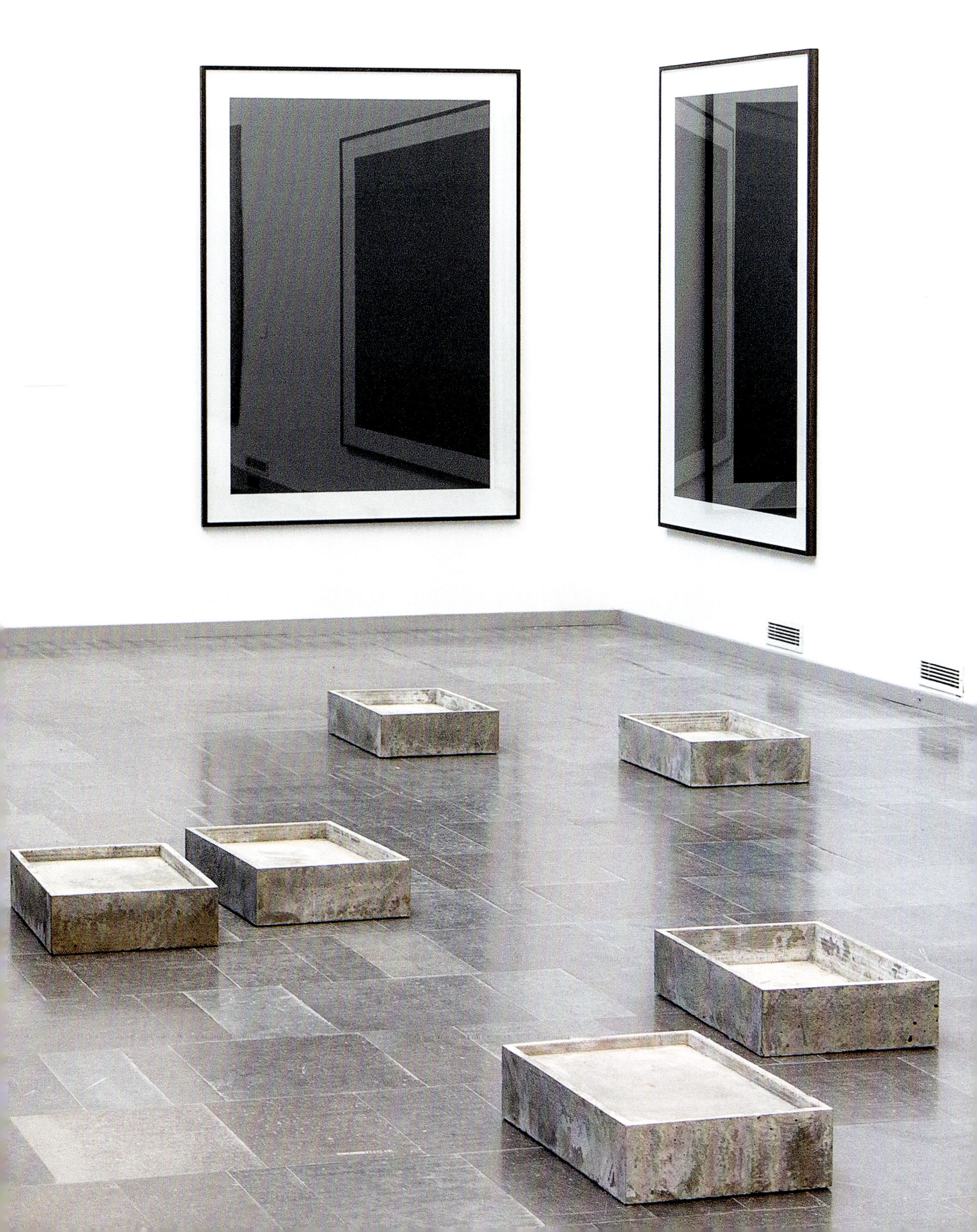

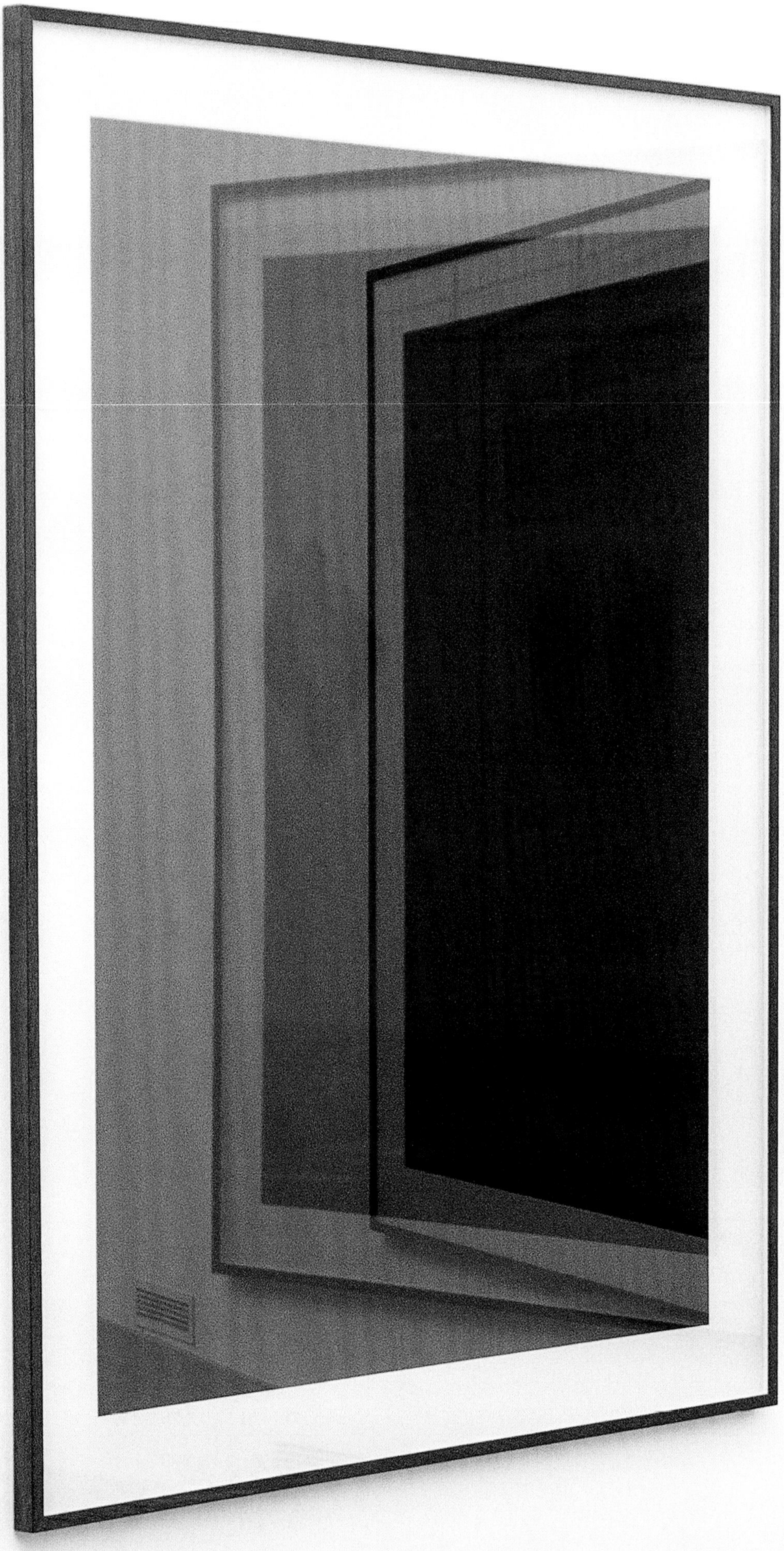

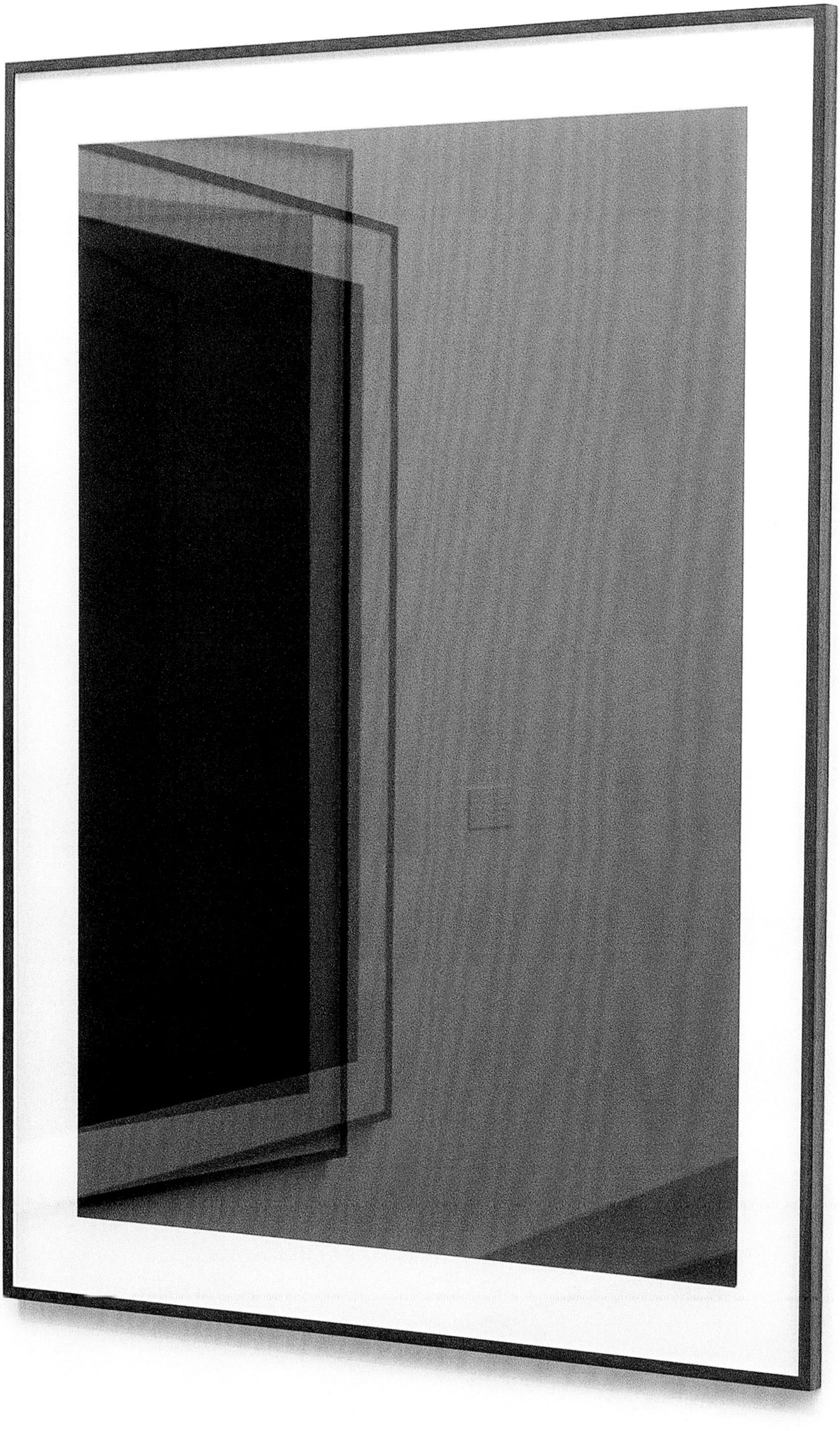

Some Works by A Kassen

Adam Carr

At speed, a wheel appears to rotate backward, albeit if the vehicle —say a car or a bicycle—is moving forwards. Several theories have tried to unpack why it appears in reverse, out of synch, with its actual direction and sometimes not moving. One such theory, which comes unsurprisingly from science, positions it as a stroboscopic effect—the spokes of the wheel appear to run untrue, caused by flickering light, that in turn makes a reverse rotation effect, or, more commonly termed, the wagon wheel effect.

This optical illusion that occurs in plain sight, along with other phenomena such as naturally distorted dimensions and objects made by clouds, resonates with the work of Danish art collective A Kassen. Indeed, much of A Kassen's work suspends belief and could be read as illusionistic, particularly given its alluring reveal of something new, something unordinary in the fabric of reality. Yet, despite the projection of an alternative worldview, it is done against the dominant mode of perceiving the world anew, whether through the internet or via the special effects occurring in the post-produced image that are engrained in our psyche through its daily use in social media.

While it might be without special effects, it is not without advanced precision that A Kassen's work is executed. Indeed, many of their pieces are underpinned by, in part, laborious processes that see collaborations with several experts, from construction workers to artisans. However, there is also a sure earnest and down-to-earth approach, in many cases literally so, that captures the spirit of their work. It dupes reality in a real way, pushing against our obsession with viewing and changing the world through digital means.

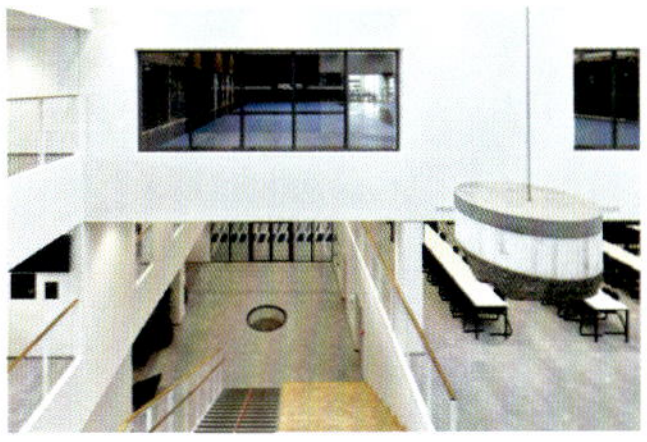

A Kassen could be thought of as ground taking in many different ways. Take *Foundation* (2021), for example, a commission for the Police Academy in Vejle, a city in the southwest region of Denmark. For this work, A Kassen had a circular section of the ground removed, dug up from the Academy's basement level, revealing the layers below the polished concrete floor; the material was then transposed to the main hall, where it now hangs as a mobile. One could think of the work in terms of its origin and subsequent potential misunderstanding. For some, it might appear as a foreign object belonging to and thrown in from a completely different context. Yet, when one approaches the basement, they soon realize a hole in the ground, and in turn, they complete what might have been a bit of a conundrum. There are many further ruminations, particularly when considering the premature status of the Academy's building. As a newly built structure, the work could be deemed a reminder of the act of construction and fabrication, which comes via deconstruction and refabrication, like cutting into a cake to reveal its layers. It might even be mistaken as an object from the design world, especially given Denmark's rich history with the invention of slightly untraditional lighting products, or, perhaps, more at home in the context of the visual arts, an anarchic nod, maybe, to the pioneering mobile work of Alexander Calder. In moving ground, it is as though A Kassen are alighting in the dual effect of historical precedent—indeed, they acknowledge it—and an entirely different, foreign reading, with which its side of interpretation depends on its receiver. Exposing its context but unveiling more of its inner workings, A Kassen also had a large circle removed from a wall so that two levels of offices are made visible in the double-height canteen space—tapping in, maybe, to our fascination with detective work that has seen the commissioning of a number of documentaries the world over, though its reality here is much more real.

A more pressing and obvious question of these two pieces perhaps: Why would a police academy commission a work by a contemporary artist? This certainly speaks to the artists' humorous angle of being anti-authoritarian, but it also underlines the long-standing commitment to culture in Denmark, allowing many of their ideas to be realized. Of more importance to the unraveling of their practice, however, the commission stands in a lineage of the artists' practice that works with, within, and at times, it seems, against contexts where the idea of art might seem peculiar.

Another unlikely marriage saw many related yet separate works produced for a Danish high school. The artists looked at the site and its history to conjure these pieces, former home to the Geological Institute of the University of Copenhagen. Inspired by a geological phenomenon, in particular plate tectonics, elements of the building were staggered, appearing as the aftermath of some kind of orchestrated earthquake. *Cut Building* (2012) had a circular building cut horizontally in half to make a top and bottom layer, with the top layer moved over slightly from its bottom section, so the two no longer marry up in perfect unison. This mode of disarray was evident elsewhere. For *Benches* (2012), sections of the concrete ground were cut out and elevated enough to form several useable benches when it was stabilized underneath. And for *Lamppost* (2012), three lampposts were shifted from the school's courtyard to the inside of the building, where they now project through various walls, floors, ceilings, and even windows where the light of the lamppost juts out of the windows like an unwanted guest.

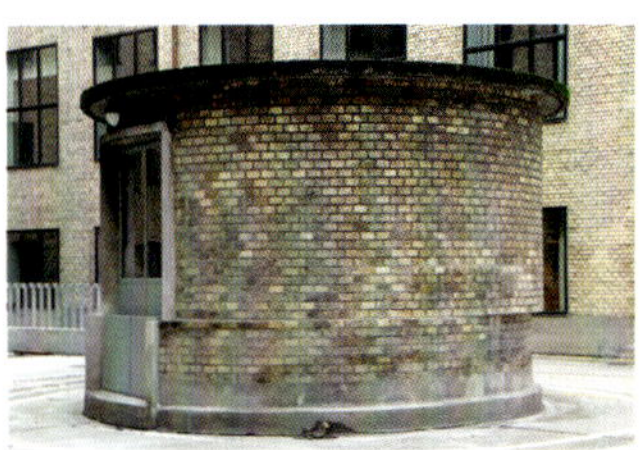

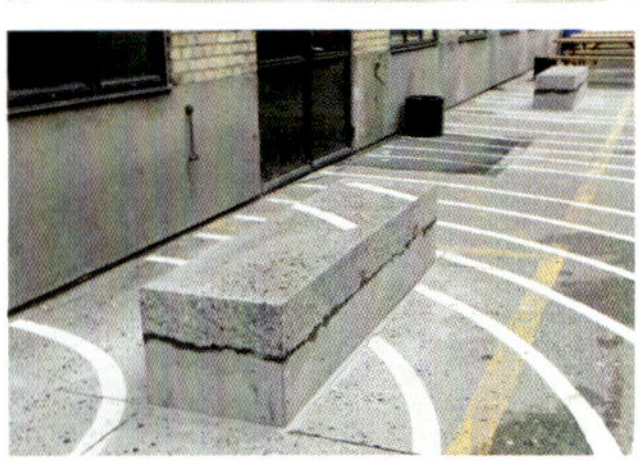

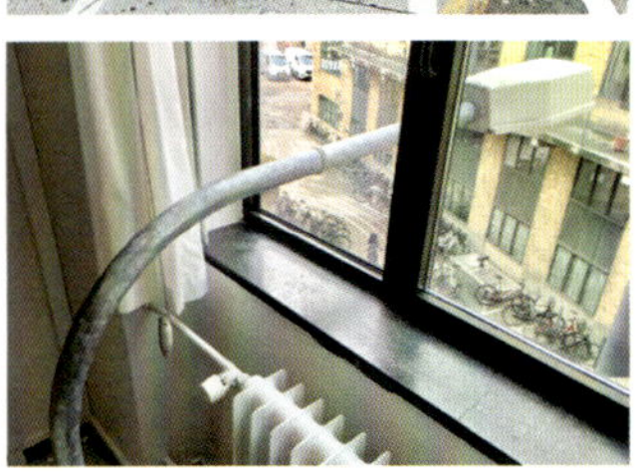

Many of these pieces, of course, infer the ground shaking movements of Land Art, from Robert Smithson to Nancy Holt. But perhaps it is the psychological inducing of Gordon Matta-Clark and the ghostly-like achievements of Michael Asher that provide a more accurate context in which to draw art historical comparisons. Indeed, A Kassen's work shares the attitude of interrupting the public sphere, as seen in the termed anarchitecture of Matta-Clark, and the reveal of varying and diverging aspects of context through removal and shifts as with Asher. Although these are crucial inlets to A Kassen's work, it is with their unique brand of humor and the particular manner of working that they seem to partly discard the possibilities found within the temporal and equally do not fully embrace a presentation of the mechanisms that guide and shape the presentation of art—after all, a considerable amount has already been done in these areas. Instead, when they seem to allude to precedent, the practice suggests the behavior of truant art students.

The works at the Police Academy and Spyken High School might envision A Kassen working exclusively on such grand, spectacle-like scales—the pieces for the Academy, for instance, are sizable in scale and clarity, and both have a pronounced public front, having been commissioned by recognized organizations. Other works come to undermine this assumption. Some are discreet, embedded, and almost disguised in their exposé.

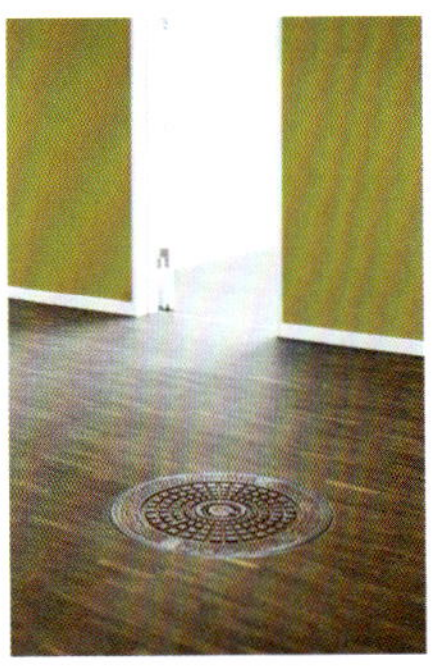

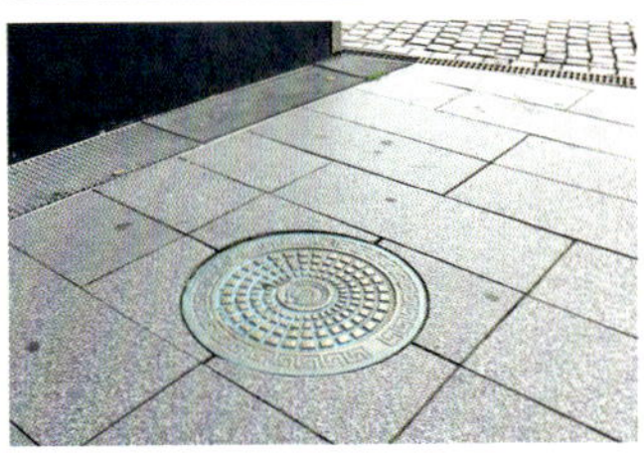

For *Manhole Cover* (2015), for example, a manhole cover was taken from a public street in Denmark's capital Copenhagen and subsequently installed in the foyer of an office across the other side of the city. The manhole cover in the street was replaced by a bronze replica. It is unbeknown to the large public that art has even taken place here, that the manhole cover had been moved, let alone replaced by a bronze cast, and that the original now lives elsewhere in the city, outside of its natural habitat. Even a bronze aficionado who might detect the green patina of the manhole cover—an essential facet of how bronze changes—would not register or even fathom the work's complete picture.

At times, this partially hidden, in-between space where some of the work performs is opened out much further, or more precisely, made more distanced. For an alternative version of *Swap* in 2016, land belonging to the 300 years old garden of Egeskov Castle was exchanged for a circular area of the same size from the nearby city of Odense. In Odense, the swap might be dismissed as a recent addition of strategic planning, but in Egeskov Castle, it was clear that the land was a direct import from elsewhere. The land from the Castle was mainly grass. However, the section from Odense included a lamppost, bicycle racks, and security surveillance signs. Another high school commission—which has become, it seems, a niche trajectory of its own in the artists' practice—for Spyken High School, Lund, Sweden, 2017, had a shorter but equally demystifying trade, where two outdoor circular areas of paving stones from the respectively new and the old part of the high school had been cut out and after that exchanged. In turn, the land falls out of sync, though it has a precise accuracy that might resemble the mundanity of the double-take.

p. 134–137

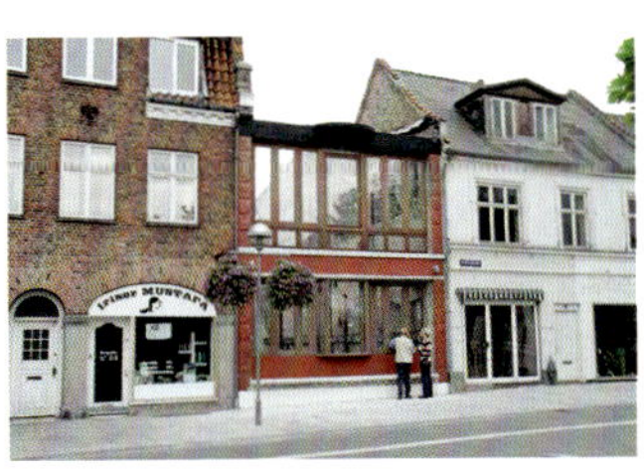

An early piece, *Flip Facade* (2010) saw another addition through subtraction of this replica-like, almost parasitic way of operating. A former building in Nykøbing Falster, a southern Danish city, was the stage for this work, a building that was burnt down some years earlier and left abandoned without restoration. The artists had the original façade rebuilt down to its minute detail. Yet, any potential promise of restoration was suspended for something that instead traverses the sharp conceptual attitude

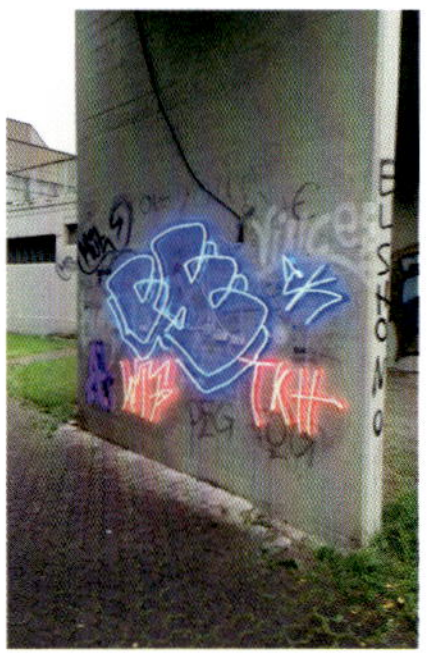

that frequents the work of many of their historical forebearers to the often-functionless statement like gestures of architects —the façade was placed in its original position but upside down. *Untitled (Neon/Graffiti)* (2015) similarly intervenes with hidden, lost, and forgotten aspects that exist in the vastitudes of our built, urban environment. Two walls of graffiti that sit underneath a railway bridge in Hagen, Germany, were copied faithfully in neon lights and mounted in place on the same wall. The temporal, ephemeral, and rapid movements of graffiti become the opposite here, and the projection of light became two-fold, making the often-disregarded mark-making of graffiti something that demanded scrutiny while appropriately giving light to an otherwise dark part of the urban environment.

One typifying element of these works is the circular shape, returning to the allegory mentioned above of the moving wheel at the start of this text. Many of their works are circular, but not only visually. A circular motion also very much defines their conceptual mode of operating, which makes use of and exists in a series of shifts and exchanges that come to simultaneously point back to themselves and project outwards. The public sphere has provided many opportunities for their ideas, and they have reveled in the endless possibilities of who or what constitutes their work's audience while going so far as to provoke the likelihood that their work might not even be recognized. Though it is not with exceptionality that they work on the outside, in public, often suggesting some form of opposition toward the traditional sanctioned contexts for art's presentation. Many of their works have used and even taken inspiration from museums, institutions, and commercial gallery spaces, underlining not only the adaptability with which they work but also an eagerness to amplify and mine, or rather undermine, aspects that come to define other contexts, in perhaps more of an acute and concentrated way.

At MUSAC, León, Spain, in 2009, the artists had several window panels from the façade of the building replaced by plywood boards as if to insinuate many breakages had occurred. The windows panels were installed in three sets of joined automatic sliding doors in the building's gallery space—in part resembling the sculptural glass of Dan Graham's pavilions—which were triggered per the movement of visitors. Only when entering the space, could one realize what had indeed occurred on the exterior. Windows have also been repurposed in many other works, which similarly collapse aspects of exterior and

p. 60–61

interior together. *Encirclement* (2012) takes inspiration from the special glass, cylindrical-like structure, which houses a staircase. The artists photographed the exterior of the building, yet in a totally unconventional artistic maneuver, they had the image framed using the panes of the curved glass of the building itself. One could think of Robert Morris's *Box with the Sound of its Own Making* (1961) and Hans Haacke's *Condensation Cube* (1965), which likewise set up a hermetic system to produce something new within materiality without adding anything, per se, to the equation. Yet, the piece perhaps most succeeds in dismantling notions of photography and sculpture—it is neither hung flat on the wall nor does it fully occupy space in a sculptural way, but instead sits, somewhat awkwardly, in between these two states, coalescing into a whole other category.

p. 150–153

Lamppost (2016) at Galleri Nicolai Wallner, Copenhagen, also caused disorientation concerning the reading of an object in terms of discipline. Here a lamppost was dislocated from its place and brought inside the gallery, though in such a way that it cut through the space entirely. The bottom appeared on one side of the wall, with its earth showing signs of its upheaval from its site of origin, and the remainder of the lamppost is visible in the space on the opposing side but such that the top of its surface can be seen straight on, appearing like some kind of painting cum sculpture, which has been left to weather and struggle with the elements of the world outside. One of their earlier pieces, which was shown in 2006, was already presented behind the scenes of Nicolai Wallner in a confusingly subtle way, here uniting sculpture with a wall drawing and site-specificity with provisional performance. *Drawer* (2006) installed a draw into the gallery wall so that it sits entirely flush and parallel with its immediate surroundings. If one opened the drawer, they would see that it has no bottom, and through this opening, they could see the gallery's storage room, making that usually placed out of view a public spectacle.

p. 68–71

The transposition of things from the outside world to a commercial context was apparent in their exhibition for Maisterravalbuena Gallery, Madrid, in 2018. *View from Below* (2018) brought two outside statues and installed them horizontally in the space so as to penetrate a wall, as with the work for Nicolai Wallner before. The intention here was focused on exposing the bottom of the statues to dizzying effect, which were only visible from the gallery's exhibition space, again confusing sculptural objects with something decidedly more painterly. The remainder of the statues could be seen in non-exhibition areas of the gallery, including the office.

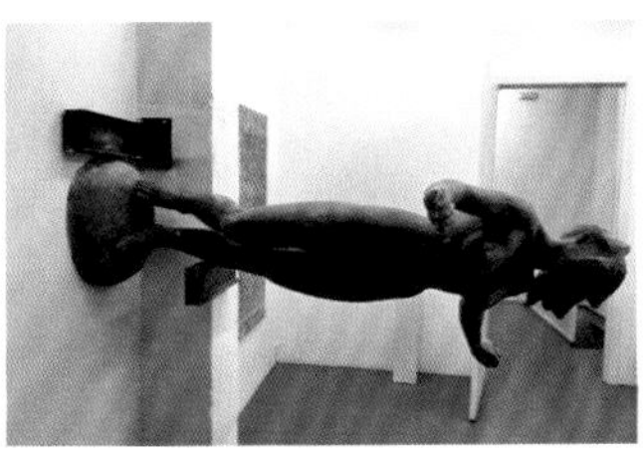

Another unnecessary but highly welcomed addition to commercial gallery architecture came from *Terrazzo* (2011). A marble statue was placed in the empty gallery space of New Galerie, Paris, and was photographed. Afterward, the statue was smashed into pieces and used as a material to make a terrazzo floor. The photograph of the entire sculpture was placed on the wall in the same gallery space. Defining the commercial context are, of course, notions of value and sale and purchase transactions. An ongoing series of photographs, *Mirror* (2013), depict mirrors and groups of mirrors. The mirrors are taken from auction house catalogs listing them for sale. In a typically humorous yet highly critical turn, A Kassen's photographs from the catalogs are then printed, framed, and auctioned via the same auction house.

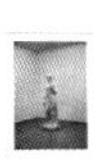

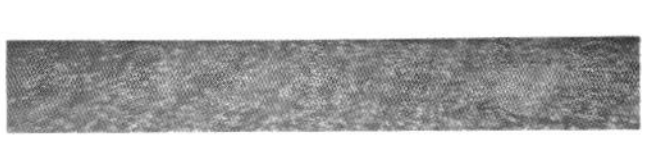

p. 74–79

If private space and its particular traits are the subjects for reordering, public exhibition space has seen equal alteration. As before, a tendency is to bring the world closer to the exhibition space, and this found its extreme point in *Pigeon's Portal* (2008), which, as its title signals, is a portal for pigeons. One could think of it as a living sculpture. A window corridor was constructed in the space of Nikolaj Kunsthal, Copenhagen, connecting two opposing windows. The work was as much about the imaginative possibilities for pigeons as humans, who could now kindly gain free entrance to the institution and cross the exhibition room.

p. 146–149

Often, A Kassen works in such a way that a highly staged event meets a provisional accident—where artistic statement collides with the curatorial. *Ponds* (2017) hones in on the world's fodder for curators over the floor plan. Coffee is spilled on a printed floor plan of an exhibition site, and in the actual space itself, the coffee spill is made to mimic the original spill in the same location, position, and shape. Yet, the spill is made much larger, taking on a gargantuan proportion. The work might recall the sheer amount of cups of coffee used to transform the once small spill into a huge pond, turning the accidental into the deliberate and working between and in between two speeds, slow and fast.

p. 90–95

Opposites tend to collide in A Kassen's work, as we have learned, though they have also entertained the possibilities located within measuring materials concerning utterly unorthodox processes that would rarely, if not at all, be placed in the same conversation, even as a dichotomy—though strangely; as a result, they end performing as so. A recent series of works, *Bronze Pour* (2016–), explores the bizarre practice of pouring bronze into water. Molds are made from the resulting process, then 3D scanned, enlarged, and cast in bronze. On the one hand, the work disrupts the artistic language of bronze and its particular use and function—which is made more impressive when considering its longwinded history—and on the other, it stands as an unconventional recording of site and place. In typical fashion, some works in the series have found homes in public spaces, museum gardens, and even embassies, while other, slightly smaller pieces have been exhibited in gallery spaces on plinths. Often working in series, it seems as though A Kassen have a penchant for exploring a given idea in its seriality, which includes its subsequent presentation and reception in contrasting environments.

p. 104–109

Contraries, converses, and counterparts are terms that could aid in neatly describing and determining A Kassen's practice. Indeed, much of their work had dealt with provoking twin modes of before and after, interior and exterior, public and private—and placed them in conversation through transportation, removal, substitution, and exchange, often using these methods simultaneously. Yet, although their work sets up and operates in a system where contrasts regularly come into contact and form a relation, the space in-between demarcates their work and the particularities in which it is enlivened.

Opening out a third dimension between time and space, creation and presentation, it is as though A Kassen are not only calling our attention toward our own cognition and understanding but also the circumstances through which they take place —to the extent of us beginning to requestion them. Even when the work feels as though it has already acknowledged the process of its own failure and embraced truncation, they continually project revelation, especially when it is in the most mundane and banal realities of things—buildings, materials, objects, and ultimately people.

Objective

A circle is cut out from the wall of the Police Academy canteen revealing the structure of the building and creating a connection between the floors. The circular cut-out leans against the canteen's wall.

Police Academy, Vejle, Denmark, 2021

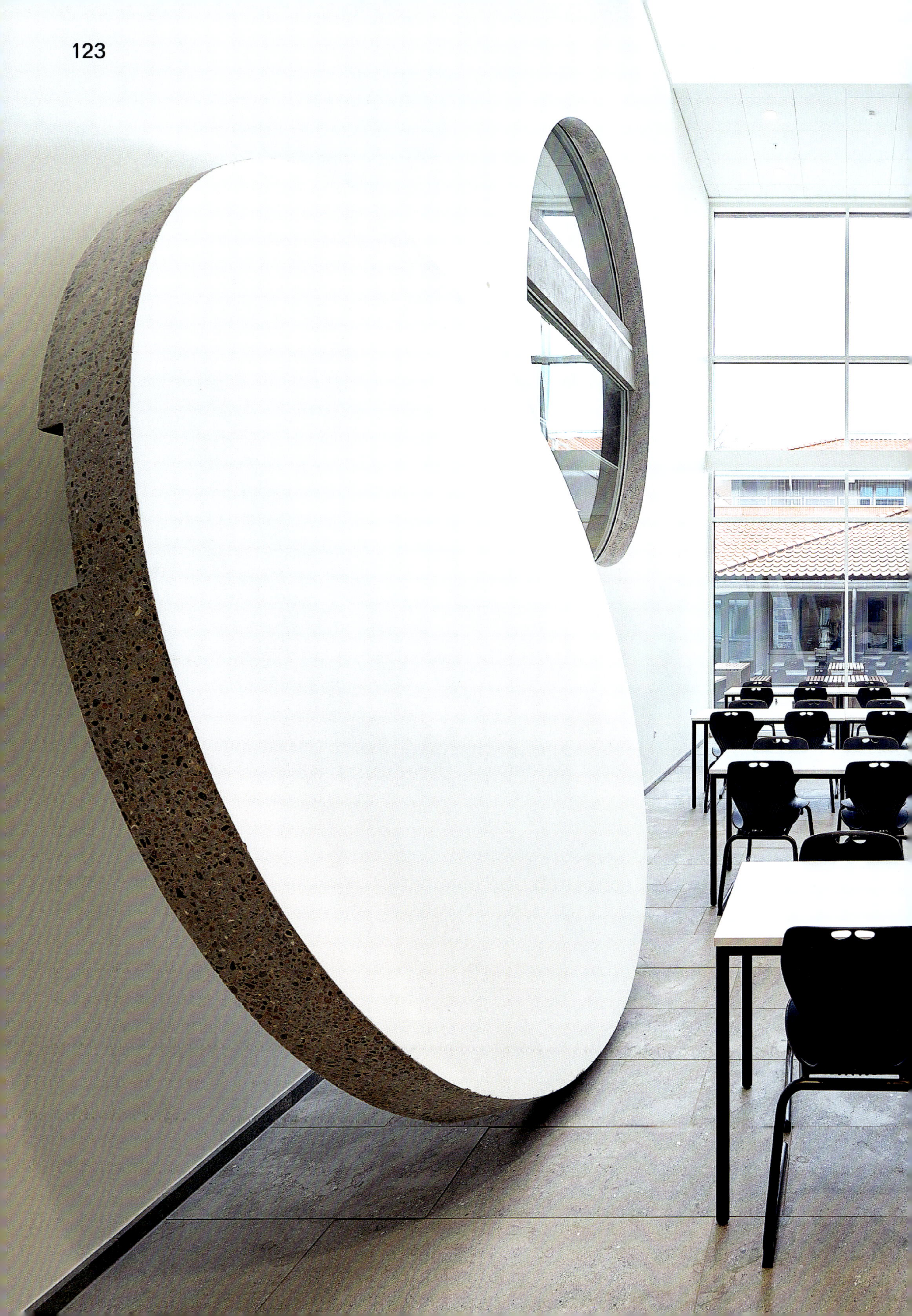

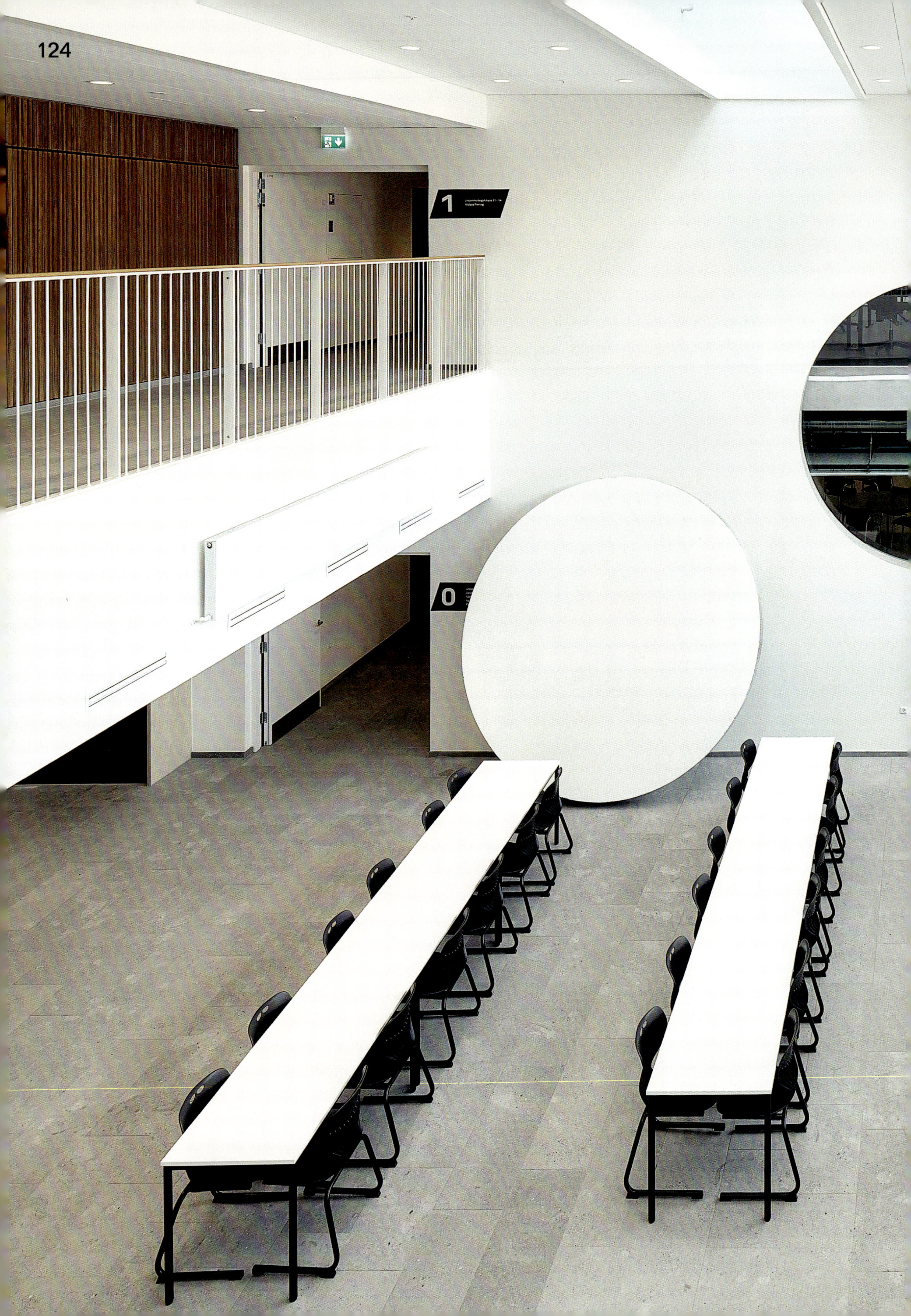
1
0

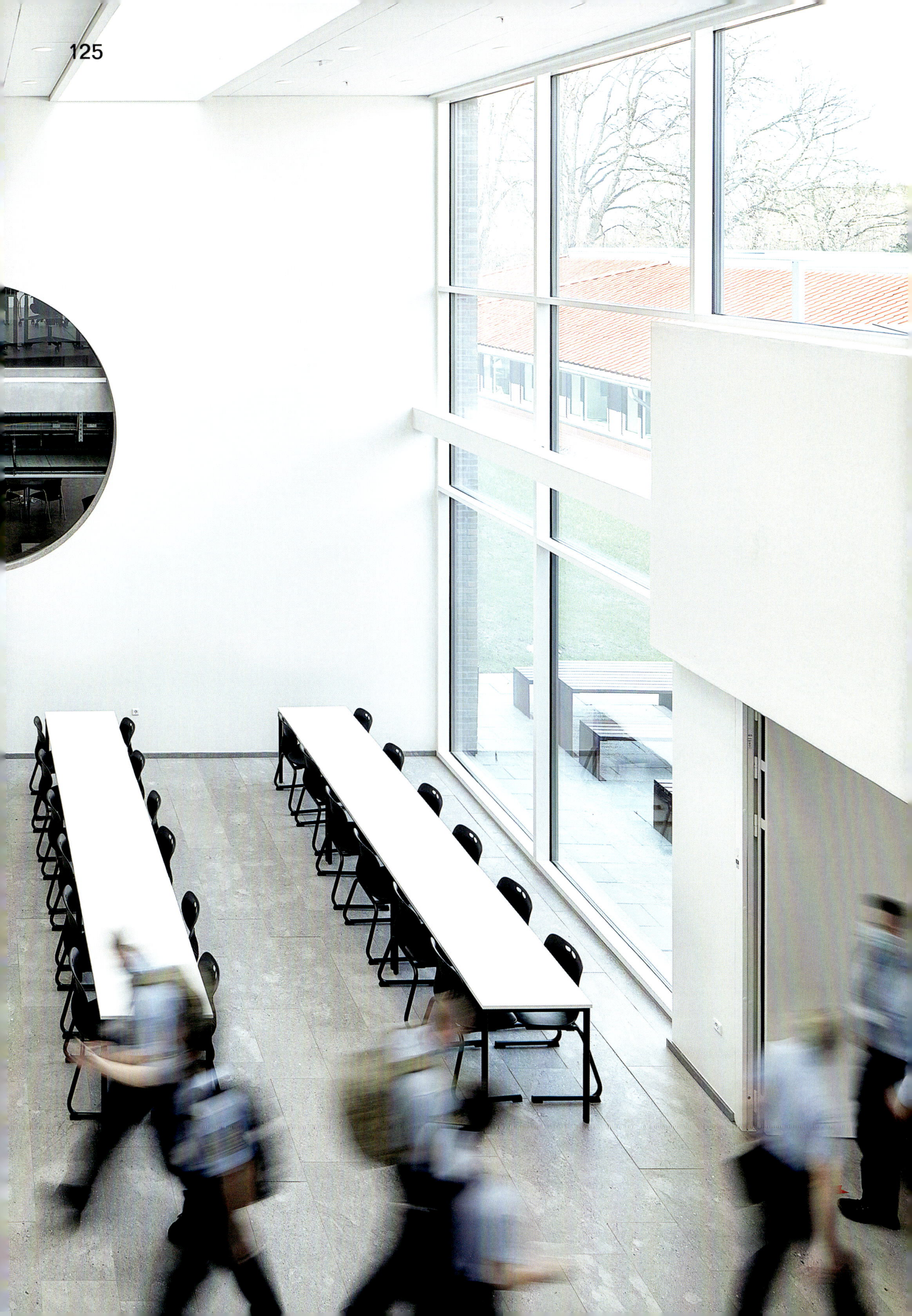

Concrete Floor

Concrete is laid on the gallery's floor and a pair of trainers is set in it. A stand-in wears the trainers during the exhibition opening hours.

Kirkhoff Contemporary Art, Copenhagen, Denmark, 2008

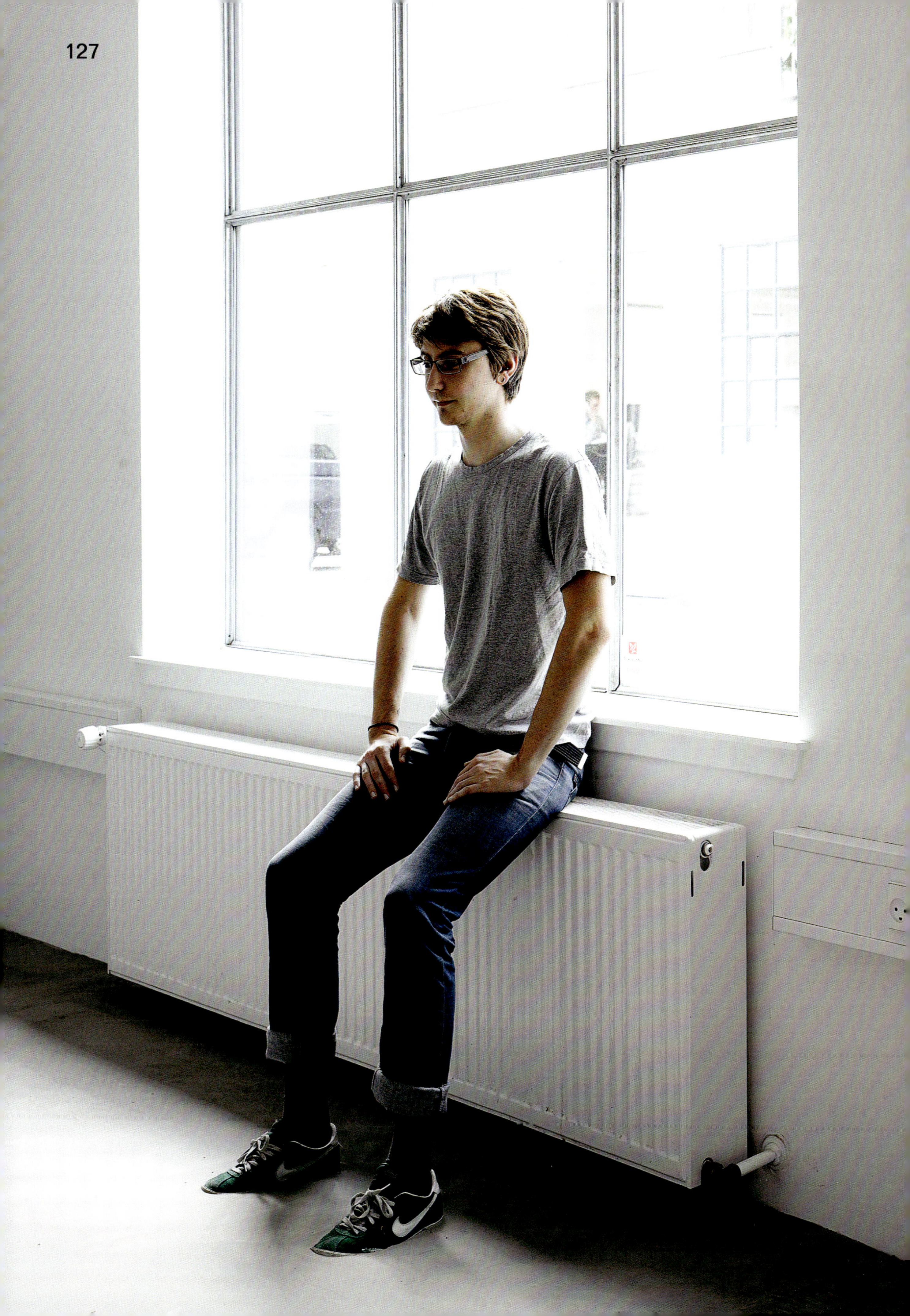

View from Below

A table and six chairs are installed perpendicularly through a wall showing the bottom of the legs. During the exhibition opening hours, a stand-in sits at the table and the soles of their shoes are visible from the exhibition space.

Kirkhoff Contemporary Art, Copenhagen, Denmark, 2008

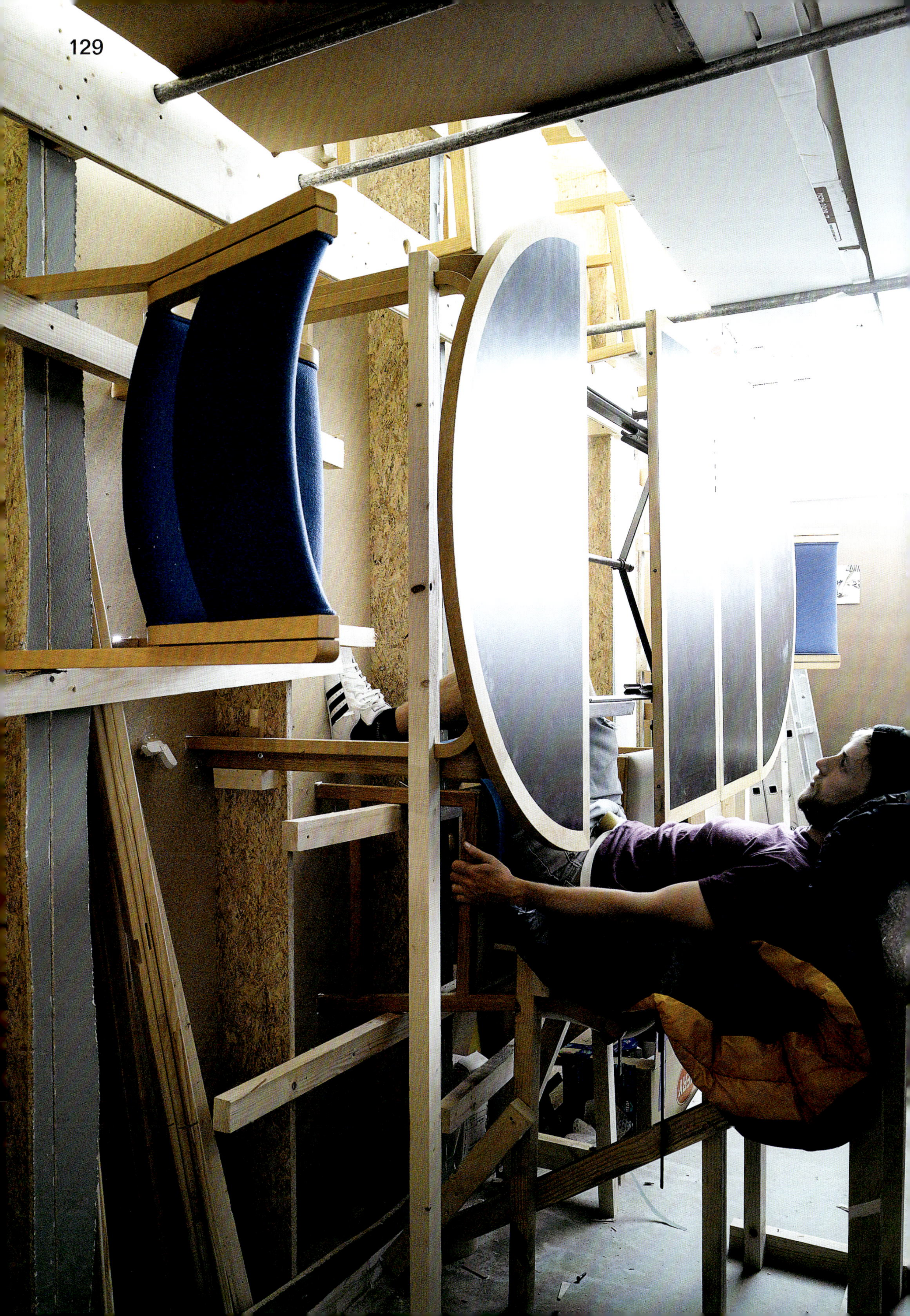

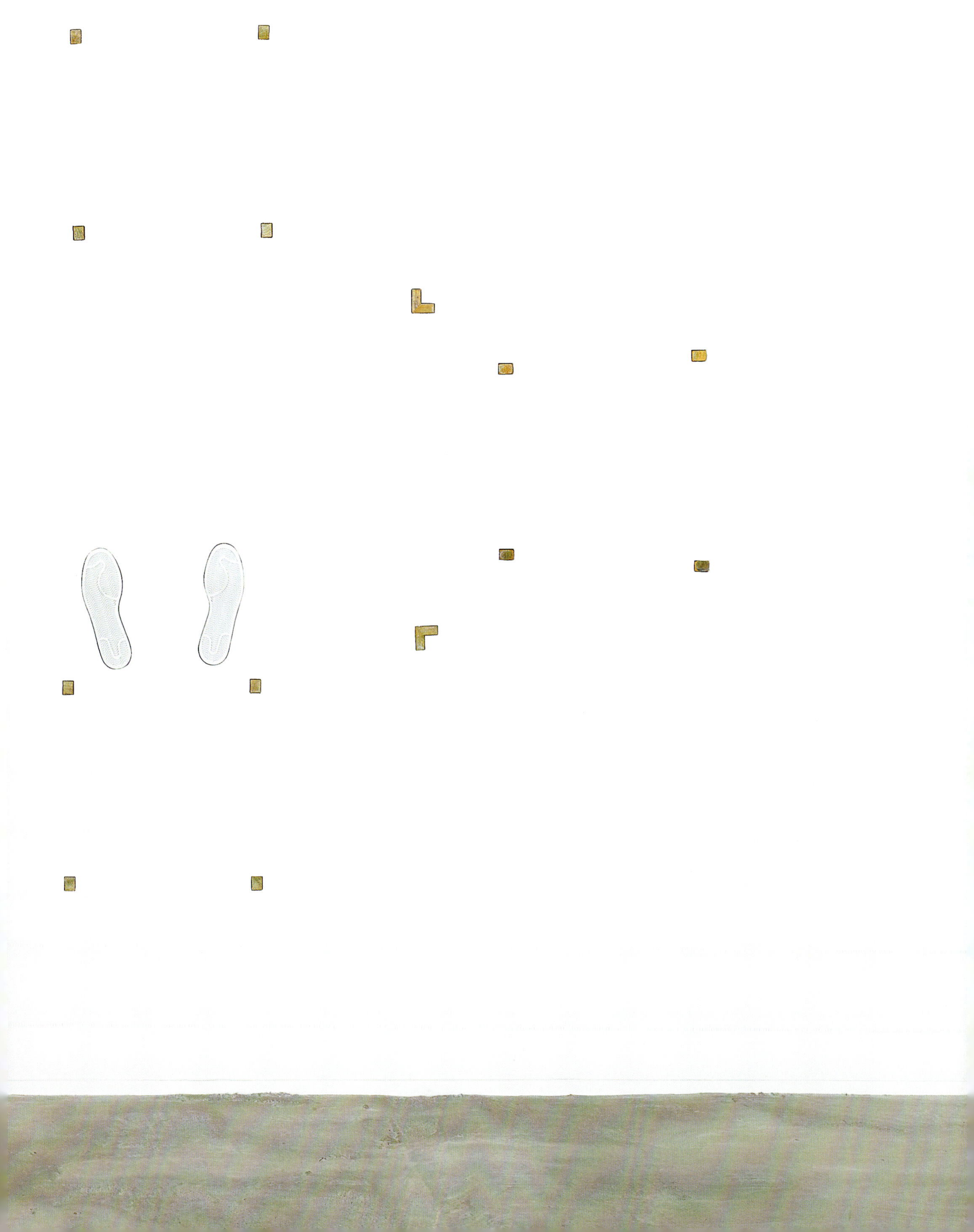

Bronze Painting

Liquid bronze is poured into open moulds and subsequently patinated.

Galleri Nicolai Wallner, Copenhagen, Denmark, 2020

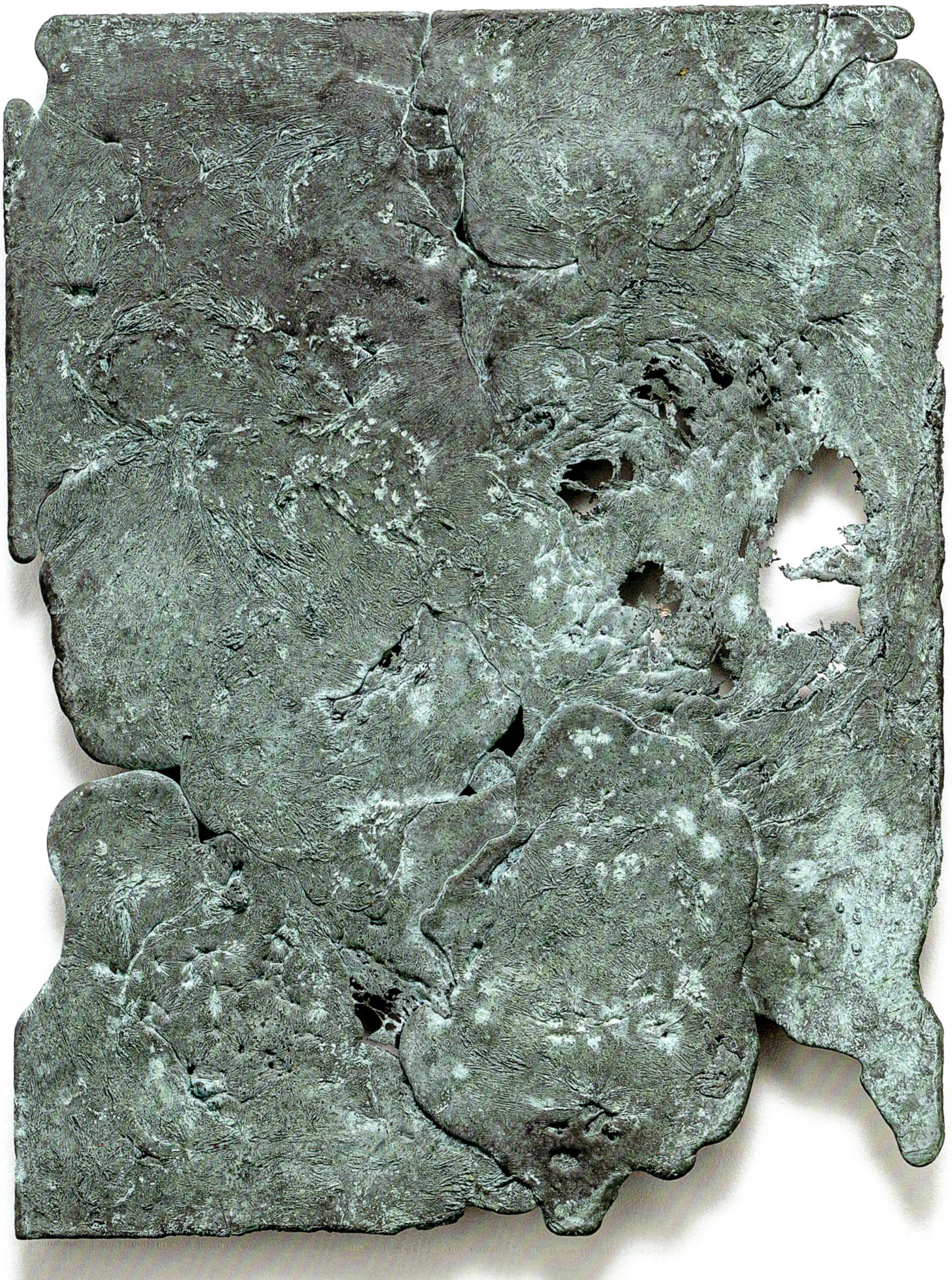

Swap

Two circular areas from the old and the new schoolyards are cut out and swapped.

Spyken High School, Lund, Sweden, 2017

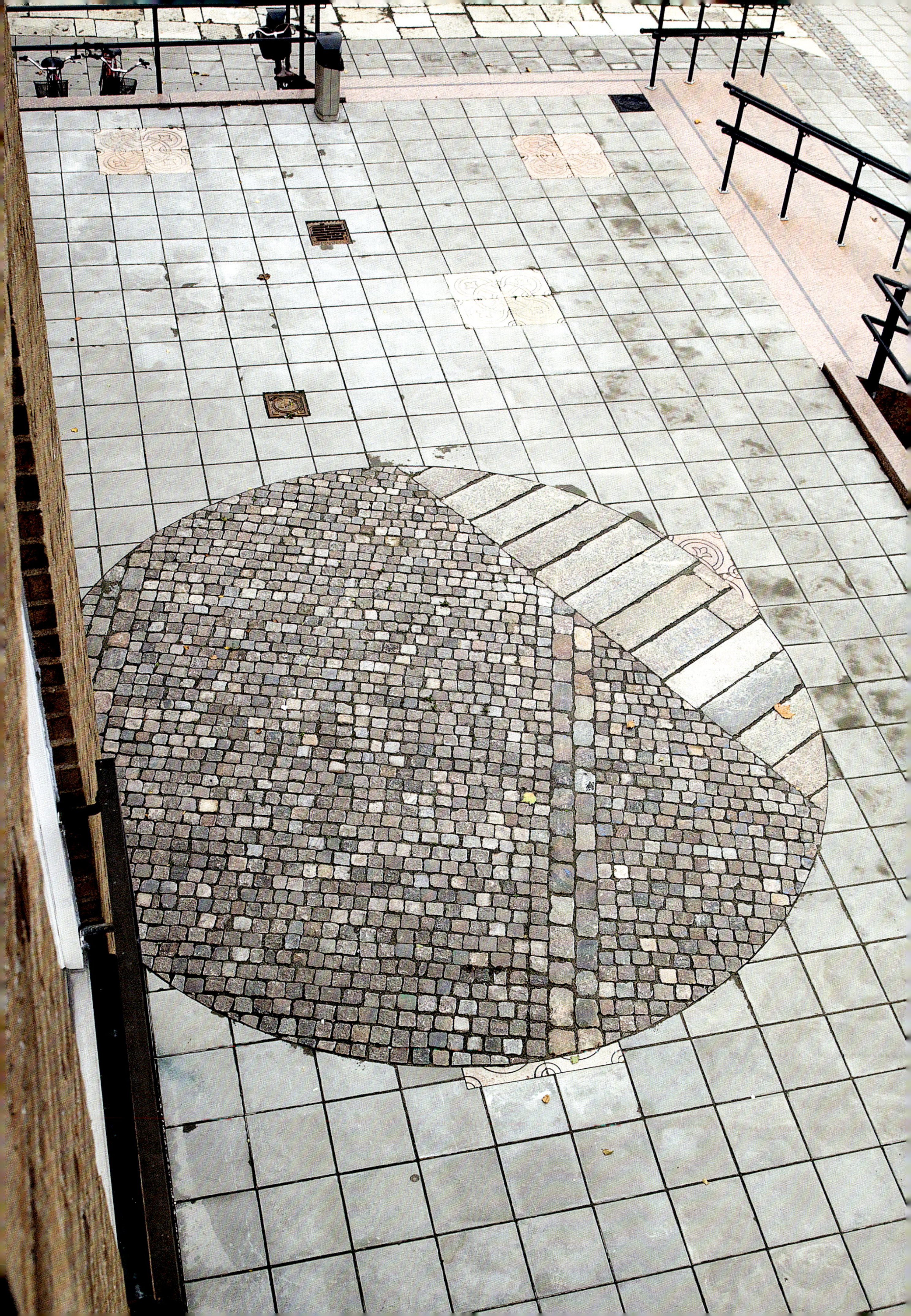

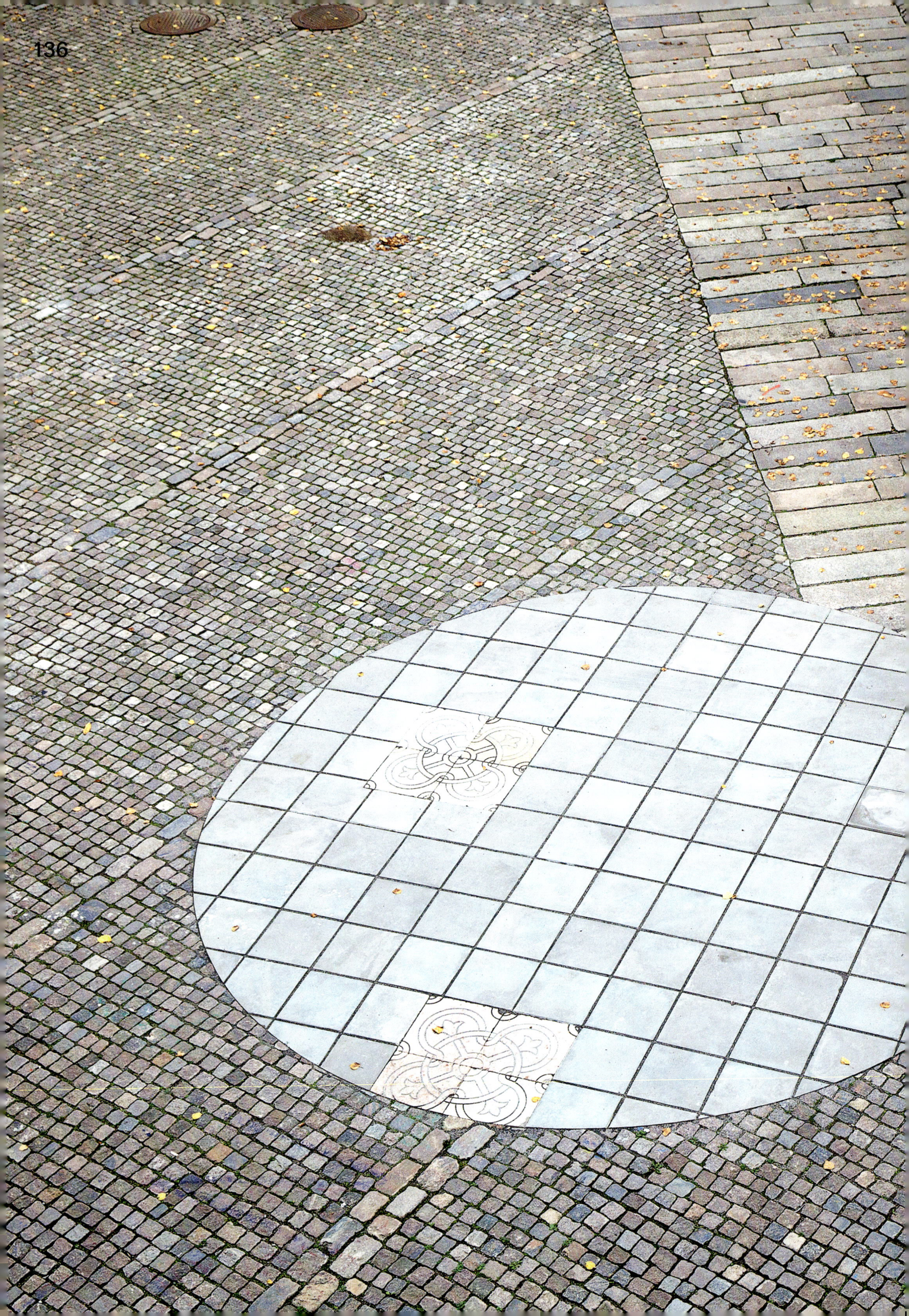

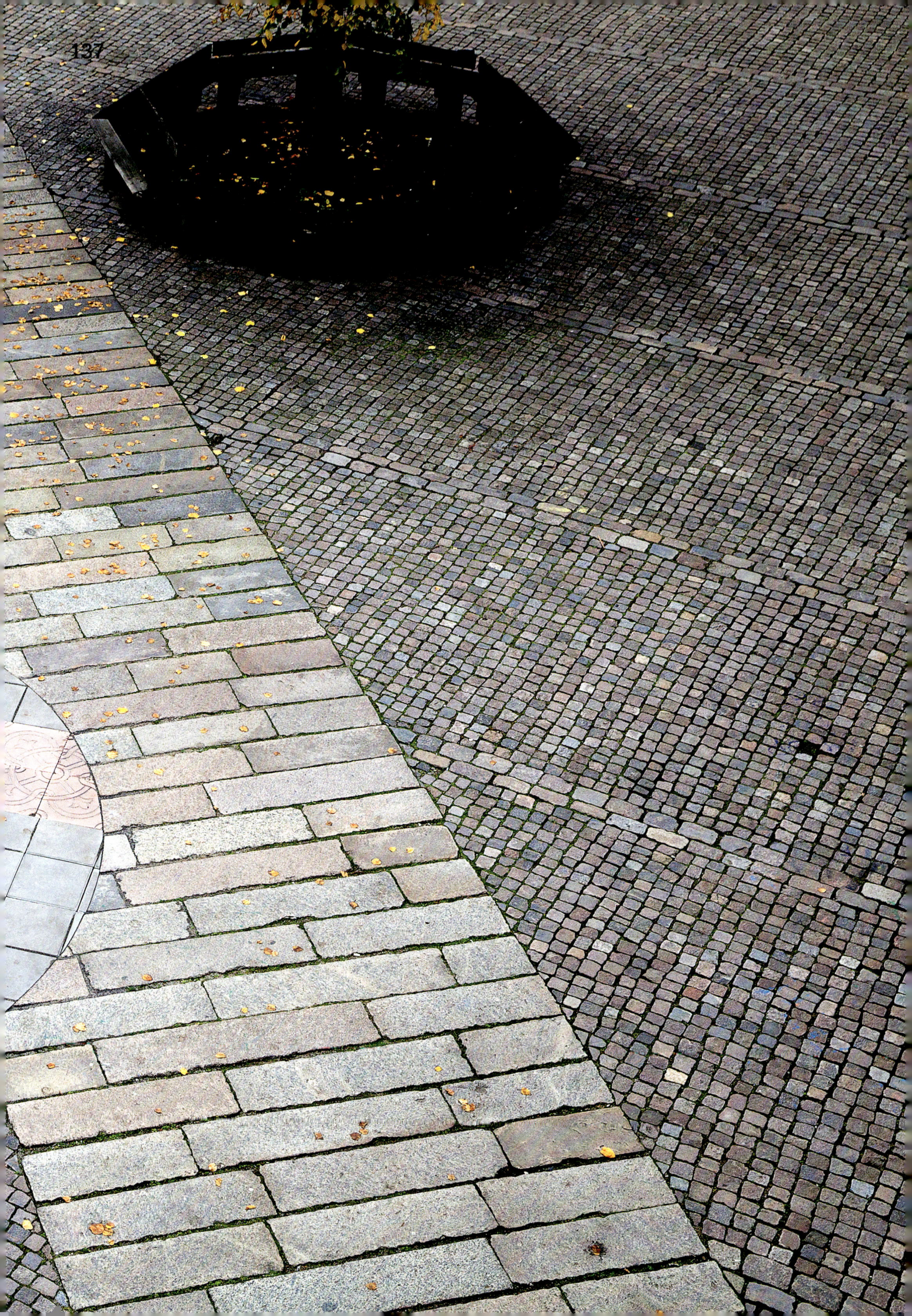

Paper Work

The upholstered seat of a chair is turned into paper.

CA2M – Centro de Arte Dos de Mayo, Madrid, Spain, 2015

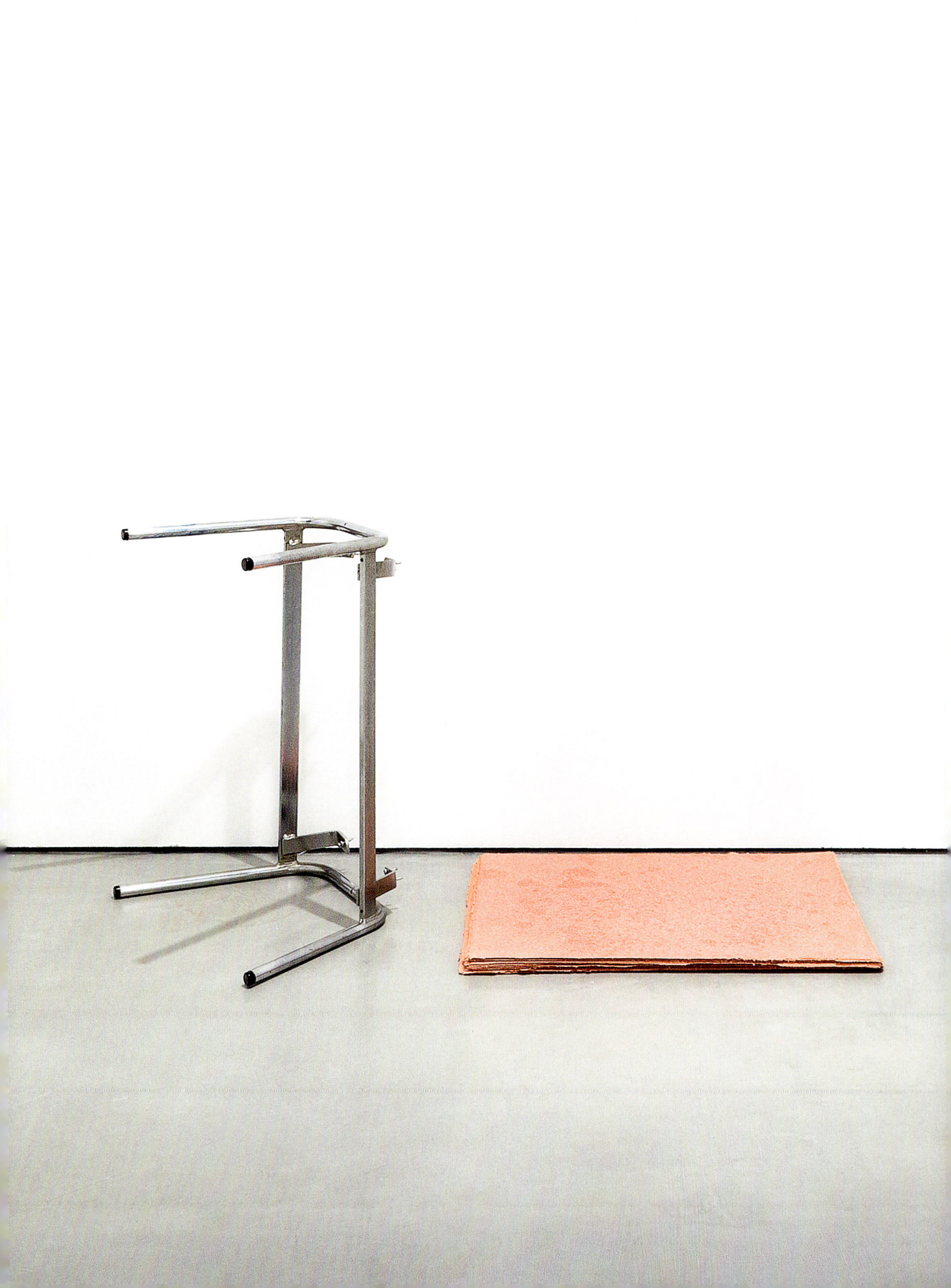

Sound of Sculpture

A bronze sculpture replaces the clapper of the church bell.

Nikolaj Kunsthal, Copenhagen, Denmark, 2015

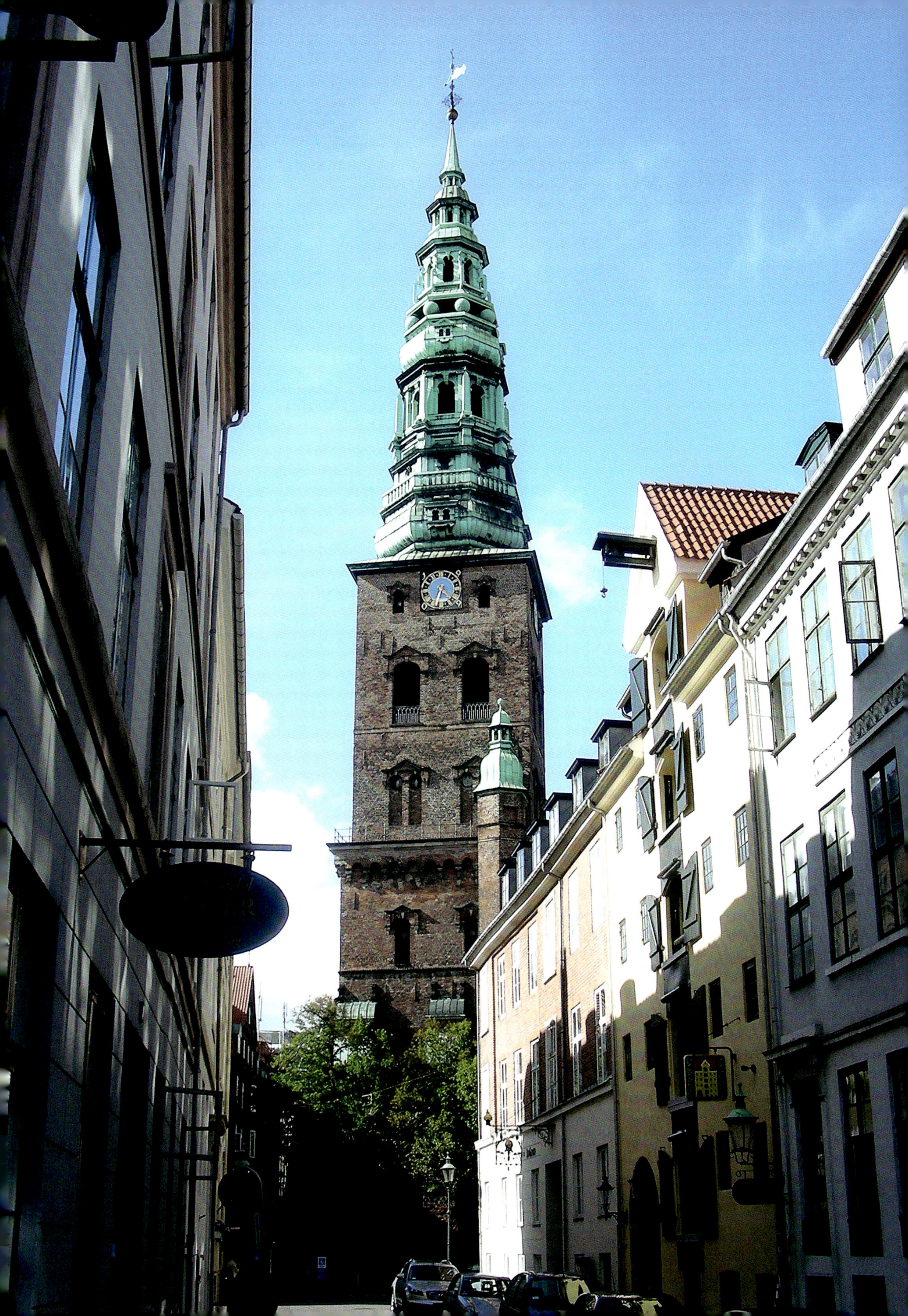

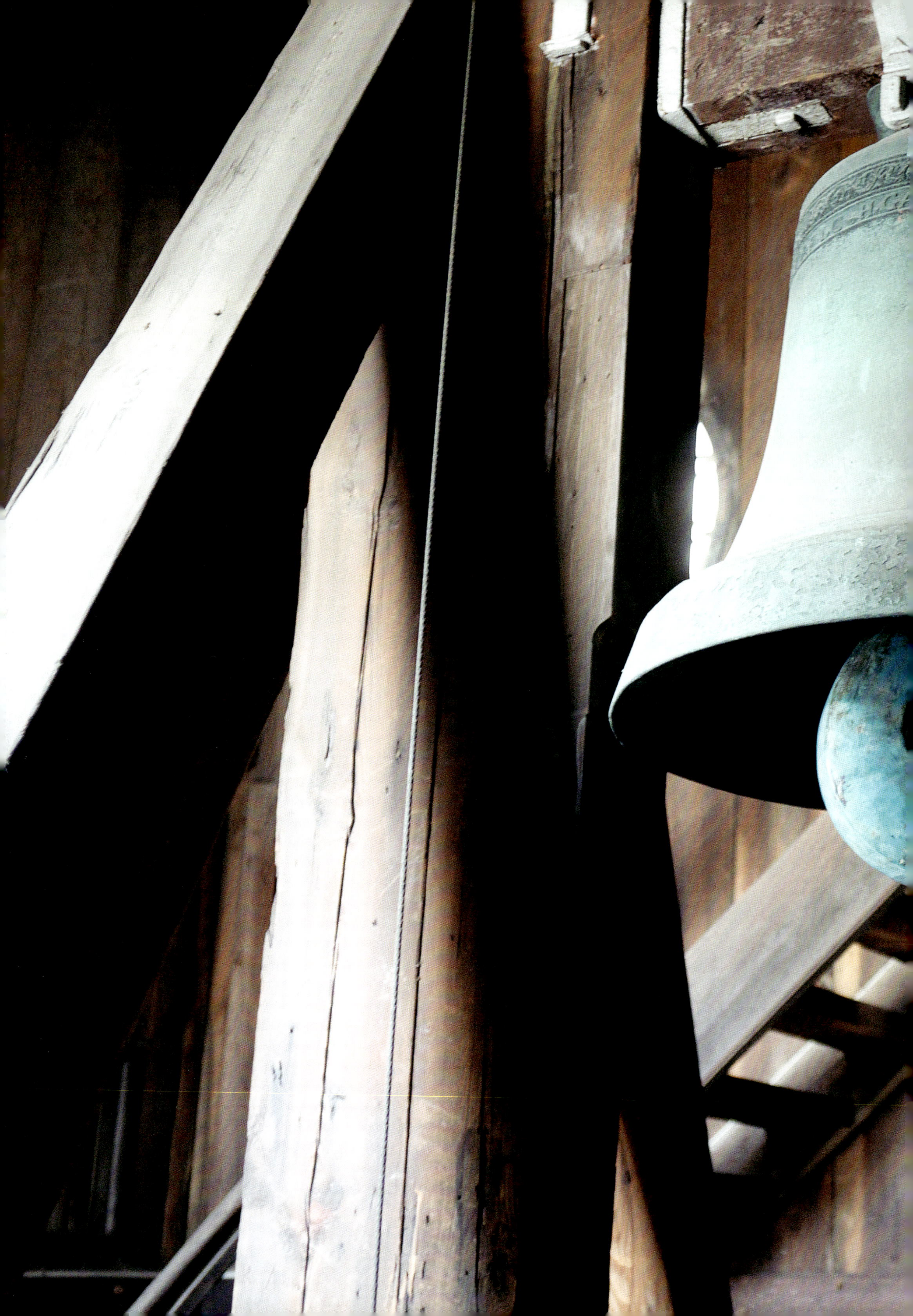

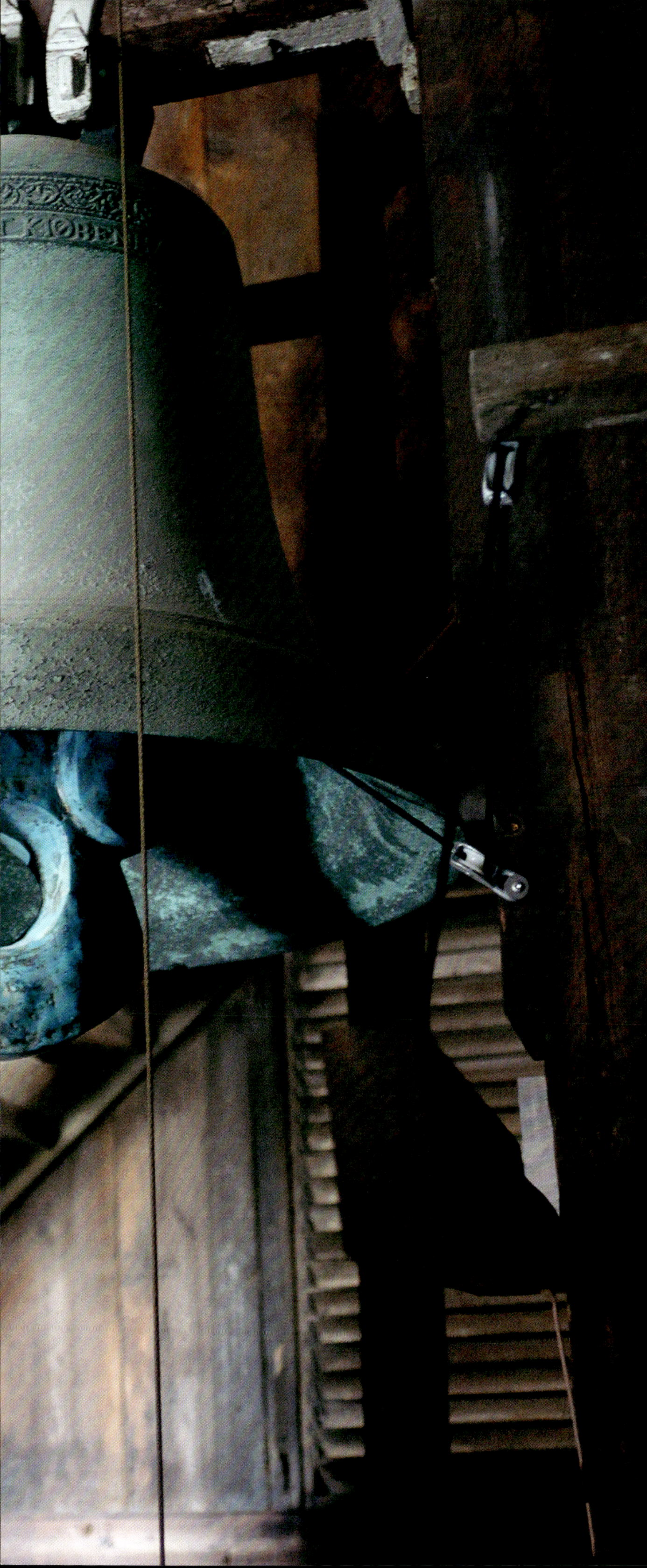

Bannister

A stand-in saws the wooden bannister during the exhibition.

Nikolaj Kunsthal, Copenhagen, Denmark, 2008

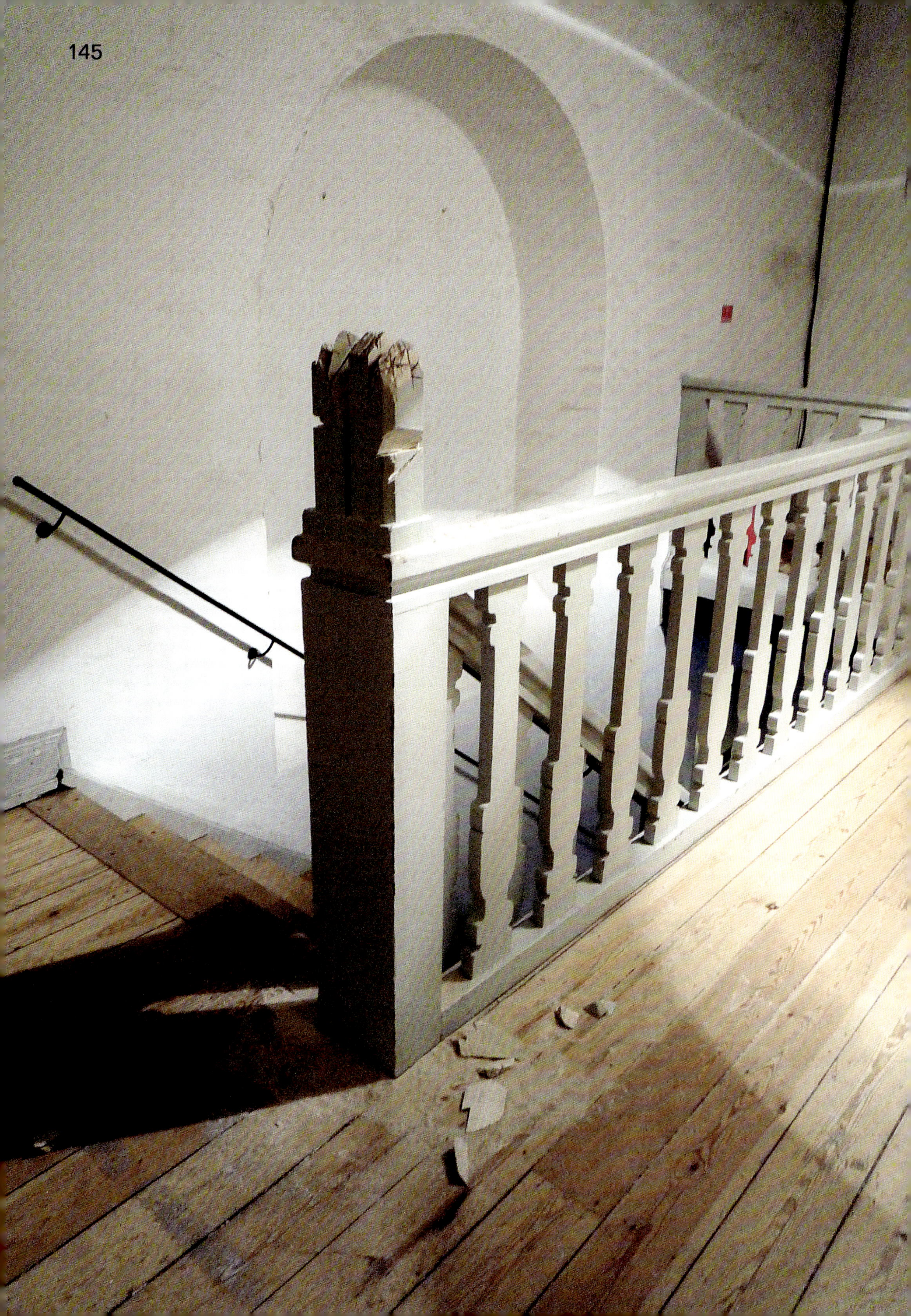

Pigeon's Portal

A corridor connects two opposite windows of the building allowing pigeons to go through the exhibition space.

Nikolaj Kunsthal, Copenhagen, Denmark, 2008

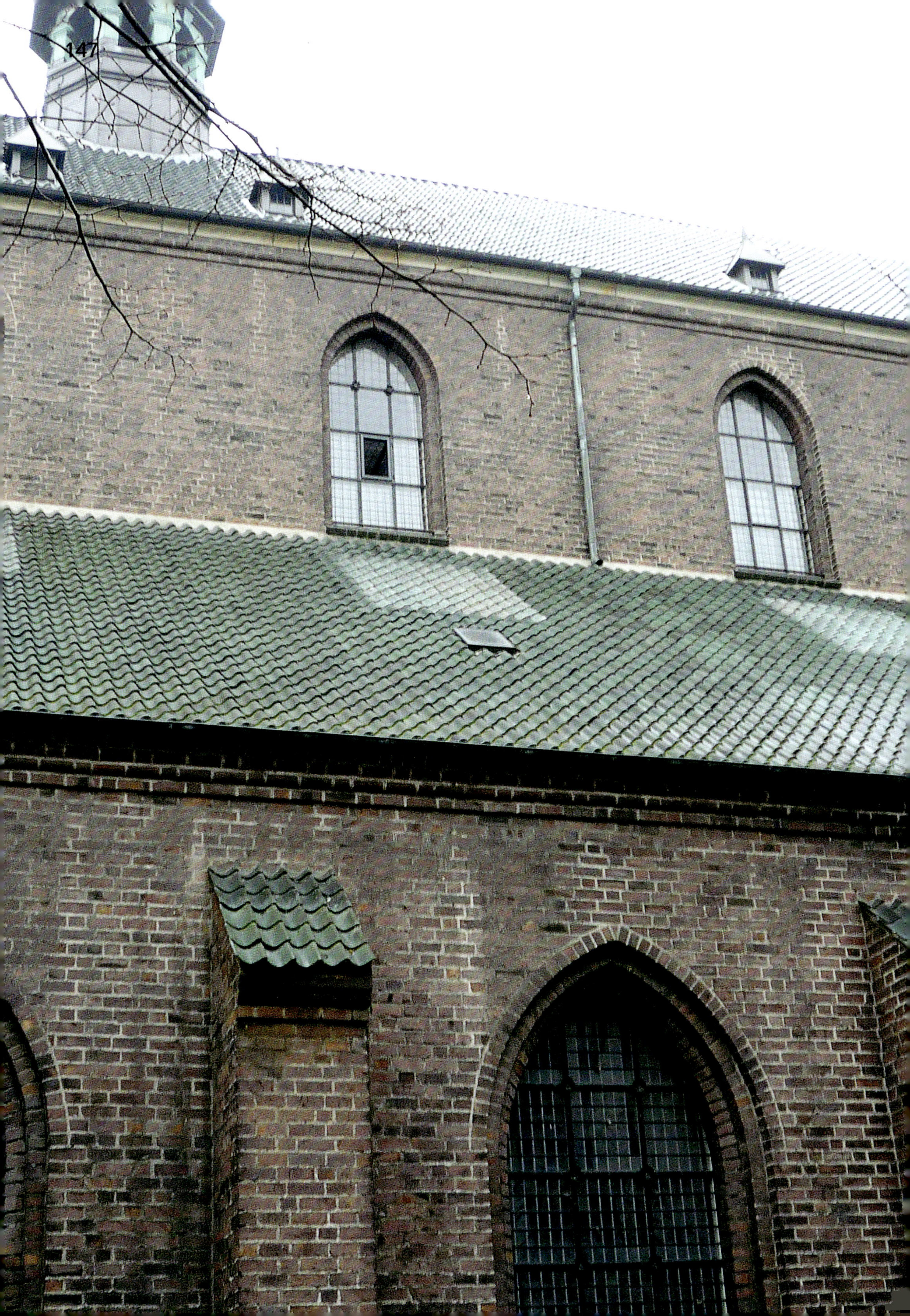

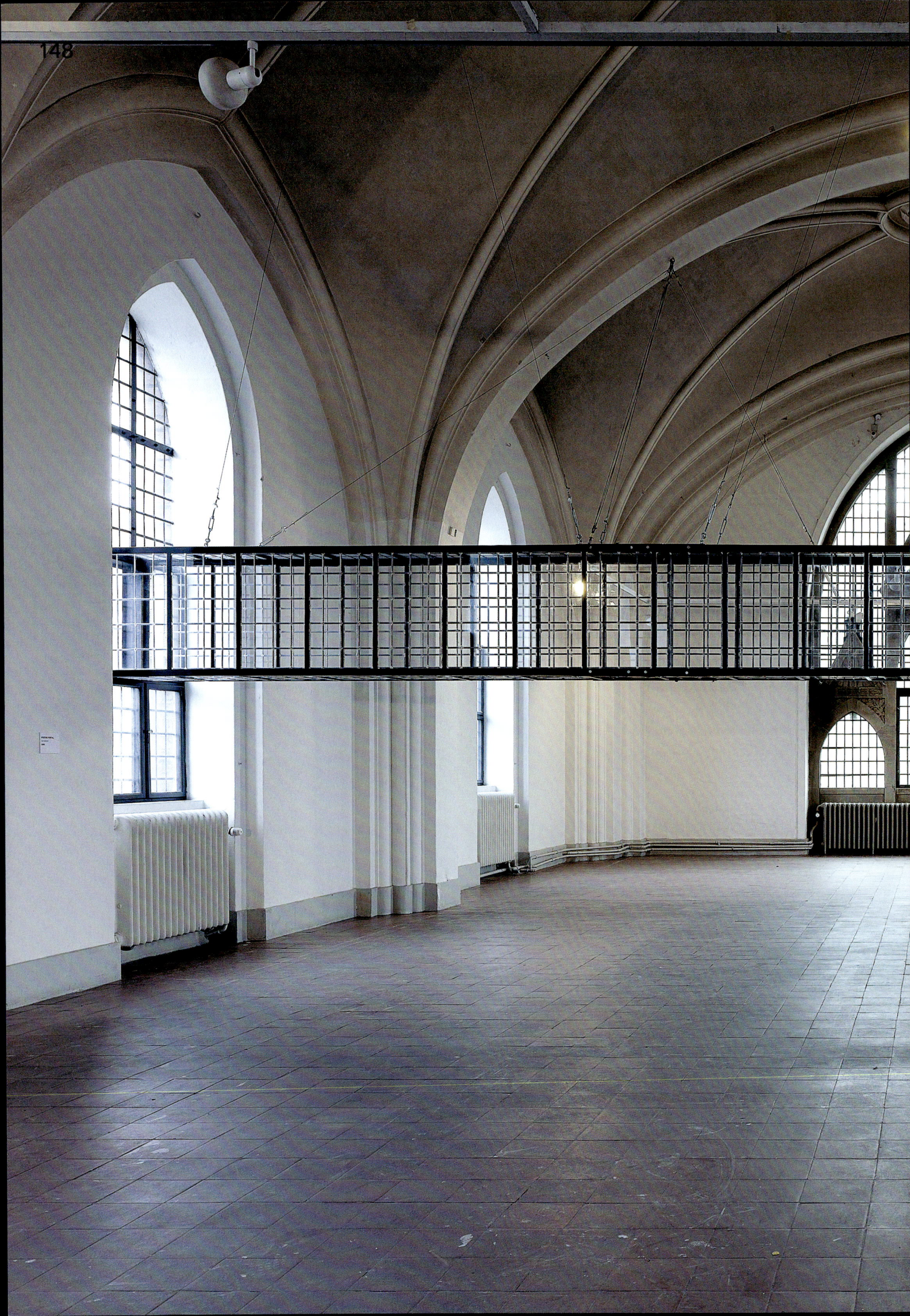

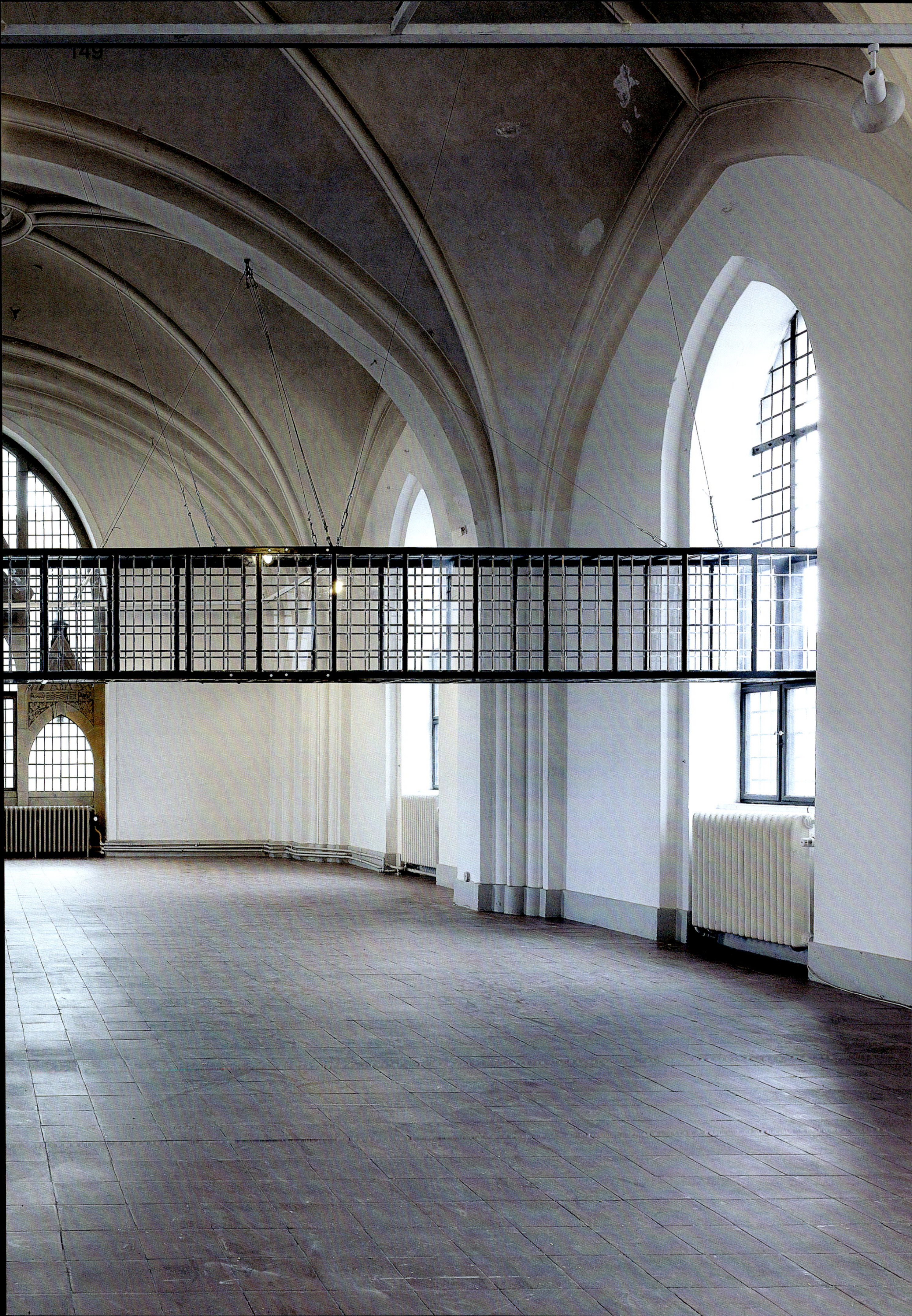

Lamppost

A lamppost is installed horizontally through the gallery wall.

Galleri Nicolai Wallner, Copenhagen, Denmark, 2016

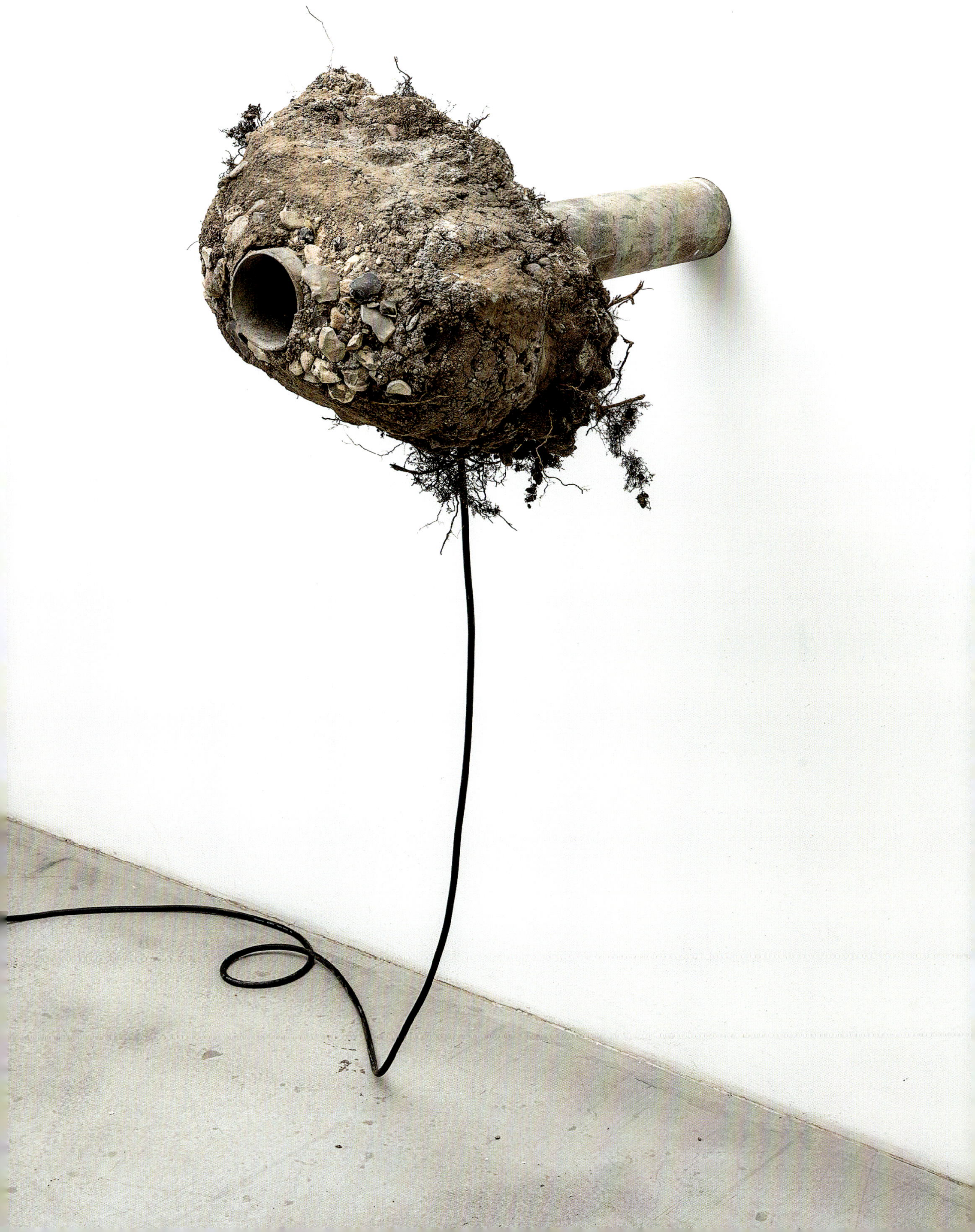

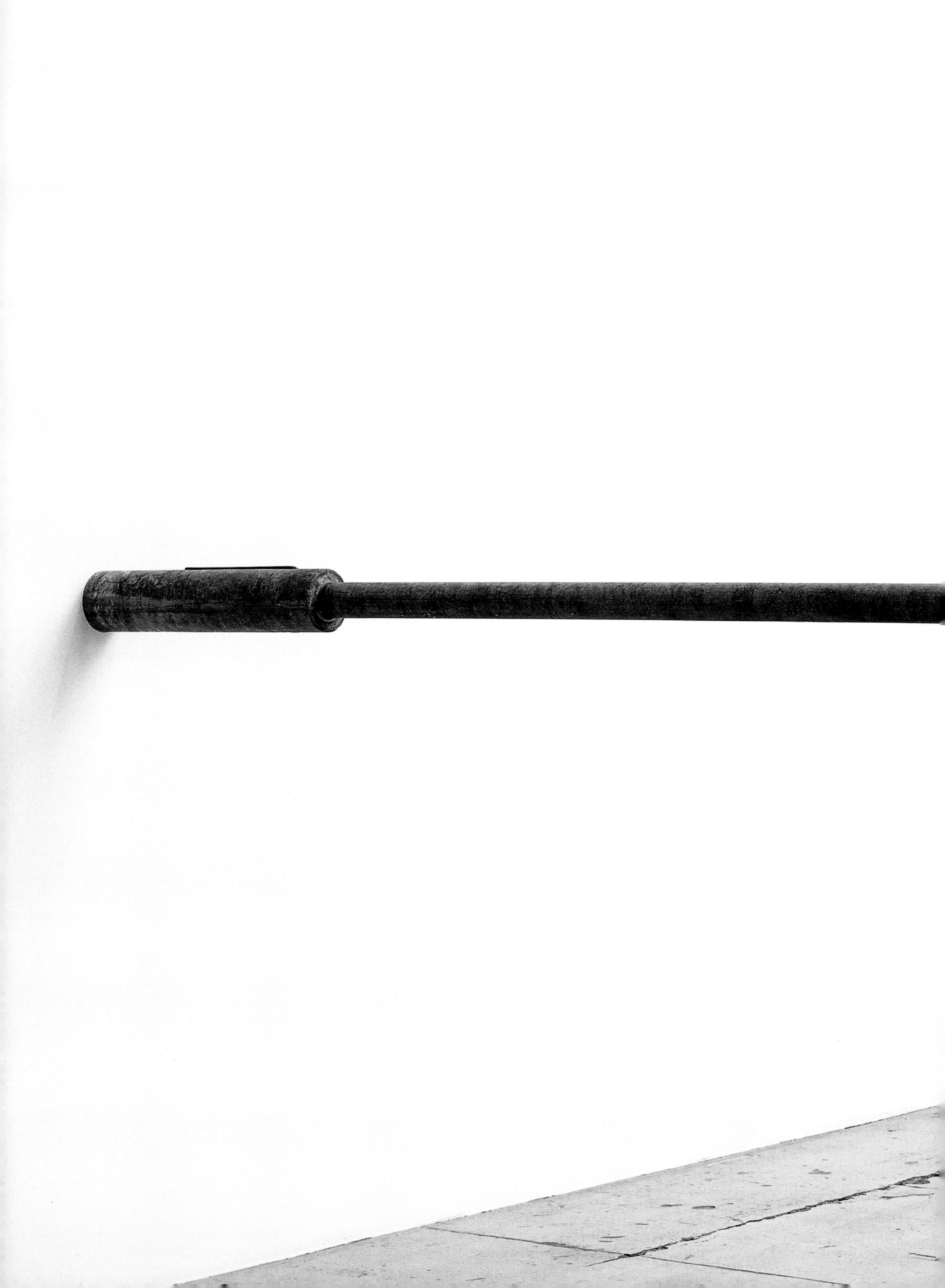

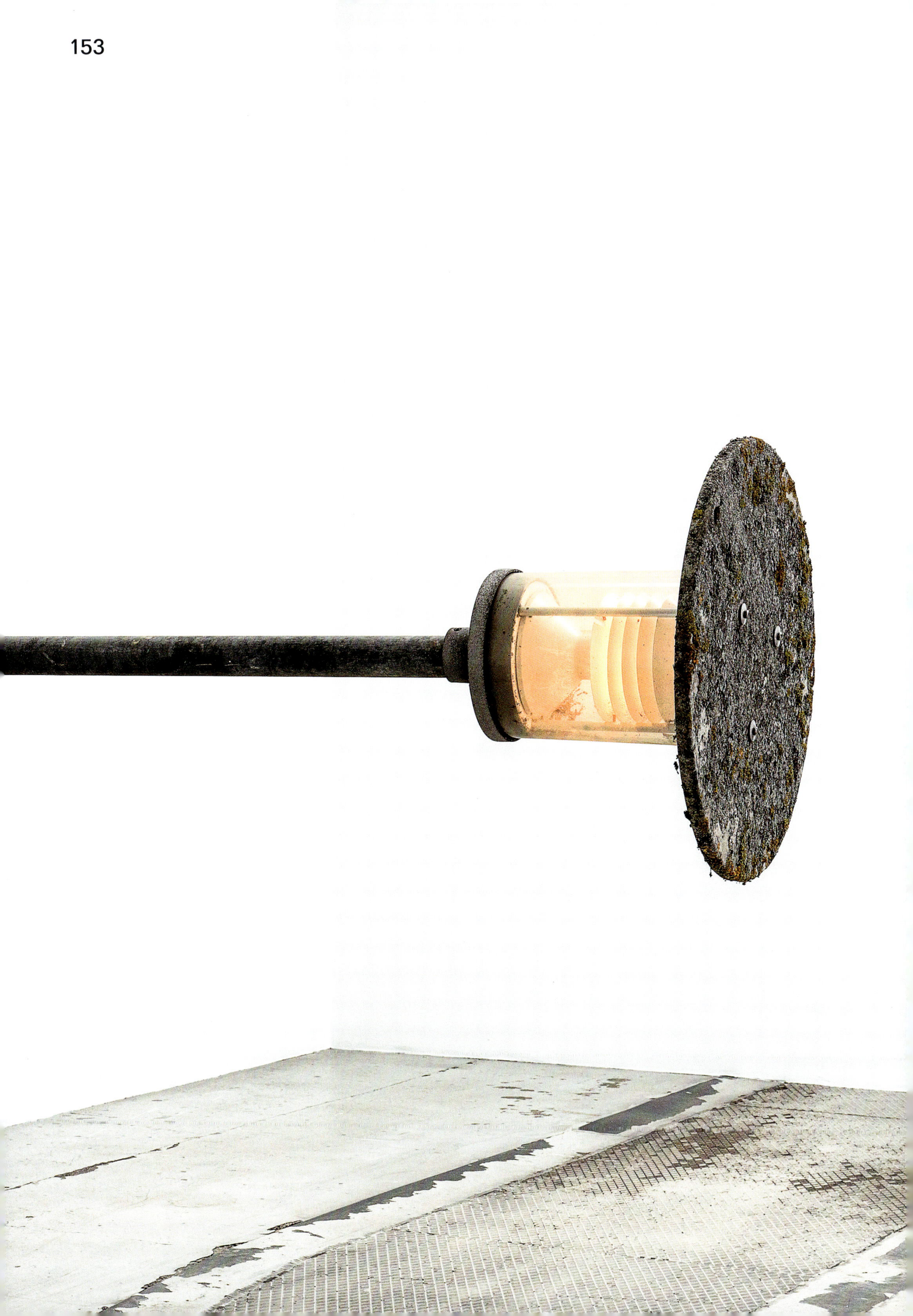

Lift

A stair lift is installed over the entrance to the gallery space and is used by the guards.

Kunstmuseum Brandts, Odense, Denmark, 2008

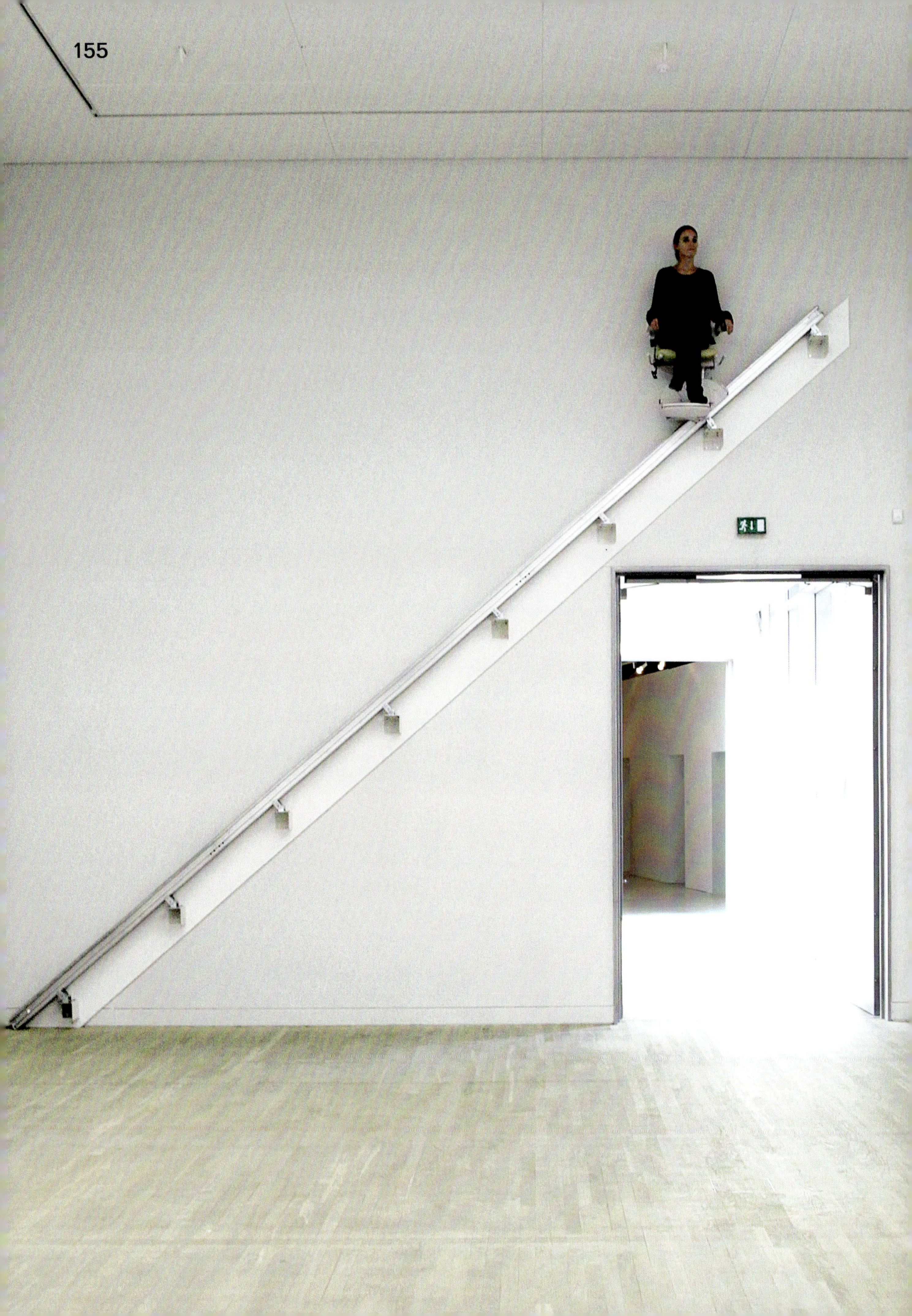

Ventilation Slide Projections

Slide shapes are cut out from the gallery window panes, placed in a projector, and shown on the gallery wall.

Galerie Édouard-Manet, Gennevilliers, France, 2016

Kodak

A Kassen

Dimensions Variable

Publishing Editor	Vittoria Mieli, Mousse
Texts	Irene Campolmi Adam Carr Jonatan Habib Engqvist
Copy editing and proofreading	Orin Bristow
Graphic design	Marcello Jacopo Biffi, Mousse
Photographs	A Kassen: cover, p. 8–9, 13, 17–19, 21, 25–27, 29–35, 37, 40, 55, 63, 73, 75–77, 81–83, 86–87, 89, 91–93, 103, 105, 116–118, 139, 141, 145, 158–159 Kling & Bang: p. 5, 10–11, 14 Ana Victoria Bruno: p. 6–7 Lilja Birgisdóttir: p. 22–23 Torben Eskerod: p. 47–53, 59, 155 Anders Sune Berg: p. 56–57, 69–71, 81–83, 94–95, 97, 112–113, 115, 123–125, 127, 129–131, 133, 147–149, 151–153 Maisterravalbuena Gallery: p. 61, 101, 119 Fondation CAB: p. 64–67 New Galerie, Paris: p. 78–79, 119 Jojo Taylor: p. 85 Niels Fabæk: p. 98–99 Frédéric Boudin, courtesy Kistefos: p. 106–109 Terje Östling: p. 111 Helene Toresdotter: p. 135–137 Owen Armour: p. 142–143 Rémy Lidereau: p. 157
Printing	Faenza Printing S.p.a., Italy
Published and distributed by	Mousse Publishing Contrappunto S.r.l. via Pier Candido Decembrio, 28 20137, Milan – Italy
Available through	Mousse Publishing, Milan moussemagazine.it DAP | Distributed Art Publishers, New York artbook.com Les presses du réel, Dijon lespressesdureel.com Antenne Books, London antennebooks.com Idea Books, Amsterdam ideabooks.nl

All works by A Kassen courtesy Maisterravalbuena Gallery, Madrid, and Galleri Nicolai Wallner, Copenhagen

Kindly supported by Beckett Fonden, Grosserer L. F. Foghts Fond, Overretssagfører L. Zeuthens Mindelegat, 15. Juni Fonden, Politiken Fonden

First edition: 2022

ISBN 978-88-6749-525-2

EUR 27 / USD 30 / DKK 200